The Po

The Possibility of Love:
An Interdisciplinary Analysis

By

Kathleen O'Dwyer

CAMBRIDGE
SCHOLARS
PUBLISHING

The Possibility of Love: An Interdisciplinary Analysis, by Kathleen O'Dwyer

This book first published 2009. The present binding first published 2009.

Cambridge Scholars Publishing

12 Back Chapman Street, Newcastle upon Tyne, NE6 2XX, UK

British Library Cataloguing in Publication Data
A catalogue record for this book is available from the British Library

ISBN (10): 1-4438-1387-7, ISBN (13): 978-1-4438-1387-7

FOR MY SISTER, MARY

TABLE OF CONTENTS

ACKNOWLEDGEMENTS

I would like to thank Dr. Paula Murphy, for her unfailing encouragement, guidance, support and kindness throughout the preparation and the writing of this work. I would like to express my gratitude, for their help and support, to all the staff at the Department of English Language and Literature at Mary Immaculate College, Limerick, particularly Dr. Eugene O'Brien and Dr. John McDonagh.

I would like to thank Carol Koulikourdi and Amanda Millar at Cambridge Scholars Publishing for their help and support.

As always, thanks to Michael, Maeve, Kate, Muireann and Nessa.

Some of the material in this book has been published in different forms in: "Jacques Lacan on Love: Realist Cynic or Inveterate Optimist" in *Crossroads: An Interdisciplinary Journal for the Study of History, Philosophy, Religion and Classics*, Vol. 11, Issue 1, 2007, pp. 47-56; "The Question of Love's Possibility Explored through the Poetry of William Wordsworth" in *Cosmos and History: The Journal of Natural and Social Philosophy*, Vol. 4, no.s 1-2, 2008, pp. 178-210; "Nietzsche's Reflections on Love" in *Minerva – An Internet Journal of Philosophy*, Vol. 12, November 2008, pp. 37-77.

INTRODUCTION

> For one human being to love another;
> that is perhaps the most difficult of all
> our tasks, the ultimate, the last test and
> proof, the work for which all other
> work is but preparation
> —Rilke, 2004: 37.

This study seeks to examine the possibility of love in human experience as a key question which forms a foundational link between the separate disciplines of philosophy, psychoanalysis and poetry. It is my contention that the question of love's possibility is an essential human question, essential in the sense that it is endemic to humanity and, therefore, endemic to any discipline concerned with the exploration of what it means to be human. In some way, and on some level, the question preoccupies the thrust and direction of the three disciplines chosen as the basis of research in this study; all three pose this question as a central and essential concern of human living, albeit that their methods and responses take different formats. According to this argument, the three disciplines are linked in their assertion that the question of love's possibility cannot be ignored even if it cannot be answered. This interconnection between the three disciplines is the focus of inquiry in the following chapters. It is explored in the literature of nine writers selected across an inter-disciplinary reading of philosophy, psychoanalysis, and poetry, and across different historical periods. The study examines how the selected writers pose, discuss and answer the question of whether the experience and communication of love is possible in inter-relational encounters, or whether such experience remains an unattainable ideal inevitably blocked and limited by personal and societal forces. An examination of this expansive question is confined to a concentration on how the concept of love has been, and continues to be, interpreted and explored in the three disciplines, and it is limited to a concentration on a small selection of writers within these areas.

This work aims at a limited and a selective reading of philosophy, psychoanalysis, and poetry, as three disciplines wherein language is the key mode of inquiry, practice, and expression; each of these disciplines is directly and indirectly concerned with questions pertaining to concepts of truth, being, and the experience of the human condition, and each strives to approach the elusive yet essential issues of subjectivity, existence and essence, and particularly the needs and deprivations which enhance or diminish the experience of human living. The concept of love pertains inevitably to these questions, and it is argued that this concept enables a significant and insightful connection between the three disciplines. There are some common ways in which the concept of love is explored in relation to the three disciplines, and some ways that are specific to particular schools of inquiry; this commonality and difference also applies to different historical periods. A focus on key figures/writers from the three areas and from three time-frames ranging from romanticism, through modernism, to contemporary postmodernism, enables an analysis of the concept of love through diverse situations, personalities and cultural/literary/philosophical contexts. The limitation of the analysis to this time-frame, which necessarily excludes an examination of the question through periods prior to romanticism results from a determination to maintain coherence and focus in the discussion.

The question has been chosen because, it is asserted, the possibility of love is a question that lies at the deepest and most secret part of humanity. It is a question that, down through the ages and across different disciplines, has intrigued, disturbed, challenged and ultimately formed the (often unacknowledged) foundation of theoretical, creative or philosophical inquiry. It is a question that, although it defies conclusive analysis and the boundaries of discipline, is firmly rooted in any concept of what it is to be human, and therefore has never been - and can never be - ignored. It is consequently central to these three disciplines which are motivated, at least in part, by the search for an understanding and an expression of the human condition and truths thereof.

The notion of love is traditionally and conventionally associated with idealistic expressions of self-denial, object-worship, self-transcendence, and god-like characteristics. Sentimentality, cliché, and consumerist depictions of human relatedness often supersede the human reality of love, in its ambivalence, its contradictions, its failures and its diversity. Humanness, the pursuit of truth, the striving for happiness, indeed the full spectrum of lived experience, is impacted to at least some degree by the concept of love; from birth to death, across cultural and historical divides, the need/urge/instinct to love and to be loved may be discerned, at times clearly and obviously, more often hidden and disguised, in diverse manifestations of human behaviour. As a result, questions relating to the concept of love have exercised thinkers and writers across many disciplines; attempts have been made to define and describe love, to provide theories of love, and to explain the meaning of love. However, this study seeks to ask how the selected writers respond to the question as to whether, in the light of philosophical insight, psychoanalytic observation and poetic inspiration, all of which attempt a realistic and truthful appraisal of human nature, and in the light of the contentious and disturbing facts of human history, love is possible at all.

"Is love possible?" It may be argued that this is a question which is too vague and too complex to be posed, explored or answered in any comprehensive way. Its analysis necessitates the construction of a definition of love which is comprehensive enough to embrace a broadly acceptable understanding of the concept; it also demands an explanation of the notion of possibility within the context of the question. I accept the complexities, limitations, and inconclusiveness pertaining to a theoretical inquiry into the question of love's possibility, and thus I seek to approach a narrower and more focused aspect of such an investigation. The study places the question within a framework of historical and disciplinary boundaries, and asks how it is explored, analysed and pronounced by selected writers within this framework. Thus, definitions and conceptual explanations are limited to those which emerge from a reading of these writers. It is proposed that the central importance of the question lies, not in such analysis or exploration, but rather in the incontrovertible evidence of the centrality of the question to human experience. Great thinkers and writers have always, in various ways, represented or anticipated the great questions of their particular age or time. In the following chapters, evidence of the centrality of the question "is love possible?" will be explored through selected writers from the disciplines of philosophy, psychoanalysis and poetry. Essentially – and crucially – this is an exploration that gains its strength from the interdisciplinary nature of the exercise.

Over the centuries, the phenomenon of love has inspired and occupied philosophers, psychologists/psychoanalysts and poets, as well as students and researchers in fields of study which are outside the scope of this work. Hence, perennial questions of philosophy such as "who am I?", "how should one live?" and "whence meaning and significance?" reflect in a direct way concepts and definitions of love. Platonic, Aristotelian and Pauline discourses on love differentiate between *eros, agape* and *philia*, and explore diverse manifestations of love in sexuality, friendship, and divine worship and adoration.[1] Subsequent philosophers analyse and

---

[1] For an exploration of these concepts, see Alan Noble's *Eros, Agape, and Philia.*

xiv   Introduction

interpret these conceptions of love, query their boundaries, and offer traditional or revolutionary understanding and conclusion. Within philosophical discourse, religious, ethical and practical aspects of the phenomenon of love are explored, and the opposition between self-love and altruism is examined and sometimes deconstructed altogether. On this point, philosophy encounters psychoanalytic theory regarding selfhood and otherness and the complex relationship between subject and object. Psychoanalysis seeks to free the human psyche from the constrictions of deception and compulsion, and, in the words of its founder, aims to liberate man "to love and to work".[2] In the clinical setting of psychoanalytical practice manifestations of mental and emotional distress are addressed with a view to their amelioration, and this is mainly achieved through an understanding of their origins. Tracing the sources of trauma or distress to the enduring influence of early childhood experience inevitably results in a portrayal of the subject's desire for love, a desire which is replicated in the phenomenon of transference in the clinical setting. Poetry, in a manner different to other literary genres such as narrative and drama, has traditionally been seen as the creative exploration and expression of individual emotion and passion, and in lifting the veil of fixed assumptions and rational limitations, it explores and expresses the common experience of love as the nucleus of human life. The vicissitudes, losses, joys and sorrows pertaining to love are approached in a unique way through the poetic word, as it simultaneously addresses these issues intellectually, emotionally and creatively. Thus, the three disciplines share a common emphasis on the question of human love; they each contribute a unique commentary on the subject. However, it is my argument that a richer exploration of the question is enabled through a combined reading of, and an attempted dialogue between, philosophy, psychoanalysis and poetry.

The concept of love has inspired much of the literature of the three disciplines, as seen through diverse personalities and historical periods. Titles such as *The Reasons of Love, The Nature of Love, the Way of Love,* and *The Psychology of Love,* form but a miniscule reflection of the existing selection. However, this study asks if, according to the writers selected, love, as defined in myriad forms and descriptions, is actually possible within the human condition. Through a reading of selected authors of philosophy, psychoanalysis and poetry, it examines some of the obstacles to such a possibility, the impact of love on the concept of the

---

[2] This phrase is attributed to Freud by Erik Erikson, in *Identity and the Life Cycle,* p.102.

individual subject, and ultimately the role of love in human living. It investigates how the concept of love has been explored not only through the three disciplines mentioned, but also through different historical periods. This impacts on and influences, the writers chosen for exploration and analysis.

The philosophical contribution centres on Friedrich Nietzsche, whose deconstructive assault on fixed forms of being rejected the separation of philosophy from lived experience, and who suggested an inescapable relationship between thought and feeling, mind and body, and philosophy and psychology; Martin Buber as a philosopher concerned with authenticity and love in human relations, with a particular emphasis on the concrete events and encounters of lived experience, and in particular the complexities and ambivalence pertaining to the encounter between self and other; and Paul Ricoeur as a contemporary philosopher concentrated on a hermeneutical approach to subjectivity, personhood, and the interpretation of human action and motivation, especially as this enables an investigation of the interrelatedness of self and other. Psychoanalytic literature focuses on Sigmund Freud as the founder and instigator of the discipline, Jacques Lacan as both an interpreter of Freud and an influential innovator of new developments in psychoanalysis, and Slavoj Žižek as a commentator and thinker in the postmodern world of psychoanalysis, and the most prominent psychoanalytic writer of the contemporary time. The selection of poetry starts with William Wordsworth as a prime figure in the development of romanticism, with its rejection of the one-sided concentration on rationalism characteristic of the metaphysical poets, and an embrace of emotion as a worthy contributor to truth; the poetry of T.S. Eliot provides an exposé of modernity and its disillusionments; and the work of Brendan Kennelly enables an examination of the global experience of postmodernism. An assertion of Kennelly's articulation of the self between local and global particularities is proposed here, but it is offered in acknowledgement of the fact that the verdict on his contribution awaits historical hindsight. The three poets have been chosen as representative of their literary eras. All nine writers provide exploration, analysis and commentary on the concept of love; each will be examined from their own perspective and from the perspective of their particular historical framework.

Definitions of love abound in myriad forms, sexual, spiritual, parental, brotherly, divine, and many more; terms such as romantic, neighbourly, reciprocal, selfish, altruistic and ethical, variously prefix the concept and appear to suggest a vital difference in their diverse descriptions. It is not my intention to outline the manifold interpretations of the experience of love, nor is it suggested that the meaning of love is reducible to theoretic abstraction, definition or signification. The study refers to inter-personal love in the broadest sense, and does not seek to extrapolate different kinds of love from each other as it is considered that they intermingle in thought and experience. Above all, love is a subjective experience, its communication is essentially personal, and thus it resists easy generalisations and proclamations; this study is undertaken in acknowledgement of the ambiguities and restrictions necessarily ensuing from this reality, and it modestly attempts, through the selected readings, to explore glimpses of an experience which is somehow universally known while also universally disputed: "This is a reality that each one of us knows all too well, even from our own meagre experience of what it means to really love" (Hederman, 2000: 105). Love is something more than the sum of its expressions and the variety of its manifestations, and it is not within the scope of this work to transcend the incommensurable nature of the concept. The subjective nature of love's experience and the difficulties inherent in its articulation and signification is acknowledged here, and thus recourse to language and theory as media of exploration is inevitably limited and incomplete. The focus on the "possibility" of love rather than on the "existence" of love is justified within this argument; the existence of love cannot be measured or validated objectively because it is a metaphysical entity. Consequently, the study is limited to an exploration of the insights of selected thinkers as an avenue towards highlighting at least some of the conditions of the *possibility* of love.

The study is structured in three sections, each dealing with a particular discipline across three historical periods. Section 1 examines, in three separate chapters, the works of Nietzsche, Buber, and Ricoeur as they relate to the thesis question. Chapter One explores a reading of Nietzsche's work concentrated on the following texts: *Beyond Good and Evil, Human, All Too Human, Will to Power, The Genealogy of Morality,* and *Zarathustra.* Within these texts, Nietzsche's arguments relating to the misinterpretation of morality and the corresponding distorted view of human nature are explored with the view to ascertaining how these deceptions and duplicities impact on the experience of love and pose obstacles and distortions to its communication. The possibility of love is explored through a reading of the proclamations articulated in *Zarasthustra,* and particularly through an analysis of Nietzsche's doctrines of eternal recurrence and *amor fati.* Chapter Two outlines Buber's vision of love and the obstacles to its experience through a reading of his works, *I and Thou, The Way of Man,* and *Between Man and Man,* as well as through the recorded memoirs of some of his contemporaries. Topics explored through a reading of these texts include the alluring attraction of crowd membership as an escape from personal responsibility, the practice of monologue as a substitute for dialogue within relationships, and the resulting alienation from the self which negates the communication of love between subjects or selves. The possibility of love, as interpreted through Buber's work, focuses on the concrete, experiential character of love's experience, and on the practical responsibilities incurred in the encounter between I and Thou. Chapter Three examines a selection of Ricoeur's work which reflects his thoughts on the fragmented nature of subjectivity, the narrowing and distorting restrictions on vision and understanding, and the fragility of identity; these are some of the obstacles to the possibility of love which are explored in his work, particularly in the aptly titled texts such as *Fallible Man, Oneself as Another*, and *The Course of Recognition*. Ricoeur's acknowledgement of fallibility and evil in human nature is explored in conjunction with his belief and hope in the possibility of solicitude as an avenue to love of self and others.

Section 2 concentrates on the work of three psychoanalytic writers and the insights into love's possibility which may be gleaned therein. Chapter Four introduces the work of Freud as the originary expression of psychoanalysis. Freud's seminal work, *The Interpretation of Dreams*, is explored, while a selection of Freudian texts is read within collected volumes of his work, such as those edited by Adam Phillips and Peter Gay; these texts are supplemented by a reading of a selection of his private letters. Freud's "discovery" of the unconscious, and his elaboration of its impact on human behaviour and motivation, his observation and description of the many manifestations of psychic conflict, and his theory of repression as a universal human phenomenon, are outlined as they relate to the possibility of love. Freud's exposition of the conflict between the happiness of the individual and the constraints of civilization, as outlined in his work *Civilization and its Discontents*, is considered in the light of the central question of this work, and his unique and often unflattering appraisal of human nature is juxtaposed with his description of the possibility of an art of living based on love. In Chapter Five, the theories and insights of psychoanalysis are further explored through the seminars and *Écrits* (a compilation of selected publications) of the French psychoanalyst, Lacan. Lacan's pronouncements on the paradox of language, the wall of language, and the law of language, suggesting the inescapable alienation and isolation of the human subject constrained by the impossibility of full or complete expression of human existence, are explored. Lacan's vision of the subject and of the human condition, and his cynical and controversial observations of human nature are outlined as possible responses to the question of love's possibility. His assertion of the potential of psychoanalysis to liberate the subject from constraints and denials, and his call for an acknowledgement of the truth of human desire as a prerequisite to the experience of love are examined and discussed. Chapter Six explores a selected reading of the contemporary theorist, Žižek, and concentrates on aspects of his work which are pertinent to the question under inquiry. Texts chosen from his prolific *oeuvre* include characteristically titled works such as *Enjoy Your Symptom!*, *The Plague of Fantasies,* and *The Neighbour*, as well as a selection of articles and essays. Žižek's affirmation of the emergence of the new big Other, an introjected and almost involuntary acquiescence to unspoken laws, rituals and behaviours, especially as they relate to the relationships between human beings, is explored as a barrier to authentic communication, and so to love. His paradoxical response to the dictum of neighbourly love is examined, and his insistence on the unknowable and ungraspable nature of the other is explored as it appears to discount the possibility of love. His demand for truth, for traversing the fantasy, leaves the question open, and his work is increasingly seen to focus on the concept of love in its diverse manifestations.

Section 3 departs from the concentration on theory and introduces a poetic exploration of the topic. Chapter Seven begins with an examination of the work of Wordsworth and his instigation of the principles of literary romanticism. His *Collected Works* is used for reference with a particular focus on his major poems such as "The Prelude", "The Immortality Ode", "Tintern Abbey", and a selection from the shorter poems. This selection is supplemented with his "Preface to the Lyrical Ballads" and with letters and essays of relevance to the topic. Wordsworth's arguments against an over-reliance on rationalism, science and logic, to the exclusion of emotion and imagination, are outlined as an elucidation of some of the obstacles to love. His portrayal of the human experience of inevitable loss and change is explored, particularly in the light of Freud's interpretation of mourning and melancholia as basic reactions to such vicissitudes. The autobiographical nature of "The Prelude" provides a poetic exposition of the relationship between solitude and attachment, self and other, past and present, and these concepts enable a commentary on the possibility of love. Chapter Eight concentrates on the poetry of Eliot as a body of work which reflects many of the characteristics of modernity while also providing a uniquely individual portrayal of the modern subject. His collected works are explored with a special emphasis on "The Love Song of J.Alfred Prufrock", "The Waste Land", and "Four Quartets". Eliot's essays are also examined for the elucidation which they provide in formulating the impetus and motivation of the poet's work. Eliot's portrayal of the modern subject as essentially fragmented, and often split between private and public realities, is analyzed as a commentary on the subject's frequent failure to express his/her needs and desires, and hence as a contributing factor to the failure of love. The failure of language to communicate the innermost depths of human being is explored and linked with the ideas of Buber and Lacan relating to language as a barrier to intersubjectivity and hence to love. The barriers erected and maintained between separate individuals are mirrored in the denial and disavowal of certain aspects of the self as portrayed in Eliot's vision. This loss of self is considered in its impact on the possibility of love, of self and of others. An exploration of the poetry of Kennelly in Chapter Nine expands the realm of the study to the experience of postmodernism, and therefore suggests comparison with the theories of Ricoeur and of Žižek. Indeed, this final chapter, in its discussion of the essential interplay between past and present, in its outline of the postmodern phenomenon of relativism and the loss of traditional meaning and authority, provides a poetic resonance with the thoughts of the writers explored in previous chapters. Kennelly's collected works are the focus of this chapter, with a broad selection across a wide chronological spectrum. This reading is supplemented by an examination of Kennelly's latest publication, *Now,* as well as recorded and published interviews. This section closes with an investigation of Kennelly's persistence and optimism in spite of the vicissitudes, happenchance and unpredictability of human being, and his eloquent celebration of life in all its messiness and elusiveness provides a chorus to the Nietzschean exhortation of *amor fati* of the first chapter.

The reading and the exploration of primary texts is illuminated by a broad contribution from secondary sources, and an attempt is made to draw from these texts a selection balanced between diverse views. While the chosen disciplines, and the individual writers selected therein, are outlined and explored in separate sections and separate chapters, the study attempts a dialogue between these independent and separate realms of thought. Agreement, disagreement, links and divergences are noted and explored. These are highlighted and discussed in the conclusion of the work, which provides an overview of the questions, insights and possible answers resulting from the research.

SECTION I:

PHILOSOPHY

CHAPTER ONE

FRIEDRICH NIETZSCHE

The discipline of philosophy is rooted in its Latin translation, "love of wisdom". The vagueness and ambiguity of this term allows for diverse concentrations in different areas of philosophy, including philosophy of mind, philosophy of language, phenomenology, metaphysics, ethics, and the history of philosophy, to name but a few. Yet the question inevitably arises: what is the wisdom which is loved, and what is its relation to lived experience as distinct from theoretical abstractions? In the words of Martha Nussbaum, this question asks 'what philosophy has to do with the world' (Nussbaum, 1994: 3). The question poses others, such as, what is the function, reason, and significance of philosophy in the realm of human life, and how do the insights and explorations of this discipline reflect, interpret, and enhance the experience of the human condition? A concentration on this question is the focus of the philosophical exploration in this study, and in particular, the philosophical reflections on the concept of love as central to human experience.

In this section, the philosophical reflections of Nietzsche, Buber, and Ricoeur, on the obstacles and barriers to the possibility of love are explored. While the philosophies of Buber and Ricoeur are particularly grounded in an emphasis on relationship as a central and pervading concept in the experience of human living, personal, communal, and political, the choice of Nietzsche, as a philosopher who contributes in a unique way to the discussion of love, is not so immediately validated. It is argued that Nietzsche's philosophy, while dealing in a more obvious way with issues such as 'truth', perspectivism, and 'will to power', is no less concerned with the Platonic and Aristotelian explorations of 'the good', 'practical wisdom', and 'the meaning of love'. Underlying Nietzsche's reflections on morality, philosophy, history, and truth, is a persistent concern with the possibilities and hindrances to optimum human living or flourishing, personal integrity, solitude and connection, happiness and sorrow, and the full spectrum of experience which promotes or diminishes the possibility of love; love of self and of others, manifested in a love of life in all its ambivalence and mystery. Nietzsche sees the enjoyment of life, the inevitable corollary of *amor fati*, or love of one's fate/life, as the most crucial purpose of human living:[1] "As long as men have existed, man has enjoyed himself too little…if we learn better to enjoy ourselves, we best unlearn how to do harm to others and to contrive harm" (Nietzsche, 2003a: 112), and he argues for a truthfulness and a comprehensiveness which would enhance rather than diminish life: "And let that day be lost to us on which we did not dance once! And let that wisdom be false to us that brought no laughter with it!" (Nietzsche, 2003a: 228). Nietzsche's reflections on enjoyment, laughter and celebration of life ("dance"), and his assertion that these experiences are closer to the truth of who we are than experiences based on "false wisdom", suggest the following possibility: the human subject, in every conceivable situation, behaviour and experience, is ultimately striving for joy. This joy is signified diversely as "happiness", "well-being", "feeling good and worthwhile", "having one's needs met", "loving and being loved", and the myriad expressions of what underlines human desire.

Nietzsche's writings, in both style and content, provide an unconventional analysis of the individual subject through a revolutionary appraisal of philosophy, humankind, morality and truth. In rejecting hitherto unquestioned assumptions regarding the human condition, Nietzsche overturns some of our most precious depictions of ourselves and our world. As a radical and revolutionary thinker confronting uncomfortable questions regarding philosophy, psychology, and a host of traditionally held convictions relating to human nature, Nietzsche continues to resound, either in agreement or debate, with all the writers explored in the following chapters. In particular, Nietzsche's writings, through revolutionising our assumptions regarding self and others, morals and values, rationality and instinct, provoke debate and reflection on the actual experience of the human condition, and this inevitably involves an analysis of the concept of love as a central element of human living.

Throughout his work, Nietzsche is critical of the narrowness and deceptions which he sees as characteristic of philosophy throughout history, but especially in his own time. He accuses philosophers of basing their convictions on a biased and distorted view of the human subject, an

---

[1] Slavoj Žižek and other contemporary theorists, offer an ironic version of this idea whereby the injunction to enjoy is exposed as a societal command, an imposition of the superego, and therefore a constraining limitation on the individual; perhaps the dilemma lies in the variously possible interpretations of the concept of enjoyment, ranging from the struggle pertaining to the 'performance' or 'appearance' of enjoyment to a personal and often private experience of joy which is independent of public validation.

assumption of absolutism and certainty in questions of truth and meaning, and an aversion to self-analysis and self-interrogation. He refers to this as "the struggle of belief in opinions, that is, the struggle of convictions" (Nietzsche, 1984: 262), and explains that "conviction is the belief that in some point of knowledge one possesses absolute truth" (Nietzsche, 1984: 261). In contrast, many of Nietzsche's proclamations evoke shock and disbelief, as they blatantly overturn long-held assumptions regarding the human being and the human condition; his philosophy denies the validity of revered concepts of truth, being, will to life, and cause and effect; he rejects conventional interpretations of values such as responsibility, guilt, power and knowledge. The impact of the shock emanating from his thought is intensified by his aphoristic style and unapologetic mode of address. The style and language adopted by Nietzsche is radically different from that of his predecessors, and often reflects his claim that "truth tends to reveal its highest wisdom in the guise of simplicity" (Nietzsche, 1984: 253).

Nietzsche rejects what he perceives as the dogmatism and arrogance of previous philosophers, which, according to his argument, often disguised dishonesty, an ostensible objectivity that is in fact highly subjective. This is the view of Maudmarie Clark: "What Nietzsche objects to in previous philosophers is not that they read their values into the world, but that they pretended to be doing something else" (Clark, 1990: 240). Nietzsche's philosophy is not proffered as a prescription or a roadmap for mankind; he constantly asserts that his thoughts are merely *his* thoughts, *his* interpretations, and *his* truths. He explains that he "came to [his] truth by diverse paths and diverse ways", he insists that "this – is now *my* way", and asks "where is yours?...for *the* way – does not exist!" (Nietzsche: 2003a: 213). The most important questions in life can never be answered by anyone except oneself. This is an assertion which he applies to all philosophy, and it is an individual perspective which is adopted variously by all the writers explored in this study: "It has gradually become clear to me what every great philosophy has hitherto been; a confession on the part of its author and a kind of involuntary memoir" (Nietzsche, 2003: 37). Furthermore, Nietzsche acknowledges the co-existence of concealment and revelation in such confessions: "Every philosophy also *conceals* a philosophy; every opinion is also a hiding-place, every word is also a mask" (Nietzsche, 2003: 216). He looks forward to the philosophers of the future who will embrace these sentiments: "these coming philosophers...will not be dogmatists...[but will assert that] my judgement is [only] *my* judgement" (Nietzsche, 2003: 71). Walter Kaufmann suggests that Nietzsche embodies the characteristics of "these coming philosophers" and that his "greatest value may well lie in the fact that he embodied the true philosophical spirit of 'searching into myself and other men'" (Kaufmann, 1974: xvi). Robert Solomon, in his existential reading of Nietzsche, concurs with this evaluation as he claims that "he is not a philosopher of abstract ideas but rather of the dazzling personal insight, the provocative comment" (Solomon, 2003: 13). Nietzsche bases his reflections, discoveries, and proclamations on actual lived experience as he perceives it, and there is an underlying awareness that his writings, in fact all literature, is secondary to individual experience in the pursuit of personal truth, as he asks: "What *I* find, what *I* am seeking – Was that ever in a book?" (Nietzsche, 1984: 268). His emphasis on actual, concrete experience of human living renders Nietzsche's philosophy vital for this study, as it is a focus often absent from the work of other philosophers, and it is fundamental in an exploration of the concept of love.[2]

Misinterpretation of Morality

> The beast in us wants to be lied to;
> morality is a white lie, to keep it from
> tearing us apart (Nietzsche, 1984: 45).

The possibility of love is a question approached directly and indirectly in Nietzsche's work as he addresses the obstacles and deceptions which militate against love of self, of others, and of life. A major impediment to the experience of love is, according to his argument, the misinterpretation of morality involving an unquestioned acceptance of a range of values and morals which suppress and distort personal truth, motivation and desire. In what is considered his most controversial work, *The Genealogy of Morality*, Nietzsche provides a critique of morality, values and philosophy. In calling for a re-evaluation of all morals, Nietzsche brings into question common assumptions regarding accepted values and moral virtues which have been extolled and encouraged as being inherent to human nature, and which have served to portray an image of humanity which is basically good, well-meaning, and other-centred. Virtues such as altruism, generosity, sympathy, and compassion, have historically been seen as the best expressions of human nature, and are encapsulated in the Christian

---

[2] Concentration on actual lived experience as distinct from abstract theorization is also deemed essential by Buber and Ricoeur, and is a pervading characteristic of all the writers explored in this study; a willingness to look honestly at personal experience is a courage and humility shared by these writers, and their insights are ultimately based on this attempted appraisal of introspection and interrogation.

dictum to love one's neighbour as oneself.[3] Nietzsche rejects the assumption that these virtues are inherent to human nature, that they are natural to humankind, and he disputes any absolutist conception of these virtues. Rather, he argues that "values" and codes of morality are "in a continual state of fluctuation" (Nietzsche, 1984: 53), and he seeks to expose the cultural and historical relativity of our values, crucially our moral values, "the utility which dominates moral value-judgements" (Nietzsche, 2003: 122); in so doing he casts a particularly critical and sceptical eye on Christian sources of morality. The deleterious effect of unrealistic codes of morality results, according to Nietzsche, in a diminishment of human experience and a distorted appraisal of the human subject: "All these moralities...[are] recipes to counter his passions" (Nietzsche, 2003: 119). This is particularly evident in the concept of love: "Christianity gave Eros poison to drink – and he did not die of it, to be sure, but degenerated into vice" (Nietzsche, 2003: 105).[4] The poet, D.H. Laurence, describes this as "the mess of love": "We've made a great mess of love, / Since we made an ideal of it" (Laurence, 2002: 387). According to Nietzsche's argument, many assumptions, norms and practices that are accepted as inevitable and unavoidable in fact have a contingent, utilitarian and relativist character. It could be argued that the importance of modern literary theory lies in its unveiling of values that appear natural and self-evident as contrived and created, whether relating to language, identity, otherness, morality or sexuality. In this way Nietzsche can be seen as precursor to this mode of thinking, and this creates a strong link between his work and that of the theorists discussed later in the study.

Nietzsche's genealogy of morals suggests that all moral values, rather than being natural and inherent to human existence, actually serve the interests of influential groups or institutions. Morality is, in this analysis, a body of rules which has come down through centuries, appropriated by a religion or a culture, and uncritically received and accepted. Nietzsche maintains that moralities are essentially instruments of social control, usually related to the establishment or preservation of the interests of one group or another. " 'Value' is essentially the standpoint for the increase or decrease of...dominating centres" (Nietzsche, 1968: 715). This critique of "dominating centres" is expanded in the deconstruction of Western

---

[3] This dictum of universal love is debated in diverse ways by many of the writers explored below, i.e., Freud, Lacan and Žižek.

[4] The distortion and perversion of love through a religious pronouncement on the superiority of divine love and the denigration of human love is a theme explored in Kennelly's poetry, while Eliot's work progressively turns to divine love as the ideal.

metaphysics undertaken by the French philosopher, Jacques Derrida. Like Nietzsche, Derrida argues that centres or hegemonies validate themselves by making their situation at the centre seem natural and fixed, and by perpetuating the illusion of binary oppositions such as male/female, nature/culture, and mind/body. He suggests that it is necessary to consider "that the centre had no natural site, that it was not a fixed locus but a function", and he looks to "the Nietzschean critique of metaphysics, the critique of the concepts of being and truth…and the Freudian critique of self-presence, that is, the critique of consciousness" in outlining his attempt to deconstruct these "centres" (Derrida, 1981: 280).

Nietzsche's attack on morality centres on its commitment to untenable claims about human nature, and on what he sees as the deleterious impact which these claims have had on the flourishing of life; deception, resentment, and guilt ensue: "how dearly the erection of every ideal on earth has exacted its payment? How much reality always had to be libelled and mistaken, how much lying sanctified, how much conscience disturbed?" (Nietzsche, 1998: 65). Nietzsche promotes his argument by insisting on a re-examination of the origins of these values, and thereby he seeks to expose their historical and utilitarian character. Thus, his attack is not centred primarily on the nature of the values and morals which are accepted unquestionably as "good" and "true"; he insists on the necessity of examining the origins of these values as a route to understanding their historical and cultural sources. According to Solomon, "Nietzsche's genealogy of morals is, first of all, a thesis about the motivation of morality" (Solomon, 2003: 54). Nietzsche argues that the true nature of morality can only be approached if one analyses and acknowledges the sources and purposes of moral teaching, and hence he calls for a more honest, a more factual appraisal of human nature. He insists that moral values do not exist in themselves; they are not absolute or transcendent, and they can be modified according to changing situations and circumstances: "Unchanging good and evil does not exist!" (Nietzsche, 2003a: 139). This appraisal would relinquish the possibility of fixed absolutes, in relation to truth, goodness, or the human being. As Richard Kearney states: "Nietzsche's project of transvaluation effected not only the moral question of good but also the epistemological question of truth. The age-old quest for absolute truth is now exposed as a hidden will to power" (Kearney, 1998: 212).

Nietzsche's question regarding our values of good and evil is, "have they inhibited or furthered human flourishing up until now? Are they are a sign of distress, of impoverishment, of the degeneration of life?" (Nietzsche, 1998: 3). Only by recognising the pragmatic nature of all morals, and by acknowledging the premise and the purpose of all ethical rules and judgements, can we, according to Nietzsche, attempt to come to terms with the multi-faceted character of life as we experience it. Such honesty, involving the abandonment of established "ideals" which act as a barrier to instinct, passion, and an appreciation of human nature as it is, inevitably results in a transitional period of nihilism, an uneasiness portrayed in the literature of the age;[5] but, it is, according to Nietzsche, prerequisite to overcoming the resentment inherent in a slave morality, whereby individual responsibility is sacrificed for the illusions of certainty and truth, social and personal guidelines, and a fixed script of rules and expectations.[6] These assumptions and limitations alienate the subject from individual truth and expression: "The first opinion that occurs to us when we are suddenly asked about a matter is usually not our own, but only the customary one, appropriate to our caste, position, or parentage; our own opinions seldom swim near the surface" (Nietzsche, 1984: 245).

Nietzsche disputes any inherent or consistent meaning pertaining to the concepts of good and evil, and suggests that such signifiers are conditioned by historical and cultural fluctuations. On this point, Alexander Nehamas, in his interpretation of Nietzsche's philosophy in *Nietzsche: Life as Literature,* draws a comparison between the thought of Nietzsche and that of Socrates: "Nietzsche argues in a manner very close to the manner of Socrates that what we commonly consider good depends essentially on the context that we implicitly introduce into our evaluation, and that it is not therefore good in itself" (Nehamas, 1985: 212). In his analysis of the history of philosophy, Nietzsche suggests an absence of honesty in relation to these matters: "The errors of the great philosophers usually start from a false explanation of certain human actions and feelings....an erroneous analysis of so-called selfless behaviour, for example, can be the basis for false ethics" (Nietzsche, 1984: 41). Solomon argues that Nietzsche's criticism of philosophy is based on the tendency of philosophers to "ignore the concrete social and psychological situations out of which ideas, ideologies, and whole philosophies are born" (Solomon, 2000: 45).

Nietzsche challenges the foundations of traditional thought; he calls for

---

[5] The sense of disillusionment, alienation and hopelessness which characterizes much of the literature of modernism is characteristic of Nietzsche's analysis of nihilism, and it is particularly captured in the poetry of Eliot.

[6] The abdication of personal responsibility and the embrace of "collective" and popular assumptions of authority and truth is also seen by Buber as an impediment to genuine relationship. Directly and indirectly, all the writers explored in this study concur with this analysis.

a questioning of everything, especially the concepts through which we have viewed the world and ourselves without seeing their underlying assumptions and deceptions. He demands that we reconsider what we have taken for granted, and that we consider afresh what a good human life consists of, by putting our usual assumptions about the world into brackets. Nehamas, in his discussion of Nietzsche's *Genealogy of Morals,* states that "Nietzsche's opposition to traditional histories of morality and his sometimes extravagant claims for the novelty and importance of his own approach are primarily caused by his aversion to this linear or static conception of the nature of values and institutions" (Nehamas, 1985: 112). The Italian poet, Antonio Porchia concurs with this critique of the narrowness of linear thinking and vision: "Following straight lines shortens distances, and also life" (Porchia, 2003: 43), while William Blake notes what is sacrificed in the attempted "improvement" of human nature: "Improvement makes strait roads; but the crooked roads / without improvement are roads of Genius" (Blake, 2004: 139). In probing the inconsistencies and deceptions which form the background of much of our convictions about ourselves and our world, Nietzsche, like Freud, calls into question our illusions of self-knowledge and self-awareness: "We remain of necessity strangers to ourselves, we do not understand ourselves, we must mistake ourselves, for us the maxim reads to all eternity; 'each is furthest from himself'- with respect to ourselves we are not 'knowers'" (Nietzsche, 1998: 1), and he suggests that self-deception is sometimes chosen, either consciously or unconsciously: "Where my honesty ceases I am blind and want to be blind" (Nietzsche, 2003a: 264).

Freud later reiterates this assertion that we can never fully know ourselves, particularly in the light of his description of the unconscious as a part of mental life over which we have little or no control, and which can be aptly described as a stranger in the house, suggesting its inaccessibility and alienation from rational thinking. Thus Nietzsche claims that "Man is difficult to discover, most of all to himself" (Nietzsche, 2003a: 212). The impossibility of complete self-transparency may be difficult to acknowledge, and this difficulty is also an obstacle to the acceptance of the alterity of the other as something which can never be fully penetrated; the state of "unknowing" discomfits the demands and expectations of human pride and propels an insistent desire to "know" and so to evaluate that which cannot be known. Derrida looks to Nietzsche's analysis of this dilemma as part of his exploration of love and friendship, and he concludes that love and friendship involve an acceptance of distance and "unknowing": "Whereby those who are separated come together without ceasing to be what they are destined to be...dissociated, 'solitarized', singularized, constituted into monadic alterities...what is proper to the *alter* ego will never be accessible" (Derrida, 2005: 54). Accordingly, love of the other is possible in an acknowledgement that one can never fully know another, and in a gracious appreciation of this difference and mystery.

Nietzsche philosophizes from "the perspective of life", from the awareness that all knowledge is ultimately based on one's interpretation of reality, on one's experience in the world. He therefore urges an expansion of this experience to include a broad spectrum of perspectives and interpretations:

> There is only a perspectival seeing, only a perspectival 'knowing'; and the more affects we allow to speak about a matter, the more eyes, different eyes, we know how to bring to bear on one and the same matter, that much more complete will our 'concept' of this matter, our 'objectivity' be (Nietzsche, 1998: 85).[7]

According to Nietzsche, our lack of self-knowledge is mirrored in our crippling dependence on overly rationalistic or metaphysical conceptions of human nature, and on external sources of value, such as religion and society. This one-sided and distorted view of human nature has, in Nietzsche's view, been mirrored in traditional philosophy, a criticism which is echoed by Nussbaum: "Philosophy has often seen itself as a way of transcending the merely human", and she suggests a different possibility: "The alternative I explore sees it as a way of being human and speaking humanly" (Nussbaum, 1992: 53). Nietzsche urges us to abandon the false certainties which we have unknowingly inherited and internalised, and concludes that there are no absolutes, no certainties, no "truth", only the unique experience of the individual. Only then, when we face the reality of our experience, of ourselves and of the world, can we begin to confront the actual obstacles to our experience of love and happiness. The absence of this honest encounter with reality ensures that we recoil from life as it is, and therefore dismiss the challenge to overcome the barriers to self-knowledge and self-fulfilment. What is not faced, acknowledged, and accepted, persists, and cannot be changed.

---

[7] This plea for the acceptance of a plurality of perspectives resounds with the other writers explored in this study, and pre-empts a central characteristic of postmodernism.

Distorted View of Human Nature

> For all too long man has regarded his
> natural inclinations with an 'evil' eye
> (Nietzsche, 1998: 65).

The desire to love and to be loved can only be genuinely pursued within an honest, albeit constantly changing, acknowledgement of human nature. Without this acceptance, the experience of love is supplanted by fantasy and pretence, where the flesh and blood reality of self and other is camouflaged by denial of certain aspects of human nature and exaggeration of more acceptable traits; the result is an array of pseudo-loving encounters which recoil from the complex and ungraspable nature of living relationships. This distorted view of human nature is necessitated and maintained by the demands and expectations of civilization and socialization, and clearly functions as an impediment or obstacle to love. Nietzsche sees the evolution of civilization, and the changes and adaptations that this has entailed, as both a blessing and a curse on the actual life of the individual. While accepting the practical necessity of some control and order which civilization inevitably imposes on the citizens of particular societies, he laments the corresponding loss of life-affirming and life-enhancing values which he ascribes to the Dionysian world-view of ancient Greece. Qualities such as power, aggression, mastery, self-advancement and the full embrace of all that humanity is, are, according to Nietzsche, since the advent of Christianity especially, denigrated as sinful and evil. Under the influence of established institutions such as Church, state, and the prevalent conventions of legal and penal systems, these values have been replaced by euphonic qualities; humility, service, pity, sacrifice, and self-effacement are now established as the ideal components of love and goodness, and are encouraged as essential guidelines in the living of a good life. Nietzsche rejects this diminishment of life as it is: "all those aspirations to go beyond, to that which is contrary to the senses, contrary to the instincts, contrary to nature, contrary to the animal…libel the world" (Nietzsche, 1998: 65). However, in attempting to uncover the origins of these values, Nietzsche rejects the possibility that they are natural, actual, or unequivocally beneficial to human life. He suggests that powerful institutions of Church and state have wittingly imposed these unrealistic ideals in order to establish and maintain their positions of power and authority. Acceptance of these values has been enabled by offering the reward of an other-worldly existence, the comfort of an all-seeing, all-knowing, all-powerful deity, and the relaxation consequent to a diminished sense of personal freedom and responsibility: "For out of fear and need each religion is born, creeping into existence on the byways of reason" (Nietzsche, 1984: 79).[8]

Hence the emergence of a herd-mentality, where morality is grounded in the anonymity of the crowd, and where security is sought in the euphoria of consensus. This compliance to the herd-mentality constricts individual spontaneity and freedom, and forbids the expression of many natural experiences: sexuality, aggression, hatred and anger are denigrated as evil; concealment and subterfuge are inevitable, and empirical experience in the here and now is devalued: "Many men wait all their lives for the opportunity to be good in *their* way" (Nietzsche, 1984: 243). Adherence to public expectations, concern with recognition and acceptance, and consciousness of image and reputation, result in loss of self: "Who has not for the sake of his reputation – sacrificed himself?" (Nietzsche, 2003: 94).[9] This need to belong, this fear of one's separateness and difference, is outlined as one of the obstacles to love by the psychoanalyst, Erich Fromm, in his exploration of the topic, *The Art of Loving*, and is referred to as "fusion without integrity" (Fromm, 1995: 16).[10] Nietzsche argues that such escapism, deception, and rejection of reality, rather than enhancing life, diminishes and weakens the human being, and thus inhibits the possibility of experiencing the full spectrum of human existence. Although he states that "there is much in man that is horrifying" (Nietzsche, 1998: 64), Nietzsche argues that the repression of this fact entails a simultaneous blindness to human goodness and potential: "Much hidden goodness and power is never guessed at; the most exquisite daisies find no tasters!" (Nietzsche, 2003a: 212). The possibility of love, as part of this spectrum, is therefore blocked and distorted.

The unquestioned acceptance of artificial dualities such as mind/body, appearance/reality, human/nature, and good/evil, is seen by Nietzsche as

---

[8] The "fear" and "need" which, according to Nietzsche, propel religious fervour and conviction, as well as other doctrines which purport to explain/guide/judge human existence, resonates in some way with Freud's theory of the superego and with Lacan's exposition of "The Big Other" as an internalized system of self-governance. Nietzsche's word choice in the phrase – "*creeping* into existence on the byways of *reason*" (emphases mine) prompts a questioning of "reason" as an infallible source of truth. It resounds with Wordsworth's arguments against an over-reliance on reason to the exclusion of feeling and imagination.

[9] Sacrifice and loss of self in pursuit of public acceptance is a theme addressed by the other writers explored here, and is given vivid expression in the persona of Eliot's "Prufrock".

[10] Buber also refers to this craving to belong, and he differentiates between collectivity, as a type of "fusion without integrity", and community, where individuals attempt to relate to each other as authentic human beings.

both originating from and contributing towards, a denial of life as it is, and particularly of humanity as it is: "The false opposites...have always been dangerous hindrances to the advance of truth" (Nietzsche, 1968: 371).[11] The resulting deception posits reason as superior to sensual experience,[12] suggests a "reality" beyond what is perceived by the senses, elevates "human" unrealistically above the realm of animal passion and instinct, and imposes impossible judgements of good and evil which disavow the inevitable ambiguity inherent in all such concepts. This critique of a distorted portrayal of human nature, which has hitherto been prevalent in Western philosophy, is the starting point for the French philosopher/psychoanalyst, Luce Irigaray, in her work, *the Way of Love*, which she introduces with a call for "a philosophy which involves the whole of a human and not only that mental part of ourselves" (Irigaray, 2002: ix). She defines this philosophy as "the wisdom of love", and argues that:

> This possible interpretation would imply that philosophy joins together, more than it has done in the West, the body, the heart, and the mind. That it is not founded on contempt for nature. That it not resort to a logic that formalizes the real by removing it from concrete experience; that it be less a normative science of the truth than the search for measures that help in living better: with oneself, with others, with the world (Irigaray, 2002: 2).

Her call for a more holistic, and a more realistic assessment of the human being concurs with Nietzsche's exhortation to see the human condition as it really is, in all its complexity and ambivalence: "we who are of a mixed nature, sometimes aglow with fire and sometimes chilled by intellect" (Nietzsche, 1984: 266), and echoes his conviction that morality and philosophy are sometimes "founded on contempt for nature", and consequently diminish life and being: "Every morality is...a piece of tyranny against 'nature'...it is a protracted constraint" (Nietzsche, 2003: 110).

In exposition of his argument, Nietzsche examines, with ruthless self-scrutiny, so-called virtues such as gratitude, pity and generosity. He probes beneath the surface interpretation of behaviour based on these values, and suggests that in many cases, self-interest, fear, and will to power provide the real motivational drive of such behaviours. In outlining this drive as "self-enjoyment", Nietzsche's description finds echoes in Freud's theory

---

[11] These "false opposites" resonate with Derrida's false binaries mentioned above.
[12] Wordsworth is also critical of the exaltation of reason above the realms of feeling and imagination.

of the "pleasure principle":

> Good actions are sublimated evil actions; evil actions are good actions
> become coarse and stupid. The individual's only demand, for self-
> enjoyment (along with the fear of losing it), is satisfied in all
> circumstances: man may act as he can, that is, as he must, whether in deeds
> of vanity, revenge, pleasure, usefulness, malice, cunning, or in deeds of
> sacrifice, pity, knowledge. His powers of judgement determine where a
> man will let this demand for self-enjoyment take him (Nietzsche, 1984:
> 75).

Nietzsche is here asserting a truth which, though often denied and debated, is somehow familiar to human experience, albeit at an unconscious level much of the time: the behaviour of the human subject, across the spectrum including selfishness, altruism, love, hatred, aggression, gentleness, is, at some level, always motivated by self-interest, by the desire to "feel good" about oneself, and by the urge to self-preservation in diverse areas of experience. Nietzsche looks behind the physical and verbal expression of an array of familiarly understood emotions – compassion, sympathy, outrage, grief - and suggests that behind the outward show of expected response lurks an ever-present concern with audience, image and impression: "Ultimately, not even the deepest pain can keep the actor from thinking of the impression of his part and the overall theatrical effect" (Nietzsche, 1984: 50). Following this assertion, Nietzsche continues to give detailed analyses of the less accepted motivational direction of a wide range of "good" and admirable behaviour. Gratitude is exposed as empowering the giver rather than the benefactor; pity is portrayed as being evoked as evidence of power within the pitiable individual;[13] and punishment is revealed as "the means to frighten others away from certain future actions" rather than having any intrinsic relation to the crime or its perpetrator (Nietzsche, 1984: 73). Nietzsche therefore expresses a warning: "distrust all in whom the urge to punish is strong" (Nietzsche, 2003a: 124), and he is adamant in his assertion of the contradictions inherent in the desire for punishment: " 'Punishment' is what revenge calls itself; it feigns a good conscience for itself with a lie [because] no deed can be annihilated: how could a deed be undone through punishment?" (Nietzsche, 2003a: 162). The duplicity, conscious or unconscious,

---

[13] Many of the writers explored in this study offer interpretations of the phenomenon of pity; these interpretations range from an analysis of pity as something which empowers the individual evoking the emotion to an assertion that pity is often motivated by a sense of superiority and disdain which is patronizing and/or disguised.

underlying many "moral" virtues, entails a contradiction between theoretic ideals and hidden motivation; the concept of love is often abused in this way, for example: "Ultimately 'love of one's neighbour' is always something secondary, in part conventional and arbitrarily illusory, when compared with fear of one's neighbour" (Nietzsche, 2003: 123). Freud also refers to the "hypocrisy" whereby *the suppression and inversion of affects* is useful…in social life" (Freud, 1997: 320), and proceeds to offer some easily recognizable examples: "If I am master of the art of dissimulation I can hypocritically display the opposite affect – smiling where I should like to be angry, and pretending affection where I should like to destroy" (Freud, 1997: 321). Public expressions of moral rectitude often belie a different personal perspective: "Men are not ashamed to think something dirty, but they are ashamed when they imagine that others might believe them capable of these dirty thoughts" (Nietzsche, 1984: 62).[14] In summary, human motivation and behaviour are often ambiguously inspired, and transcend the polarities of good and evil: "Our actions shine alternately in differing colours, they are seldom unequivocal – and there are cases enough in which we perform *many-coloured* actions" (Nietzsche, 2003: 148).

The deception involved in denying the self-serving impetus underlying much of one's virtuous behaviour militates, according to Nietzsche, against authentic confrontation with self and others; the experience of love, friendship, and mutuality is forfeited through an embrace of "safer", less-demanding, weaker forms of pseudo-intimacy and approval-seeking performances; dismissal of one's ambiguity diminishes one's engagement with life, and muffles one's experience with a cloak of security and fear. Nietzsche sees in this willingness of the subject "to let itself be deceived", a rejection of alternative possibilities and perspectives:

> a sudden decision for ignorance, for arbitrary shutting-out, a closing of the window, an inner denial of this or that thing, a refusal to let it approach, a kind of defensive posture against much that can be known, a contentment with the dark, with the closed horizon, an acceptance and approval of ignorance (Nietzsche, 2003: 161).

The passive and outward acceptance of a world view which suppresses much of our natural inclinations, and the ensuing frustration of life, results in an ongoing cycle of resentment, guilt, and atonement, "where universal slow suicide is called – life" (Nietzsche, 2003a: 77). The repression of the

---

[14] In a similar vein, Lacan is sceptical of the professed motivation of philanthropic acts.

individual's human nature does not obliterate it: "All instincts that do not discharge themselves outwardly *turn themselves inwards*" (Nietzsche, 1998: 57); as Freud later discovered, what is repressed finds expression in intra-psychic and inter-relational conflict, personal and social discontent, and private and public negation of life and love. A reluctance to embrace a more realistic and integrative appraisal of the motivation of human behaviour is accepted as understandable and predictable by Solomon in his discussion of Nietzsche's theories, but he admits a recognition of the truth of these theories: "Much of what Nietzsche says about pity is quite outrageous, but at least some of what he says strikes us as exactly on the mark. How often is our supposed compassion a mask for our sense of superiority, or at least, our relief that the victim wasn't us?" (Solomon, 2000: 208). In a poem exploring "the fruit of Deceit", William Blake echoes this sentiment: "Pity would be no more / If we did not make somebody poor" (Blake, 2004: 76). Ricoeur makes a similar point when he differentiates sympathy from "simple pity, in which the self is secretly pleased to know it has been spared" (Ricoeur, 1992: 191). Solomon argues from this analysis that Nietzsche's exposure of deception and pretence inherent in much of human behaviour paradoxically, and simultaneously, enables a more honest and realistic acknowledgement of the baseness and the greatness which constitute the potential of human being (Solomon, 2000: 208). Light *and* shadow are essential components of human being. Nietzsche argues for a comprehensive integration of all aspects of human nature, free of moralistic and guilt-inducing judgements of good and evil: "The great epochs of our life are the occasions when we gain the courage to rebaptize our evil qualities as our best qualities" (Nietzsche, 2003: 97).[15] Only thus – and not in a vacuum of deception and pretence - can love of self and other be experienced.

Fear of Freedom and Responsibility

> We wish that there will one day no
> longer be anything to fear! (Nietzsche,
> 2003: 124).

Fear of confronting the complex, ambiguous, and contradictory nature of being human, has, according to Nietzsche's philosophy, diminished and

---

[15] The work of the Italian poet Antonio Porchia, *Voices*, has many Nietzschean echoes, both in its aphoristic style and in its embrace of apparent contradictions: "That in man which cannot be domesticated is not his evil but his goodness" (Porchia, 2003: 31).

weakened human life by cutting off the joys and tribulations of experiencing all that a person is. "For fear – that is man's original and fundamental sensation" (Nietzsche, 2003a: 312). Fear of embracing the potentiality and danger, the uncertainty and ambivalence of individual freedom and responsibility, curtails the possibility of love, as priority is directed towards the attainment of security, recognition and identity through externally imposed standards and definitions. The child-like yearning for an external authoritative and protecting figure, the rejection of instinctual and sensual realities, and the exclusive emphasis on rationality as characteristic of human nature, is fuelled by the forces of civilization and by the constraints of individual and private concerns: "As soon as we imagine someone who is responsible for our being thus and thus, etc. (God, nature), and therefore attribute to him the intention that we should exist and be happy or wretched, we corrupt for ourselves the *innocence of becoming*" (Nietzsche, 1968: 299). As Sartre later argued, man is afraid of his freedom, he is terrified of his own power to choose, and he seeks refuge in the safety and anonymity of the crowd. Seeking security in conformity, "the cowardly man always said 'no' inwardly, [and] he always said 'yes' with his lips" (Nietzsche, 1984: 59). The hidden conflict of this contradiction is the price of this pseudo-belonging, and Nietzsche suggests as a more life-enhancing alternative the welcoming acceptance of difference and diversity: "rather than making oneself uniform, we may find greater value for the enrichment of knowledge by listening to the soft voice of different life situations" (Nietzsche, 1984: 256).

Afraid to face the reality of himself or herself, the subject prefers to attain consolation from distorted versions of "mankind", and promotes rules and judgements in an endeavour to keep these distortions in place: "Thus they have eliminated the affects one by one…[and] placed reality in the negation of the desires and effects" (Nietzsche, 1968: 309). The individual refuses a more comprehensive awareness of what he/she is, and similarly prevents an encounter with the full range of possibility inherent in others. The result is a negation of life in all its complexity and possibility, a resentment which opposes a love of life in all its manifestations and results in "the tired pessimistic glance, the mistrust toward the riddle of life, the icy 'no' of disgust at life" (Nietzsche, 1998: 43). Mistrust and fear result in avoidance of life in its complexity and richness, and the possibility of love is averted because, "love desires; fear avoids…love acknowledges no power, nothing that separates, differentiates, ranks higher or subordinates" (Nietzsche, 1984: 252).

Nietzsche urges an integration of all the complexities and ambiguities of the individual subject, rather than a selective and exclusive depiction. In the words of Nehamas, "in Nietzsche's view every aspect of the personality is equally essential to it" (Nehamas, 1985: 159). What is not welcomed and accepted as laudable and "good" is often projected onto others, whether in the guise of criminality, madness, or evil.[16] Nietzsche explains the attraction of this phenomenon as the desire to escape from the reality of the self:

> When, as happens so often, we let our annoyance out on others, while we are actually feeling it about ourselves, we are basically trying to cloud and delude our judgement; we want to motivate our annoyance *a posteriori* by the oversights and inadequacies of others, so that we can lose sight of ourselves (Nietzsche, 1984: 253).

The individual therefore attempts to escape from the demands of personal responsibility, and seeks refuge in the bland mediocrity of "normal" humanity, "the inevitable dominion of the average" (Nietzsche, 1968: 364), where less acceptable traits and drives are disowned and denied: "To this end, they need an appearance of justice, i.e., a theory through which they can shift responsibility for their existence, for their being thus and thus, on to some sort of scapegoat" (Nietzsche, 1968: 400).[17]

Kaufmann, in his prolific commentary on Nietzsche's philosophy, traces the origins of many contemporary ideas on subjects such as alienation, depression, resentment and guilt back to Nietzsche's insights, and he credits Nietzsche with counteracting "the ostrich prudery of his age" (Kaufmann, 1974: 274). Release from the fear of responsibility, however, necessitates a simultaneous release from the fear of freedom. The freedom which is feared is the freedom to create oneself and one's life, to be master of oneself in all one's humanness, and to embrace with honesty and courage what one is at any moment. Nietzsche accepts the presence of fear as a pervading experience of living, but he argues for the necessity of meeting this fear with courage and honesty: "He possesses heart who knows fear but masters fear; who sees the abyss, but sees it with pride" (Nietzsche, 2003a: 298). Solomon gives the following appraisal of

---

[16] This concept of projection, a hall-mark of psychoanalysis, is radically explored by Michel Foucault, in his analysis of institutions such as Church, state, education, judiciary and medicine, as sources of manipulation and control.

[17] The evasion of responsibility and the projection of evil onto convenient scapegoats is a recurring theme in the works explored below; for example, Kennelly's epic poems, "Cromwell" and "The Book of Judas". It is also explored in Richard Kearney's *Scapegoats, Gods, and Monsters*, and Julia Kristeva's *Strangers to Ourselves*.

Nietzsche's thoughts on fear and courage:

> Courage, for Nietzsche, refers not so much to over-coming fear (the
> standard account) or having 'just the right amount' of fear (Aristotle's
> account), and it certainly doesn't mean having no fear (the pathological
> conception of courage). Rather, as in so many of his conceptions of virtue,
> Nietzsche has a model of 'over-flowing' – overflowing with an
> assertiveness that overwhelms fear (Solomon, 2000: 183).

In contrast to this courage, the selective rejection of aspects of one's
humanness precludes a genuine encounter with oneself, and consequently
prevents an encounter with another in the fullness of his/her being; the
experience of love is therefore blocked and thwarted.

The dichotomy between human nature as it is and the ideals which are
promoted as human aspirations is attacked by Nietzsche as a negation of
life. He abhors the elevation of one aspect of being human to the detriment
of another, and he advocates an embracing of the totality of life, with all
its uncertainties and frustrations. He calls for a translation of "man back
into nature; to master the many vain and fanciful interpretations and
secondary meanings which have been hitherto scribbled and daubed over
that eternal basic text *homo natura*" (Nietzsche, 2003: 162). He tells us
that "there is more reason in your body than in your best wisdom"
(Nietzsche, 2003a: 62), that our senses are the instruments whereby we
relate to the world: "All credibility, all good conscience, all evidence of
truth comes only from the senses" (Nietzsche, 2003: 100), and that our
instincts, all of them, are central to our nature and cannot be successfully
denied or censored; they are, like all of life, "beyond good and evil".

Acknowledgement of human nature as it is, acceptance of
contradiction and uncertainty in human living, and accommodation of the
reality of personal freedom and responsibility, opens the way, according to
Nietzsche, for the emergence of an affirmative nihilism, whereby we
construct our own values, our own truth, our own life, our own self: "To
live as I desire to live or not to live at all" (Nietzsche, 2003a: 285). In the
words of Solomon, "Nietzsche insists that each of us must find our own
way" (Solomon, 2003: 139). This ideal of self-creation, "become what you
are!" (Nietzsche, 2003a: 252), explored by Nietzsche through the
prophetic reflections of *Zarathustra*, confronts the joys and tribulations of
personal freedom which insists that the subject "must become judge and
avenger and victim of its own law" (Nietzsche, 2003: 137). It insists on the
necessity of self-belief: "Only dare to believe in yourselves – in yourselves
and in your entrails! He who does not believe in himself always lies"
(Nietzsche, 2003a: 146). Genuine self-belief involves an acceptance that

one is not supernaturally wonderful or hopelessly despicable, but humanly complex and indefinable. It demands a rejection of the illusions of external sources of values and authority and the defences of projection and conformity; it accepts the self as the ultimate creator and evaluator of one's life: "One should not avoid one's tests...tests which are taken before ourselves and before no other judge" (Nietzsche, 2003: 70).

Self-Acceptance and Amor Fati

> Go out to where the world awaits you
> like a garden (Nietzsche, 2003a: 236).

Confronting the obstacles and difficulties which diminish human living enables Nietzsche to affirm the possibility of love within this imperfect realm. His critique of morality, duplicity and conformity is motivated by an insistent assertion of love's central force in human life: 'Good nature, friendliness, and courtesy of the heart are ever-flowing tributaries of the selfless drive and have made much greater contributions to culture than those much more famous expressions of this drive, called pity, charity, and self-sacrifice' (Nietzsche, 1984: 48). Acceptance of the multi-faceted nature of the self enables an acceptance of the experience of life in all its manifestations, and opens the way towards the possibility of love, of self, of others, and of life, *amor fati*.

In his doctrine of the eternal recurrence Nietzsche offers a theoretical formulation of a "test" whereby life is embraced and loved. According to Nehamas, "the eternal recurrence is not a theory of the world, but a view of the self" (Nehamas, 2002: 150), and Solomon argues that Nietzsche presents "eternal recurrence...as a 'test' of our attitudes towards life" (Solomon, 2003: 14). Anticipating Ricoeur's theory of narrative identity as fluid and ongoing, Nietzsche claims that the individual's life is a continuum of creation, and that it is constructed and reconstructed again and again: "Existence begins in every instant" (Nietzsche, 2003a: 234). He sees life as the ongoing creation of the self. Accordingly, the idea of a fixed self, ego or soul is a mere fiction; there is no being, only becoming. Life is synonymous with change; avoidance of the risks inherent to change may provide illusory comfort and security, but only at the cost of stagnation and death. An affirmation of life necessitates an acceptance of this fluidity, and a simultaneous acknowledgement of the individual's unique power of self-creation as a continually evolving endeavour. This is not a static response to selected experiences, but rather a love of life in its totality; a positive response to life must embrace and integrate every experience, joyful and sorrowful, proud and shameful, loving and hateful, for, Nietzsche argues, one can only accept a particular experience if one accepts that all of the events and experiences of one's life have directly or indirectly led to this moment. Thus, nothing can be denied or regretted; everything is essential to the process of becoming, and what one is at any moment encompasses all of one's experience, past and present. Nietzsche poses the question:

> What if some day or night a demon were to steal into your loneliest loneliness and say to you: 'This life as you now live and have lived it you will have to live once again and innumerable times again; and there will be nothing new in it, but every pain and every joy and every thought and sigh and everything unspeakably small or great in your life must return to you, all in the same succession and sequence – even this spider and this moonlight between the trees, and even this moment and I myself....the question in each and every thing, 'do you want this again and innumerable times again?' would lie on your actions as the heaviest weight! Or how well disposed would you have to become to yourself and to life *to long for nothing more fervently* than for this ultimate eternal confirmation and seal? (Nietzsche, 1974: 341).[18]

The frightening possibility of endlessly replaying the single life we each have, and the demand that we affirm everything that we have experienced in that life, is, according to Nietzsche, an approach by which we can strive towards a celebration of life as it is. In a poem titled "A Dialogue of Self and Soul", Yeats echoes the possible connection between the eternal recurrence and *amor fati*:

> I am content to live it all again
> And yet again....
> I am content to follow to its source
> Every event in action or in thought;
> Measure the lot; forgive myself the lot!
> When such as I cast out remorse

---

[18] While many commentators, such as Maudmarie Clark and Robert Solomon, stress the "theoretical" nature of Nietzsche's question, I query another aspect of its interpretation: is Nietzsche calling for an affirmative acknowledgement of all of one's actions throughout one's life, or is he demanding a joyous acceptance of all the events which have been experienced by the individual? The former is a recipe for genuine self-acceptance, but the latter is, in my view, often impossible, self-contradictory and overly simplistic. An application of this interpretation of eternal recurrence to human tragedies, natural and man-made, personal and global, private and public, suggests the absence of an easy answer.

> So great a sweetness flows into the breast
> We must laugh and we must sing,
> We are blest by everything,
> Everything we look upon is blest (Yeats, 1967: 145).

The theoretical and conditional nature of the eternal recurrence – "if", "would", etc. – is given more concrete form as Nietzsche particularises the question: "Did you ever say Yes to one joy?...then you said Yes to *all* woe as well. All things are chained and entwined together, all things are in love" (Nietzsche, 2003a: 332). According to Clark, the eternal recurrence is "a test of affirmation…one's affirmation of life" (Clark, 1990: 270). This affirmation of life, *amor fati,* implies an acceptance of one's fate,[19] a delight in all aspects of life, an accommodation of chance, accident and uncertainty. This is a life lived without regret, remorse or guilt, but open to love, of self, others, and the world as it is experienced in all its manifestations; the possibility of love is closely related to acceptance and love of life: "we love life, not because we are used to living but because we are used to loving" (Nietzsche, 2003a: 68). Nietzsche believes in the interconnectedness of all our actions; what one is at any moment is influenced and created by all of one's past. To live one's life in such a way that one wants it again, helps us to make a selection of what is important and significant for us in our lives. It also fosters appreciation of the moments of genuine wonder which speckle "the symphony of real life" (Nietzsche, 1984: 247). Nietzsche includes the experience of love in his depiction of these moments:

> Life consists of rare, isolated moments of the greatest significance, and of innumerably many intervals, during which at best the silhouettes of those moments hover about us. Love, springtime, every beautiful melody, mountains, the moon, the sea – all these speak to the heart but once (Nietzsche, 1984: 247).

These "rare, isolated moments" may be rare and fleeting, but when life is experienced as an interconnected process, such glimpses of love and beauty can "hover about us" and impact on all of life.

This is the task of self-creating, self-mastery, self-overcoming; to work out what an affirming life could be, and to develop a life-affirming

---

[19] Nietzsche's advocation of *amor fati*, love of one's fate, appears paradoxical, as it is complemented by his insistence on the need for self-creation, responsibility. This is the apparent paradox between determinism and autonomy, and is an issue central to philosophy and psychoanalysis. (The question is explored in my MA thesis, "Amor Fati or Melancholia?" 2006).

world view which has no remorse, no melancholy, no end; it is a process
of becoming and creating, "*processus in infinitum*" (Nietzsche, 1968: 552).
In this life-affirming stance, the past is embraced, mistakes, losses and
disappointments are acknowledged, as are joys, achievements and
fortuitous encounters and occurrences, and the future is seen as the
offshoot of the present. Nietzsche acknowledges that this is a difficult
path, as it necessitates the humility of self-honesty and the courage of
individual responsibility in place of the comfort and security of the 'herd':
"One has to get rid of the bad taste of wanting to be in agreement with
many" (Nietzsche, 2003: 71). Self-honesty, self-direction and self-
empowerment enable one to be the artist of one's own life, and to answer
affirmatively Nietzsche's question: "Do you possess courage?...Not
courage in the presences of witnesses, but hermit's eagles' courage, which
not even a god observes any more?" (Nietzsche, 2003a: 298). In his
discussion of the doctrine of eternal recurrence, Hans-Georg Gadamer
states that Nietzsche 'was a great moralist',[20] and that he was posing the
question, 'to what extent can human life endure truth at all?':

> This is a question which Nietzsche formulated and it represents one of the
> provocative challenges which his thought poses for our epoch with ever
> greater force. In his despair at the ability of the enlightenment and of
> modern science to answer the most fundamental human questions,
> Nietzsche arrived at his provocative doctrine of the eternal return of the
> same...with this doctrine he wanted to show how in the face of absolute
> hopelessness we must learn to be resolute...what he demanded of us was
> genuine morality (Gadamer, 1996: 160).

Gadamer's response to Nietzsche suggests the crucial necessity of a
personal morality, and this acknowledgement of the sovereignty of the self
is intrinsic to the possibility of love. Taking responsibility for the creation
of one's life diminishes the perceived necessity to seek refuge, recognition
and acceptance in the "herd"; it promotes a constant re-evaluation of the
values one chooses to adopt, and it defines one's life as an ongoing
process of becoming.

The possibility of striving towards this affirmative engagement with
life is glimpsed in Nietzsche's description of the *Ubermensch*. The
overman succeeds in overcoming himself[21] and all the illusions which

---

[20] Gadamer's description of Nietzsche as "a great moralist" echoes Philip Rieff's
study, *Freud: The Mind of the Moralist'*
[21] The overcoming of the self, in particular the illusions and deceptions of the self,
is central to the psychoanalytic process as outlined by Lacan and Žižek.

constitute this falsity, as he takes responsibility for his life at every moment and in every action. This life-affirming perspective leaves no room for remorse or melancholy; it sees "truth" as the practice of one's own values – the way one lives one's life – and it recognises a continuity between the values which are espoused and the actions which characterize one's life experience: "A human being's evaluations betray something of the structure of his soul" (Nietzsche, 2003: 206). The process of self-overcoming is the expression of the "will to power", as Nietzsche sees everything alive as seeking to perfect itself and to become stronger. Thus the human subject is never satisfied with his/her "self", but is constantly driven by the urge to grow, to flourish, and to surpass what he/she is at any moment.[22] The will to power, the desire to grow beyond what one is, is inherent in the moments of life which are fully lived; its absence or denial results in melancholy, ennui, or any other attempted withdrawal from the fullness of life: "Need forces us to do the work whose product will quiet the need…but in those intervals when our needs are quieted and seem to sleep, boredom overtakes us" (Nietzsche, 1984: 254).[23]

Deception, fear, denial and repression are constant impediments to authenticity, self-creation, freedom and responsibility. The overman resists such limitation and restraint; he refuses to deny the multiplicity of drives which propel him, drives which vary in strength and direction in various circumstances. He acknowledges his aggression, selfishness, greed, sexuality, as well as his power, autonomy, uniqueness and energy. Nietzsche asserts that "Life itself is *essentially* appropriation, injury, overpowering of the strange and weaker, suppression, severity, imposition of one's forms" (Nietzsche, 2003: 194). The overman does not deny his animal nature, he does not repress his basic instincts, and he does not use a splitting mechanism to overcome his impulses. Rather, he embraces the truth of his humanity, and in so doing, he is enabled to achieve what Kaufmann refers to as "an organic harmony" (Kaufmann, 1974: 227). The

---

[22] Nietzsche's description of the insatiability of the will to power, and its constant striving to overcome resistance, resounds with Lacan's insistence on desire as the key propellant of life.

[23] Nietzsche's assertion that "will to power" is the basic driving force of human life, and his description of this drive as a ceaseless striving to overcome all that resists it, bears a strong relevance to Freud's reflections on the competing motivations of the pleasure principle, the reality principle, and the death drive. The pleasure principle, according to Freud, is motivated, at least in part, by the desired avoidance of pain, and thus seeks an equilibrium of minimum resistance, but this is countered by an opposing drive which is never quite satisfied with the ensuing stagnation congruent with this state.

overman, rather than denying aspects of himself, rejoices in his full humanity, and by overcoming his illusions and deceptions, his complaints and excuses, he achieves self-mastery; he overcomes himself. In his willingness to integrate the totality of his personality, he accepts the ambiguity inherent in being human: "the wickedest in man is necessary for the best in him" (Nietzsche, 2003a: 235), and acceptance of this reality enables a joyous celebration of life: "One must have chaos in one, to give birth to a dancing star" (Nietzsche, 2003a: 46).

In this ideal of human living, Nietzsche rejects universal definitions of "mankind"; the overman is not a specimen of "everyman", but an ideal of the individual person creating and living a unique life. Nietzsche acknowledges the tremendous difficulty of living within such expansive honesty, and he offers it as an ideal which is worth striving towards. The acknowledgement and integration of all aspects of life enables a celebratory love of life, and, according to Solomon, this is Nietzsche's "cardinal virtue...he will not deny that cruel reality or human tragedy but rather see past our suffering to the miracle of life itself" (Solomon, 2003: 11). Thus, Nietzsche claims that "though woe be deep: Joy is deeper than heart's agony" (Nietzsche, 2003a: 331). Nietzsche is non-prescriptive in suggesting an account of how to live a fuller life as he merely offers the possibility. His perspectivism extends to his own work, and he repeatedly asserts that these are merely his ideas: "these are only – my truths" (Nietzsche, 2003: 163). This avowal of "personal truth" correlates to the experience of love itself, as love is essentially subjective, primarily personal, and necessarily experiential rather than theoretic, objective or measurable.

Nietzsche's philosophy attempts to reveal the deceptions and duplicities which characterize much of life, of philosophy, and of human relations. It offers a different perspective which embraces what he sees as a more realistic appraisal of human life and human being, and through this he envisages the possibility of a life where love, of self, of others, and of life, is possible. It is a life which embodies self-acceptance, self-responsibility, and self-created values: "To have and not have one's emotions, one's for and against...to remain master of one's four virtues, courage, insight, sympathy, solitude" (Nietzsche, 2003: 214). Dichotomies of mind and body, instinct and reason, heart and soul, good and evil are dissolved, the co-existence of solitude and connection – 'sympathy' – is embraced, and the way for love's possibility is cleared, because "That which is done out of love always takes place beyond good and evil" (Nietzsche, 2003: 103).

Nietzsche ascribes the experience of love to "the genius of the heart"[24] which integrates the "gold" and the "mud" of human experience, and which exudes its richness and blessing in the spirit of Derrida's gift,[25] wherein neither giver nor receiver consciously interpret the gift as gift:

> The genius of the heart...who divines the hidden and forgotten treasure, the drop of goodness and sweet spirituality under thick and opaque ice, and is a divining-rod for every grain of gold which has lain long in the prison of much mud and sand; the genius of the heart from whose touch everyone goes away richer, not favoured and surprised, not as if blessed and oppressed with the goods of others, but richer in himself, newer to himself than before, broken open, blown upon and sounded out by a thawing wind, more uncertain perhaps, more delicate, more fragile, more broken, but full of hopes that as yet have no names (Nietzsche, 2003: 219).

The juxtaposition of images in the above quotation, blessed/oppressed, opaque ice/thawing wind, broken open/full of hopes, suggests the ambiguity, risk and vulnerability which the experience of love necessitates, the fullness of life which it embraces, and the enrichment which it proffers to both the lover and the loved. This experience entails the humility of ignorance co-existing with the reception of otherness, an openness to life which Nietzsche describes in one "who shares profusely in others' joy, who wins friends everywhere, who is touched by everything that grows and evolves, who enjoys other people's honors and successes, and makes no claim to the privilege of alone knowing the truth" (Nietzsche, 1984: 255). According to this view, love is rooted in attention and interest, devoid of judgement and expectation, receiving the other in its irreducible alterity:

> Whoever wants really to get to know something new (be it a person, an event, or a book) does well to take up this new thing with all possible love, to avert his eye quickly from, even to forget, everything about it he finds inimical, objectionable, or false...by doing this, we penetrate into the heart of the new thing, into its motive centre; and this is what it means to get to know it (Nietzsche, 1984: 257).

---

[24] This phrase resonates with Wordsworth's philosophy, as expressed poetically and personally.

[25] Derrida outlines his theory of the gift in *Given Time: 1. Counterfeit Money*, where he explains, "For there to be a gift, there must be no reciprocity, return, exchange, counterfeit, or debt...At the limit, the gift as gift ought not appear as gift: either to the donee or to the donor" (Derrida, 1994: 12, 14).

Engaging with life, with self and others, "with all possible love", is enabled through a divestment of deception and disguise, distortion and image, projection and defensiveness, and the willingness to stand in a naked vulnerability and a courageous simplicity: "Where one can no longer love, one should – pass by!" (Nietzsche, 2003a: 198). In such moments of personal honesty and agenda-free encounters with life, love is possible, joyous and life-enhancing: "Fine, with one another silent, Finer, with one another laughing" (Nietzsche, 1984: 268). The possibility of love suggested in these lines, evoking ease and acceptance, joy and silence, enables the experience of a relationship engaging the full expression of who one is, and the open reception of who the other is; this is the subject of Buber's philosophy outlined in the "I/Thou" encounter which is the starting point of the next chapter.

CHAPTER TWO

MARTIN BUBER

The philosophy of Buber evolves through the idealistic and romantic involvements of his early years to a personal and political realism inevitable in the light of the historical developments of his mature years.[1] He has been criticized for his overly optimistic opinion of human nature, for example in the work of Irving Singer in his analysis of love as explored by various philosophers: "we may also be repelled by Buber's simpleminded, and possibly delusory, vision. He depicts the cosmos as an expression of God's love; he says little about the existence of suffering, hatred, or brutality" (Singer, 1987, 338).[2] Iris Murdoch, while acknowledging positive and illuminating aspects of Buber's work, also gently criticizes its simplicity and exclusiveness: "Buber's memorable distinction between the I – Thou and the I – It relation seems too simple and exclusive, and may indeed suggest the old fascinating division of fact from value, which makes nothing of the greater part of our ordinary life of knowings and actings" (Murdoch, 1993: 478). Throughout his work, lectures and letters, Buber persistently answers his critics, mainly by insisting that his philosophy is founded on the actual, lived experience of the individual in his world, including suffering, hatred and evil. Buber later renounced his adolescent euphoria on encountering Nietzsche's work, and endeavoured to distance himself from what he came to see as Nietzsche's extremism and exaggeration. In his analysis of Nietzsche's philosophical contribution outlined in section five of *Between Man and*

---

[1] Buber describes this change as a "conversion" which he experienced after an encounter with a young man who sought his help; while Buber "conversed attentively and openly with him", he was not "there in spirit". Shortly afterwards he learned that the young man had died; believing that he had failed the individual in his hour of need, Buber made a decision: "Since then I have given up the 'religious' which is nothing but the exception, extraction, exaltation, ecstasy...I possess nothing but the everyday out of which I am never taken" (Buber, 2004: 16).

[2] Irving Singer refers to Buber as one of the "idealistic existentialists", in his commentary on the philosopher, in Volume 3 of *The Nature of Love*.

Man, Buber is critical of the limitations of Nietzsche's anthropology; yet he is lavish in his praise for what he sees as Nietzsche's achievements: "like no other previous thinker, he brings man into the centre of his thought about the universe...The questionableness of man is Nietzsche's great theme...in elevating, as no previous thinker has done, the questionableness of human life to be the real subject of philosophizing he gave the anthropological question a new and unheard-of impulse" (Buber, 2004: 176, 182). For Buber, this "anthropological question" can only be pursued through an exploration of the relationships which constitute human being: "The question of what man is cannot be answered by a consideration of existence or of self-being as such, but only by a consideration of the essential connexion of the human person and his relations with all being" (Buber, 2004: 214). Thus, Buber's concept of the self is essentially relational, intersubjective and situated within the world of others.

Buber and Nietzsche explore questions relating to self and others, responsibility and freedom, good and evil, and in their unique and disparate reflections, they initiate and expand upon existential dilemmas and conflicts. Their approach to philosophical inquiry is similar in its concentration on lived experience rather than abstract theory: "All philosophical discovery is the uncovering of what is covered by the veil woven from the threads of a thousand theories" (Buber, 2004: 216). It may be counter-argued that "theories" can illuminate as well as disguise their objects of study, particularly when they resist definitive conclusions and remain open to ongoing interrogation and revision, and when they are constantly focused and tested in the diverse and changing concreteness of lived reality. An examination of Buberian texts suggests a Nietzschean influence, both in the aphoristic and poetic style of his literature and in his insistence on an embrace of the totality of what it is to be human. Maurice Friedman, colleague, interpreter and biographer of Buber, refers to Nietzsche's influence on his philosophy:

> In one of his earliest articles Buber spoke of Nietzsche as 'the first pathfinder of the new culture', 'the awakener and creator of new life-values and a new world-feeling'. Nietzsche's influence may account in part for the dynamism of Buber's philosophy, for its concern with creativity and greatness, for its emphasis on the concrete and actual as opposed to the ideal and abstract, for its idea of the fruitfulness of conflict, and for its emphasis on the value of life impulses and wholeness of being as opposed to detached intellectuality (Friedman, 2002: 39).

While Buber necessarily developed his own unique philosophical thought, many of his pronouncements resound with those of Nietzsche, particularly on issues such as morality, human nature, deception, freedom and responsibility.

In his writings, most notably *I and Thou*, Buber expresses his belief that the deepest reality of human life lies in the relation between one being and another and that human understanding is a communal process: "The fundamental fact of human existence, according to Buber's anthropology, is man with man" (Friedman, 2002: 98). In his invitation to a dialogue between author and reader, in his observance and honouring of the ordinary, and in his assault on unquestioned conventions of thought and language, Buber challenges the reader to reassess one's encounter with oneself and with the surrounding world. His philosophy is concerned with diverse issues of human living, personal, sociological, educational, and political: "Buber proceeds to set up philosophical anthropology as a systematic method which deals with the concrete, existential characteristics of man's life in order to arrive at the wholeness of man" (Friedman, 2002: 91). Buber examines the concrete situations of the individual's life in the world, with a view to both the nature of the human being and the nature of the world in which he/she lives, and the inevitable relation between the two. Buber sees this relation as indissoluble, and through it he seeks the essence of humanness, personhood, and love. His writings centre on the ever recurring encounter between the self and all that lies outside it, between the subject and other subjects, between the individual and nature, between the human being and what he/she divines as "God". These encounters are, according to Buber, the expression of the human condition, and their manifold characteristics of mutuality and withdrawal, embrace and rejection, subjectification and objectification, reflect, in their sometimes alternating, sometimes contemporaneous experience, the potentialities and limitations of human existence in the world.

The modern world which forms the backdrop of Buber's observations and reflections is characterized by the necessity to confront anew questions regarding humanity, nature, technology, and society, as political and cultural developments effect reactions of alienation, disillusionment, and despair.[3] Friedman refers to "four types of evil of which the modern age is particularly aware":

> The loneliness of modern man before an unfriendly universe and before men whom he associates with but does not meet; the increasing tendency

---

[3] These reactions are evident in the literature of the modern age, and are uniquely portrayed in the poetry of Eliot.

for scientific instruments and techniques to outrun man's ability to integrate those techniques into his life in some meaningful and constructive way; the inner duality of which modern man has become aware through the writings of Dostoyevsky and Freud[4] and the development of psychoanalysis; and the deliberate and large-scale degradation of human life within the totalitarian state (Friedman, 2002: 15).[5]

The work of Buber engages with the reality of these issues while maintaining a conviction that their acknowledgement does not preclude their opposites: dialogue, relationship, integration and love are realistic goals which, though never experienced in a fixed and absolute attainment, are potentially present to each new moment of being: "none of the contacts of each hour is unworthy to take up from our essential being as much as it may" (Buber, 2004: 26).

Avraham Shapira, in his study of Buber's life and work, argues that "polar duality...occupies a central place in all of Buber's writings" (Shapira, 1999: 193), and lists these as "Distance - Relation, Vortex - Direction, Moment - Eternity, and I-It – I-Thou" (Shapira, 1999: 8). According to Buber, these dualities and the tensions between them characterize human life; they co-exist in varying degrees of discord and harmony, and are never mutually exclusive: "behind the common pairs of opposed concepts, good and evil, beautiful and ugly, there stand others in which the negative concept is intimately bound to the positive" (Buber, 2004: 87). Thus, in the interplay between Distance, wherein the self is experienced as a separate and private entity, and Relation, whereby this same self is also experienced as interacting with and relating to the outer world, the polarities of human existence are embodied. Interpersonal relationships are also the canvas upon which is drawn the conflicts and questions, the dreams and solutions, the certainties and disruptions, which originate in, and belong to, the inner psychic experience of one's relationship with oneself.[6] In his attempts to comprehend the complexities and contradictions observable throughout history and in his own time,

---

[4] Buber was critical of some of Freud's theories and methods and suggested that the psychoanalytic encounter should approach the I-Thou relationship. These ideas are outlined in *Martin Buber on Psychology and Psychotherapy*, 1999.

[5] The work of Lacan is also fore-grounded in the reality of totalitarianism, its emergence, maintenance, power, control and destructiveness, and he attempts, through psychoanalytic insight, to approach an explanation and an understanding of this phenomenon.

[6] Buber's reference to inner conflict and the difficulties involved in over-coming internal oppositions echoes Freud's description of the mind as a tripartite apparatus, often in conflict with itself.

Buber concludes, similarly to Nietzsche, that understanding can only begin with personal truth. Only thus is it possible to confront otherwise theoretical abstractions, such as good and evil, love and hate, self and other: "A man should himself realize that conflict-situations between himself and others are nothing but the effects of conflict-situations in his own soul" (Buber, 2002: 21). Thus, while Buber's philosophy is essentially a philosophy of dialogue, of relationship, it also supports Nietzsche's concentration on introspection, self-honesty, and self-acceptance, as it insists on an examination and an awareness of the self as the starting point of all genuine encounters, and for any realization of the possibility of love.

The Crowd as an Escape from Responsibility

> A man in the crowd is a stick stuck in a
> bundle moving through the water,
> abandoned to the current or being
> pushed by a pole from the bank in this
> or that direction (Buber, 2004: 74).

The philosophy of Buber is primarily concerned with the possibility of genuine relationship, mutuality and love, and it therefore examines the personal and societal, political and historical obstacles to these ideals. Murdoch sees Buber's analysis of relationship as an illumination of the concept of love: "The well-known contrast made by Buber between I – Thou and I – It relations can illuminate morality, the dealings of people with each other, can serve as commentary upon the concept of love" (Murdoch, 1993: 469). One such obstacle to genuine relationship, according to Buber, is the tendency of the individual to seek safety and companionship in the crowd; the "crowd" resonates with Nietzsche's "herd", with popular opinion, and with the assumed validity of the majority. Buber refers to "the historical paradise of crowds" where "uniformity is the real thing", and describes the crowd "as non-truth'" and "unfreedom" (Buber, 2004: 74, 75). He realistically offers an analysis of the individual as a being inevitably existing in relationship with his/her society and community. He is interested in the constitutive correlation and tension between society and community, and between individual and social experience. While Buber sees the goals of authentic relationship, dialogue, and love, as being sought and attained in community – communication between self and others – he is critical of the more common misrepresentations of the experience of community, which foster a false sense of belonging and contributing. Buber distinguishes between community as "being no longer side by side but *with* one another of a multitude of persons" (Buber, 2004: 37), and its counterpart, collectivity. Friedman outlines this distinction:

> In opposition to true community stands not only individual monologue, but the collectivity, the totalitarian states of left and right in which, bundled together without Thou and without I, hostile and separated hosts march into the common abyss. True community emerges only out of the breakthrough from the repressed and the pedestrian to the reality of the between (Friedman, 1988: 116).

Collectivity, whether expressed through religion, morality, or politics, whether glorified in the group, the institution, or the ideology, is based, according to Buber, on a renunciation and a distortion of personal existence, responsibility and freedom, and it cancels any genuine encounter with self or other: "Collectivity is based on an organized atrophy of personal existence" (Buber, 2004: 37). Here, as in Nietzsche's depiction of herd morality, the individual takes refuge in the security of obedience to the dictates of the group, adheres to a "simplified mode of valuation" (Buber, 2004: 36), and turns away from the possibility of a personal response to life's questions: "[this] marks the beginning of the paralysis of the human search for the truth" (Buber, 2004: 96). Responsibility is evaded "by a flight into a protective 'once-for-all'" (Buber, 2004: 82).

In his personal recollections of Buber, Aubrey Hobes states that "he was completely against any dogma or system imposed upon the individual...because a dogma states as absolute truth a conclusion in advance of any given situation, it stifles the individual response which has in it the power of creating a dialogue with life" (Hobes, 1972: 33). Immersion in the opinions and dictates of the crowd or the group releases the individual from the responsibility of finding his/her own answers, undergoing his/her own tests, and responding to Nietzsche's challenge of the eternal recurrence: "everything is decided. What you once thought – that you had to answer ever anew, situation by situation, for the choice you made – is now got rid of. The group has relieved you of your...responsibility. You feel yourself answered for in the group" (Buber, 2004: 79). According to Friedman, reneging on the responsibility "to answer ever anew" in the uncertainty of each experience and encounter, withdrawing into the illusory security of fixed judgements and responses, and avoiding the vulnerability of "unknowing" and exposure, obliterates the possibility of real relationship: "the various types of 'once for all'...make unnecessary the 'ever anew' of real response to the unique situation which confronts one in each hour. This false security prevents us from making our relationships to others real through opening ourselves to them" (Friedman, 2002: 131). Recalling Nietzsche's exposition of the dubious nature of traditional codes of morality, Buber claims that adherence to such codes precludes the possibility of encountering the humanity of the other: "there is nothing that can so hide the face of our fellow-men as morality can" (Buber, 2004: 21).[7] As Shapira notes, "Buber is wary of ideologies whose human subject is not kept in view, of a 'progress' based on the masses, in whom the 'human visage' disappears" (Shapira, 1999: 33). The desire for certainties and absolutes and the aversion to doubt and ambivalence restricts the possibilities of open and vital relationship, because, as the German poet Rilke states: "fear of the inexplicable has not alone impoverished the existence of the individual; the relationship between one human being and another has also been cramped by it" (Rilke, 2004: 118). Avoidance of the challenge of living with doubt and uncertainty originates in the illusory attractions of control and protection, but results in the denial of personal freedom:

> a man tries to find a system in the universe around him, a pattern that he
> can apply to a solution of the problems of his existence. He seeks a
> formula, a governing rule. And he thinks this will make him free. But the
> formula imprisons him. He lives with only one part of his being,
> surrendering the quest and insecurity which alone can make him truly free
> (Hobes, 1972: 33).

The attempt to avoid the inescapable aloneness of the individual is often expressed in the striving to belong, to be part of the group/crowd/collectivity, with its illusions of connection and uniformity. The outcome of this reliance on the palliative offerings promised by membership of the crowd is also seen by Fromm as an obstacle to the possibility of love:

> Human relations are essentially those of alienated automatons, each basing
> his security on staying close to the herd, and not being different in thought,
> feeling or action. While everybody tries to be as close as possible to the
> rest, everybody remains utterly alone, pervaded by the deep sense of

---

[7] Žižek says something similar when he argues that abstract notions of universal human rights are often assumed as convenient, self-congratulatory theories which maintain others/foreigners/strangers at a comfortable distance which precludes responsibility or recognition.

insecurity, anxiety and guilt which always results when human separateness cannot be overcome (Fromm, 1995: 67).[8]

This attraction to the comfort of the crowd, reminiscent of Nietzsche's depiction of a "herd-mentality", involves the renunciation of personal freedom and responsibility, the refusal to respond creatively to that which presents itself to one in the concrete experience of each moment, and the "flight from the vital dialogic, demanding the staking of the self, which is in the heart of the world" (Buber, 2004: 37). Acquiescence with general, universal, and absolutist interpretations of the individual's life in the world is based, according to Buber, on an unquestioned acceptance of *a priori* assumptions and definitions of the human subject, and is far removed from the actual, concrete experience of each moment, with its ever-new challenges and possibilities; it is an evasion of personal responsibility which demands that 'I answer for my hour. My group cannot relieve me of this responsibility' (Buber, 2004: 80). The price of this acquiescence, of this illusory belonging, is the suspension of individual thought and responsibility and the assumption of externally imposed opinions and convictions; consequently, the alterity of the other is averted:

> I am either completely excused from forming an opinion and a decision, or...convicted...of the invalidity of my opinions and decisions, and in their stead fitted out with ones that are approved as valid. By this means I am not in the least made aware of others since the same thing happens to them and their otherness has been varnished over (Buber, 2004: 74).

Rejecting the pseudo-security and illusory comfort offered by conformity and uniformity, Nietzsche expresses the hope that "perhaps a future survey of the needs of mankind will reveal it to be thoroughly undesirable that all men act identically" (Nietzsche, 1984: 31), and concurs with Buber's claim that "Mankind's great chance lies precisely in the unlikeness of men" (Buber, 2002: 10).[9] Acceptance of difference, of otherness, of the other-than self is essential to the experience of love wherein "I wish his otherness to exist, because I wish his particular being to exist" (Buber, 2004: 72).

The craving to belong, to be an accepted part of something larger than

---

[8] The paradox of loneliness, isolation, and alienation amid the crowd, the multitude, and the city, is a central theme of Eliot's poem, "The Wasteland".

[9] The "unlikeness" or difference between individuals is stressed here by Buber and by Nietzsche; while this reality is acknowledged by the other writers outlined in the study, Wordsworth and Ricoeur assert that these differences are less significant than the likenesses and links that also exist between human beings.

oneself, necessitates the real or imaginary erection and maintenance of a defining boundary, protecting and insulating the collective – family, group, institution, nation, or party – against the perceived threat of what is different, the other, the foreigner. The illusory camaraderie of the group or the crowd is only maintained by a projection of society's ills onto convenient scapegoats, strangers, outsiders. The price to be paid for the construction of the "happy crowd" is often the ostracizing of some outsider or difference; this was blatantly obvious to Buber with the rise of Nazism and the corresponding condemnation of the Jewish world. In this sense, inclusion is based on exclusion of the different. The splitting off of the "unacceptable" and its convenient projection onto some demonic other resounds with the findings of psychoanalysis, and particularly with the writings of Carl Jung, who described what is split off as the "shadow", and who suggested that the result of such an artificial division is psychic conflict and self-alienation (Jung, 2005: 75). Friedman also makes reference to this practice of demonizing the "other" in his discussion of Buber's work: "The demonic Thou sees the beings around him as Its, as machines capable of various achievements which must be taken into account and utilized in the cause" (Friedman, 1988: 345). This resounds with Hegel's master and slave theory, in which the other is objectified by the self, becoming a slave or an "It"; but as Hegel explains, the duality of master/slave, I/It, obliterates the reality and humanity of both, as the self cannot find recognition in a demonized or diminished other. The identity of self and other is jeopardized, as it is splintered into convenient but illusory oppositions of good/bad, strong/weak, friend/foe.

The unquestioned adherence to popular values and morals as ends in themselves results in an alienation from personal response to concrete experience, and a simultaneous restriction of the other to fixed and distorted images. Arguing for a courage which would embrace "that dangerous insecurity [which] is so much more human", Rilke claims that "only someone who is ready for everything, who excludes nothing, not even the most enigmatical, will live the relation to another as something alive and will himself draw exhaustively from his own existence" (Rilke, 2004: 119). Agreeing with Nietzsche, Buber rejects the authority and the validity of externally created codes of morality which are unquestioningly accepted as absolute and complete: "Morality and piety, where they have in this way become an autonomous aim, must also be reckoned among the show-pieces and shows of a spirit that no longer knows about Being but only about its mirrorings" (Buber, 2004: 51). The concept of "mirrorings" resonates with Lacan's theories regarding self-knowledge, identity and image. According to Lacan, the subject, in the mirror stage of development, defines his/her identity by identifying with its reflection in the mirror; "the transformation that takes place in the subject when he assumes an image" (Lacan, 1977: 4). This is the start of a life-long process of identifying the self in terms of the other. The influence of this Buberian analysis is also evident in the work of the psychoanalyst, R.D. Laing, in which he focuses on the impact of environmental conditions on mental health. Echoing Buber's reference to a "simplified mode of valuation", Laing describes "normality" as a state of unwitting complicity in "social phantasy systems", wherein shared assumptions about reality define the perspectives of a particular group, culture, or any powerful majority: "We see the shadows, but take them for the substance" (Laing, 1999: 33). Buber suggests that our acceptance of the constrictions inherent in collectivity is enabled by the "perversion of thought" and by "chatter", portrayed in our duplicitous use of language itself (Buber, 2004: 36). The use of words such as "comradeship", "obedience", "sacrifice", and "achievements", is based on the attempt to conceal the escapism involved in marching to the popular drum: "Collectivity is not a binding but a bundling together: individuals packed together, armed and equipped in common, with only as much life from man to man as will inflame the marching step" (Buber, 2004: 37).

This critique of an adherence to already defined meanings, to a dependence on a rigid conception of language, is echoed by Irigaray. She, like Buber, rejects speech or language which "submits body and spirit to already pronounced words which paralyze life, breath, energy, and prevent a living communication with the other" (Irigaray, 2002: 84). For Buber, this paralysis of communication is far removed from the possibility of authentic encounter with the world, it precludes a genuine dialogue between self and other, and it remains a serious obstacle to the experience of an I-Thou relationship, and so to the experience of love. According to these arguments, the conditioning influence of collectivized society, with its unquestioned values and rules, its accepted demands and expectations, depersonalizes the human being, generalizes the human condition of the individual, and reduces the immeasurable complexity of the human person to an abstract concept of "mankind". Irigaray points to the repercussions of this mode of thinking: "Man always wanders further away from himself towards some remote universal [and is] more and more chained by a priori constructions that conceal from him a possible perception of himself, and of his environment" (Irigaray, 2002: 91). Such abstractions, applied to complex issues such as subject, truth, friendship and love, often fail to symbolize the concepts in any meaningful way; as Derrida urges in his discussion of love and friendship, "Let us cease speaking of friendship, of

the *eídos* of friendship, let us speak of friends" (Derrida, 2005: 302).
Buber's analysis of civilization and society resounds with Nietzsche's
exhortation to consider "man" rather than "mankind",[10] and also with
Freud's portrayal of the constraints of civilization on the potential and
happiness of the individual,[11] and his assertion of "the gulf between an
actual individual and the concept of a species" (Freud, 1995: 644).
Simplistic generalisations of the human subject and of human society,
expressed in political, social, religious or ideological platitudes, disavow
the diverse multiplicity and in definability of the human condition, the
human subject, and the relations between individuals, and reduce human
experience to abstraction and stagnation: "If a culture ceases to be
centered in the living and continually renewed relational event, then it
hardens into the world of *It*, which the glowing deeds of solitary spirits
only spasmodically break through" (Buber, 2004a: 46).

Monologue as Pseudo-Dialogue

> There are not merely great spheres of
> the life of dialogue which in appearance
> are not dialogue, there is also dialogue
> which is not the dialogue of life, that is,
> it has the appearance of dialogue but
> not the essence of dialogue. At times,
> indeed, it seems as though there were
> only this kind of dialogue (Buber,
> 2004: 22).

In his outline of human relationships, Buber posits another polarity and
contrasts two different approaches and attitudes in the subject's encounter
with existence. He contrasts the I-Thou relationship of openness,
mutuality, and presence with the more common mode of experience
whereby the other is encountered as an object – 'It' – without the intention
of genuine connection. The former is the approach of genuine relation,
dialogue, and love, and the pervasiveness of the latter is a serious obstacle
to this experience. In many encounters between human beings, there may
be the appearance of communication, yet the other remains an object

---

[10] Nietzsche repeatedly points to the incompatibility of the concepts "man" and
"mankind": "society, where one hears a lot of talk about men, but none at all *about
man*" (Nietzsche, 1984: 39).
[11] Freud outlines the tensions between civilization and the individual in his work
Civilization and its Discontents, where he argues that the "good" of society is often
at variance with the "good" of the individual.

unconnected with the self– an "It". As Friedman explains, "In general, people do not really speak to one another. Each turns to the other, to be sure, but he speaks in reality to a fictitious audience which exists only to listen to him" (Friedman, 2002: 144). The reference to "audience" here resounds with Nietzsche's interpretation of human behaviour as being largely motivated by impression, image and performance. The deceptions involved in many experiences of human encounter are analyzed by Buber as being inherently limited to an I-It relationship, whereby the reality of the other is negated either by an effort to impose an element/concept/desire of the self, or by a need to satisfy a lack in the self through appropriation of the other. This echoes Nietzsche's observations: "You cannot endure to be alone with yourselves and do not love yourselves enough, [so] one man runs to his neighbour because he is looking for himself, and another because he wants he wants to lose himself" (Nietzsche, 2003a: 87). Either way, the other is not embraced in his/her alterity, but rather is reduced or subsumed as a means to an end.

Denial of the radical alterity of the other, which is an inevitable counterpart of the I-It relationship, also cancels the ethical phenomenology which derives from this concept. The consequence of a life without a real reaching out to the other is a life where love, of self or of other, is not possible, because, as outlined by Friedman

> The monological man is not aware of the 'otherness' of the other, but instead tries to incorporate the other into himself. The basic movement of the life of monologue is not turning away from the other but 'reflexion', bending back on oneself. 'Reflexion' is not egotism but the withdrawal from accepting the other person in his particularity in favour of letting him exist only as one's own experience, only as a part of oneself (Friedman, 2002: 103).

Buber refers to this withdrawal of the self from a genuine encounter with the other as self-contradiction, because in his view it contradicts an essential aspect of being human: "Self-contradiction...Buber uses that concept to designate a life of monologue that, in his opinion, contradicts human nature. The end of a monologic life, he claims, is self-immolation" (Shapira, 1999: 55). Buber gives concrete examples of pseudo-dialogue, apart from the practical necessity of gaining and exchanging information which is inherent in much human interchanges, i.e. "technical dialogue...which is prompted solely by the need of objective understanding" (Buber, 2004: 22). Echoing Nietzsche's statement that "I and Me are always too earnestly in conversation with one another" (Nietzsche, 2003a: 82), Buber points to the intrinsic preoccupation with self which often underlies the pretence at genuine communication:

> A *debate* in which the thoughts are not expressed in the way in which they
> existed in the mind…a *conversation* characterized…by the desire to have
> one's own self-reliance confirmed by marking the impression that is
> made…a *friendly chat* in which each regards himself as absolute and
> legitimate and the other as relativized and questionable; *a lovers'* talk in
> which both partners alike enjoy their own glorious soul and their precious
> experience…what an underworld of faceless spectres of dialogue! (Buber,
> 2004: 22, 23).

The possibility of expressing thoughts as "they existed in the mind" is
explicitly or implicitly questioned by all the writers explored in this study.
For example, Lacan argues that as our thoughts are mediated through
language, they are inevitably changed by that language. Lacan refers to
this everyday language as "empty speech" and suggests that it reveals little
about the real self. In contrast, he argues that full speech is the language of
the unconscious – before it has been distorted and formalized – and as
such it exists in any way in which the unconscious is brought to the fore,
such as symptoms of illness, in dreams, in language spoken under
hypnosis (Lacan, 1977: 46). Perhaps full, transparent expression is
impossible, but perhaps there are degrees of distortion and of revelation.
The difficulties inherent in the use of language is acknowledged by Buber
as he refers to attempted expression and response as "stammering
perhaps", but he suggests that the effort, the "stammering", while
imperfectly voicing the inner world, nevertheless may attain its goal: "the
soul is but rarely able to attain to surer articulation – but it is an honest
stammering, as when sense and throat are united about what is to be said"
(Buber, 2004: 20).

For Buber, the appearance of relationship, of dialogue, is merely the
public play of parallel monologues, where neither partner hears, nor is
interested in hearing, what the other says: "The most eager speaking at one
another does not make a conversation" (Buber, 2004: 3). Nietzsche is even
more emphatic in his analysis of "social dialogue", where "three-quarters
of all questions and answers are framed in order to hurt the participants a
little more" (Nietzsche, 1984: 50), and he points to the potential of speech
to disguise and distort: "Speech is a beautiful foolery: with it man dances
over all things" (Nietzsche, 2003a: 234). The duplicity and distortion
underlying this masquerade of relationship reflects and maintains internal
and external conflict, because, as Buber states, "The origin of all conflict
between me and my fellow-men is that I do not say what I mean, and that I
do not do what I say. For this confuses and poisons, again and again and in

increasing measure, the situation between myself and the other man" (Buber, 2002: 22). This pseudo-encounter cancels any possibility of meeting with the person/presence/reality of the other, whether this is expressed in words or silence, in action or stillness, in expectation or despair. Hence, growth, of self-understanding and self-awareness, and of appreciation and welcome of the otherness of the other, is absent from the experience. Irigaray echoes Buber's analysis of pseudo-dialogue, and says that "our rational tradition has been much concerned with 'speaking about' but has reduced 'speaking with' to a speaking together about the same things" (Irigaray, 2002: 7).

Buber realistically accepts the necessity of the I-It relationship in one's dealings with the world, and observes that we could not live unless we, to some extent, manipulated nature in order to meet our basic needs; he accepts the criticism of the I-Thou relationship as idealistic and only imperfectly attainable; he sees the reality of human relationships as inevitably oscillating between the two; but he warns against the limitations inherent in an exclusive and one-sided concentration on the separation and incompatibility of subject and object. As Donald Berry asserts in his analysis of Buber's vision, "Fundamental to an appreciation of Buber's thought is the recognition that the mutuality of which he speaks admits of degrees" (Berry, 1985: 41). Buber argues that when we allow the "I-It" way of viewing the world to dominate our thinking and actions, we are spiritually emaciated and pauperized, and our lives are a narrow reflection of what they could be. The potential of the human being, and his/her potential relationship with his/her world, is thus restricted and distorted:

> The fulfilment of this nature and disposition is thwarted by the man who has come to terms with the world of *It* that it is to be experienced and used. For now instead of freeing that which is bound up in that world he suppresses it, instead of looking at it he observes it, instead of accepting it as it is, he turns it to his own account (Buber, 2004a: 37).

A similar reference to what is lost to human experience through a concentration on the world of It is made by Irigaray: "the ability to say oneself to the other without for all that forcing upon the other one's truth. The ability to listen to the other as well, to hear a meaning different than the one from which a world of one's own has achieved its course" (Irigaray, 2002: 8). In the absence of communication in dialogue, in the withholding of one's presence from the other, in the recoiling from the unfamiliarity and difference of the other, the narrow complacency of the self is carefully guarded, and the possibility of reciprocity, connection, and love is averted and denied. According to Buber, this is a rejection of life's possibilities, a distortion of relationship, and a negation of the reality of human living:

> When a man withdraws from accepting with his essential being another person in his particularity – a particularity which is by no means to be circumscribed by the circle of his own self, and though it substantially touches and moves his soul is in no way immanent in it – and lets the other exist only as his own experience, only as a 'part of myself'…then dialogue becomes a fiction, the mysterious intercourse between two human worlds only a game, and in the rejection of the real life confronting him the essence of all reality begins to disintegrate (Buber, 2004: 28).

The rejection of the real life confronting the individual is, in Buber's view, a withholding of the self on some level from the ambiguity and unpredictability of a fully-embraced encounter, it entails a guarded and partial address to the other, and it sets limits on the reception and response to the call of the other in all its possibilities, dangers, and challenges.

Alienation from Self

> Man…must find his own self, not the
> trivial ego of the egoistic individual,
> but the deeper self of the person living
> in a relationship to the world (Buber,
> 2002: 22).

Buber insists that one cannot become a person by oneself, that life is essentially relational, and that "I become through my relation to the *Thou*; as I become *I*, I say *Thou*. All real living is meeting" (Buber, 2004a: 17). However, Buber also accepts the inevitable solitariness of the human condition, whereby each person "goes the narrow way from birth towards death, tests out what none but he can, a wrestling with destiny, rebellion and reconciliation" (Buber, 2004: 146). In asserting emphatically that "one is alone", Rilke argues "that even between the *closest* human beings infinite distances continue to exist, [but] a wonderful living side by side can grow up, if they succeed in loving the distance between them which makes it possible for each to see the other whole and against a wide sky" (Rilke, 2004: 34). Various experiences, historical, political, and cultural, can portray this essential solitude as a burden to be evaded, and thus attempt to alienate the subject from responsibility for himself or herself and the world. An attempted escape from the self, with all its contradictions and ambiguities, results "from the fear of being left…to rely on themselves, on a self which no longer receives its direction from eternal values...the unconscious desire to have responsibility removed from them by an authority in which they believe or want to believe'"(Buber, 2004: 137). Nietzsche's assessment of "a necessary nihilism" following the "death of God", is echoed here.

Buber argues that meeting of selves or of 'I's is only possible when one has recognized the necessity of attaining a sense of one's own self, when one has honestly encountered all of one's humanity, and when one has accepted that encounter, presence, and communication only occur in the immediate, concrete situations which involve the self in all its complexity and ambiguity, and what lies beyond it: "in order to be able to go out to the other you must have the starting place, you must have been, you must be, with yourself" (Buber, 2004: 24). Otherwise, in an obvious or repressed alienation from the self, one meets the other either as a threat to one's fragile, false, identity, or as an object which might be utilized as a supporting prop to this false self.[12]Avoidance of contact with the self results in limitations to attempted connection with others. This analysis is clearly summarized by Irving Singer, in the third volume of his treatise on *The Nature of Love,* where he states that "Buber frequently denies that beings can be related to one another as I and Thou if either is absorbed in the other or deprived of ultimate independence" (Singer, 1987: 334).

A focus on concrete examples of lived experience in order to explore questions regarding relationship, dialogue and communication is a persistent element of Buber's philosophy; it examines particularities such as marriage, family, work, politics, and the many areas of influence and reaction which impact on the individual. As Shapira notes, "Buber repeatedly glorifies 'the infinite ethos of the moment'. For him the transitory situations of the stream of life receive a particular gravity of their own" (Shapira, 1999: 3). When Buber outlines his criteria for teaching and education he insists on the necessity of the I-Thou relationship. As in other caring professions to which he refers, such as psychotherapy, Buber cautions against the dangers of resorting to technique and formulae in an effort to remain distant from the self. In a discussion on "the self-education of the educator" as it applies to the psychoanalyst, Carl Jung makes a similar point: "He will discover that the ultimate questions which oppress him as well as his patients cannot be solved by any amount of 'treatment'", and he insists that "the physician may no longer slip out of his own difficulties by treating the difficulties of others" (Jung, 2004: 53). The importance of self-awareness and self-

---

[12] The quest for recognition, affirmation, validation and reflection in the other is a theme explored, albeit in different directions, by Ricoeur and Lacan, and is poetically portrayed in Eliot's "Prufrock".

honesty in the person of the carer/educator/psychoanalyst is crucial according to Nietzsche: "A genuine physio-psychology has to struggle with unconscious resistances in the heart of the investigator" (Nietzsche, 2003: 53), and is explored by Freud as the phenomenon of countertransference. In these, as in all human relationships, Buber insists that mutuality is essential, the mutuality of persons meeting each other without presumption, conviction, or the superiority of a one-sided expertise.[13]

Reminiscent of Freud's theory of defence mechanisms, Buber's reference to the dulling of awareness and consciousness, particularly with regard to one's ultimate aloneness and individual responsibility for one's life (Buber, 2004: 131), suggests that in an attempted flight from the reality of the self, one necessarily refuses the immediate experience of life itself: "But the risk is too dangerous for us...we perfect the defence apparatus...Each of us is encased in an armour which we soon, out of familiarity, no longer notice" (Buber, 2004: 12).[14] In this position of self-alienation, genuine encounter is precluded, and the possibility of love is thwarted. Instead, according to Buber, we approach the other either as an object of our observation in an attempt to measure and categorise, or with the interest of the onlooker detached from any personal relation, "the aloof fields of aesthesis" (Buber, 2004: 11). The use of this defence apparatus sets between the individual and the world a rigid religious dogma, a rigid political belief and commitment to a group, or a rigid wall of personal values and habits. Thus, we seek to avoid the nakedness of risk and vulnerability which would result from the shedding of these defences.[15] Limited by this protective armour, the subject seeks security in illusions of sameness and denial of difference, and thus loses sight of the potential and

---

[13] Buber insists on the necessity of mutuality in all real relationships whilst acknowledging that in areas such as education and psychotherapy this mutuality cannot be fully developed.

[14] Buber's reference to the gradual incorporation of an "armour" which is no longer discerned by the individual evokes reflection on the relationship between the real and the false self, between inner and outer realities, and in particular the various interpretations of "the mask" as a conscious or unconscious disguise adopted in order to hide the reality of the self, or as an integral component of the integration of the public and private expression of being. (These issues are explored by writers as diverse as Yeats and Žižek).

[15] Richard Kearney explores this avoidance of vulnerability in his work, *The God Who May Be*, and explains: "this reality of the ego's fundamental insecurity and frailty is something most prefer to ignore, compensating instead, from childhood on, with fantasies of power and omnipotence" (Kearney, 2001: 12).

mystery of his or her unique self.[16] Echoing Nietzsche's reference to "slow suicide" and his observation that "the most exquisite daisies are never tasted", Buber describes the consequence of self-alienation: "Most of us achieve only at rare moments a clear realization of the fact that they have never tasted the fulfilment of existence, that their life does not participate in true, fulfilled existence, that, as it were, it passes true existence by" (Buber, 2002: 30). Concurring with Nietzsche's thesis of self-actualization, Buber states that "Every man's foremost task is the actualization of his unique, unprecedented and never-recurring potentialities, and not the repetition of something that another, and be it even the greatest, has already achieved" (Buber, 2002: 9). When individuals are alienated from themselves, when they are concerned with the impression made on the other, they favour seeming over being, opt for approval over authenticity, and refuse to proceed from what they really are.

Buber acknowledges the duality of being and seeming, and realistically accepts the vacillation between the two modes of living. The human being inevitably dons a variety of masks in an attempt to protect the vulnerability of the self, and in the quest for recognition and affirmation from the other: "Man wishes to be confirmed in his being by man, and wishes to have a presence in the being of the other. The human person needs confirmation because man as man needs it" (Buber, 1999: 16). Concern with appearance, performance, and the perceived effect of one's self-presentation on the other has its source in "man's need for confirmation", and the fear that one's real self would fail in this quest, according to Friedman: "It is no easy thing to be confirmed by the other in one's essence; therefore, one looks to appearance for aid" (Friedman, 2002: 99). This phenomenon of human behaviour suggested in terms such as 'seeming', appearance', 'mask', 'persona', 'false self' or 'public self', is an issue explored in diverse ways by all the writers explored in this study. According to these analyses the motivation underlying the various manifestations of this behaviour lies in a commingling of fear and desire; the desire for recognition, affirmation, confirmation, acceptance and belonging, and fear of exposure, rejection, denial, ridicule and misunderstanding. All the writers validate this motivation as understandable, and Nietzsche and Žižek, particularly, suggest that authenticity may involve an interplay of the two modes of being, and an eventual

---

[16] Eliot's "Prufrock" is a poetic expression of the loss of self in the attempt to merge with the social world.

integration of being and seeming, essence[17] and mask, inner and outer experience.

Where One Stands

> There is something that can only be found in one place. It is a great treasure, which may be called the fulfilment of existence. The place where this treasure can be found is the place on which one stands (Buber, 2002: 30).

Buber situates the event of dialogue, of genuine meeting, in the particular, concrete experiences of daily life, rather than in the high moral ground of generalized platitudes and easy clichés: "The life of dialogue is not one in which you have much to do with men, but one in which you really have to do with those with whom you have to do" (Buber, 2004: 23). This concentration on the particular and the concrete, on the demands and responsibilities of the face-to-face encounter with actual lived experience in the present moment, is central to the possibility of love, according to Buber, and his assertion that, "I know no one in any time who has succeeded in loving every man he met" (Buber, 2004: 24), resounds with the opposition of Nietzsche, Freud, Lacan and Žižek to the dictum of universal love.

Buber insists that "the essential thing is to begin with oneself", but this is only the start; the ultimate direction is a departure from the exclusively subjective and exclusively objective points of view, and is an embrace of both polarities and what is possible between them: "to begin with oneself, but not to end with oneself" (Buber, 2002: 25). This is a movement which is necessarily outward, intersubjective, relational, and it is an attempt "to breach the barriers of the self and to come out from ourselves to meet with essential otherness" (Buber, 2004: 213). This is where the possibility of love is enabled: "Love is responsibility of an *I* for a *Thou*" (Buber, 2004a: 20). In the words of Shapira, "the importance of individualization [is] as an anticipation of a life of communion" (Shapira, 1999: 148), because

---

[17] The concept of "essence" is used here in an acknowledgement of its elusive, ambiguous and open-ended interpretation. It resounds with ideas which are similarly complex and ambivalent, such as "real self" and "core self". It is not asserted here that 'essence' is an unchanging, static form of being; however, it is suggested that the potential existence of a "mask" implies a phenomenon/reality which is being "masked".

"someone who concentrates on his individuality, must, in Buber's view, realize that the formation of personality is not an end in itself but rather a stage prior to a life of relationship, to dialogical existence" (Shapira, 1999: 126). The poet, Brendan Kennelly, puts it simply: "Self knows that self is not enough" (Kennelly, 2004: 425).

This "dialogical existence", the authentic relationship between persons, and the experience of love, are glorified concepts devoid of meaning as long as they remain confined to theoretic and absolutist abstractions. As such, they are easily espoused, gain popular adherence, and fit comfortably with ideals of what life and love should be as distinct from what it is on a personal and experiential level. Buber does not situate his vision of authentic relationship and genuine conversation in this unreal realm but asserts its possibility, "the break-through", as contingent on an acceptance of the imperfect nature of human existence: "I am not concerned with the pure; I am concerned with the turbid, the repressed, the pedestrian, with toil and dull contraryness – and with the break-through. With the break-through and not with perfection" (Buber, 2004: 41). Belief in the possibility of authenticity, genuineness, and relationship implies a belief in the possibility of love, and Buber asserts his conviction that this experience is open to the human being in spite of and perhaps because of the complexity and imperfection of human nature: "You are really able. There are no gifted and ungifted here, only those who give themselves and those who withhold themselves" (Buber, 2004: 40). With a resounding echo of Nietzsche's view, Buber states that: "Man is not good, man is not evil; he is, in a pre-eminent sense, good and evil together...that is the nakedness in which he recognizes himself" (Buber, 2004: 92).

Buber's acknowledgement of the complex "nakedness" of human being is enabled by a concentration on concrete, actual situations of lived experience: "Into nothing exalted, heroic or holy, into no Either or no Or, only into this tiny strictness and grace of every day" (Buber, 2004: 41). It is here, away from the comforting protections of morality, ideology and academic rationalizations that Buber situates the ever-new challenge of loving relationship: "where we really stand, where we live, where we live a true life...the little world entrusted to us...in that section of Creation entrusted to us" (Buber, 2002: 33). The practical experience of encounter in these terms is open to what is yet unfamiliar, unknown, and unpredictable, it is a manifestation of interest and attention and care, and it is far removed from prescriptive assumptions and absolutist guidelines which prohibit the possibility of growth and new understanding: "The highest culture of the soul remains basically arid and barren unless, day by day, the waters of life pour forth into the soul from those little encounters to which we give their due" (Buber, 2002: 32). When encounter, with experience, with the other, with life, is based on assumption and fore-knowledge, understanding and meeting is negated because "what is untypical in the particular situation remains unnoticed and unanswered" (Buber 2004: 135). Relationship, openness to the other, demands an appreciation of "the uniqueness of every situation" (Buber, 2004: 134):

> In spite of all similarities every living situation has, like a newborn child, a new face, that has never been before and will never come again. It demands of you a reaction which cannot be prepared beforehand. It demands nothing of what is past. It demands presence, responsibility; it demands you (Buber, 2004: 135).

According to Buber, "genuine responsibility exists only where there is real responding…to what happens to one [in] each concrete hour allotted to the person" (Buber, 2004: 18, 19). He rejects the "illusion of a responsibility without a receiver" (Buber, 2004: 53), and implicitly discounts the validity of "convictions" and "values" that are proclaimed in the vacuum of distance and theory.[18] Conviction and responsibility become real and meaningful in the concrete experiences of human relationships: "Only one thing matters, that as the situation is presented to me I expose myself to it as to the word's manifestation to me" (Buber, 2004: 80).

Awareness of personal responsibility and potentiality as distinct from the dictates of "the crowd", persistent attempts at genuine dialogue and openness to the other as distinct from the many faces of monologue, ongoing acceptance and integration of the self in complexity and ambivalence, and a willingness to respond openly and unknowingly to the present moment, with its particular demand, its unique encounter, and its unpredictability, enable the possibility of genuine meeting, I-Thou relation, and the experience of love: "Everything is changed in real meeting" (Buber, 1999: 242).[19] Here everything is possible because dialogue in the Buberian understanding of the term takes place: "dialogue in my sense implies of necessity the unforeseen, and its basic element is surprise, the surprising mutuality" (Buber, 1999: 190). "The unforeseen", the "surprise", entails the reality of uncertainty and the risk of

---

[18] Buber's dismissal of "responsibility without a receiver" is similar to Žižek's interpretation of virtuous-sounding phrases such as "human rights" and "neighbourly love".

[19] Jung reiterates Buber's assertion: "the meeting of two personalities is like the contact of two chemical substances: if there is any reaction, both are transformed" (Jung, 2004: 49, 50).

unpredictability: "There is no certainty. There is only a chance; but there is no other. The risk does not ensure the truth for us; but it, and it alone, leads us to where the breath of truth is to be felt" (Buber, 2004: 83). In this mode of being the "magic of life" is embraced:

> Believe in the simple magic of life, in service in the universe, and the meaning of that waiting, that alertness, that 'craning of the neck' in creatures will dawn upon you. Every word would falsify; but look! Round about you beings live their life, and to whatever point you turn you come upon being (Buber, 2004a: 20).

This magic does not negate the imperfection and incomprehension pervading life; it insists that one "must put his arms around the vexatious world" (Buber, 2004: 76) because "the man who has not ceased to love the human world in all its abasement sees even today genuine form" (Buber, 2004: 70). This embrace of "the vexatious world" echoes Nietzsche's call for *amor fati*, and also resounds with Nussbaum's view of philosophy and education: "Abandoning the zeal for absolute perfection as inappropriate to the life of a finite being, abandoning the thirst for punishment and self-punishment that so frequently accompanies that zeal, the education I recommend looks with mercy at the ambivalent excellence and passion of a human life" (Nussbaum, 1994: 510). The possibility of love emerges in the celebration of the beauty and mystery of that which is imperfect and incomprehensible.

Buber's proposition that the I-Thou relationship occurs only in rare moments and is inevitably replaced by the necessity of the I-It relationship is the subject of Kaufmann's criticism of Buberian philosophy (Kaufmann, 2002: 263). However, Kaufmann justifies his inclusion of Buber as one of the philosophers who have contributed to "discovering the mind", and hence to self-knowledge and self-awareness, by concentrating his admiration of Buber's work on translation and hence on interpretation: "his theory of translation is his most enduring contribution to the discovery of the mind. It only needs to be extended beyond the art of translation to the art of interpretation not only of written materials but also of human beings – others as well as oneself" (Kaufmann, 2002: 279). The topic of translation, of interpretation, and of hermeneutical philosophy is one of the central contributions of the philosopher Paul Ricoeur, and the following chapter examines how this dimension of thought can enhance an understanding of the possibility of love.

CHAPTER THREE

PAUL RICOEUR

The philosophy of Paul Ricoeur, like that of Buber, has a strong theological aspect which is outside the exploration of this study. Ricoeur has repeatedly stated his intention to maintain the autonomy and integrity of his theological and philosophical work as separate: "I am very committed to the autonomy of philosophy".[1] While his work ranges over diverse subjects – the problem of evil, the meaning of identity, human will, and human fragility - his philosophical writings have increasingly centred on hermeneutics as the key instrument in the search for meaning; he sees human experience as inherently interpretive; and he asserts that language is both the foundation and the form of one's encounter with reality and one's attempt to make sense of the world:

> The decisive feature of hermeneutics is the capacity of world-disclosure yielded by texts. Hermeneutics is not confined to texts nor to authors of texts; its primary concern is with the worlds which these authors and texts open up. It is by an understanding of the worlds, actual and possible, opened up by language that we may arrive at a better understanding of ourselves (Ricoeur, 1991: 490).

William Hall explores Ricoeur's work with the focus on "what his writings tell us about what it means to be human", and he argues that "his philosophy can be viewed as a singular project which is centrally concerned with this question of human meaning" (Hall, 2007: 4). Therefore, Ricoeur's philosophy aims at greater understanding, of the

---

[1] This is a statement from Ricoeur quoted by William David Hall in *Paul Ricoeur and the Poetic Imperative: The Creative Tension between Love and Justice*, p. 4. In an essay, "Ricoeur's Philosophical Journey: Its Import for Religion", David Tracy asserts Ricoeur's achievement of this aim: "Ricoeur always keeps the genres clear in order not only to allow figurative and conceptual forms their distinct but dialogically related roles but also to keep properly distinct religion, philosophy and theology...Unlike some of his admirers, Ricoeur himself never allows philosophy or theology to be confused or conflated" (Tracy, 1996: 202).

world, of the subject, and of the relationship between them; it resonates with Nietzsche's theory of "perspectivism" which states that all knowledge is based on interpretation, and with Buber's contention that life is essentially dialogical.

Ricoeur's examination of the role of language in human experience, its inevitable translation both across different language usages and within same-language contexts, and its power to reveal and to conceal the truth of who we are and how we live, forms the nucleus of his analysis of the human subject as ambiguous, fallible, and mysterious, but also as potentially powerful, loving, and creative. The expanse of this spectrum is noted by Richard Kearney as he addresses Ricoeur with the reflection: "It is remarkable that you should begin your philosophical career by reflecting on the nature of *l'homme fallible* (*fallible man*) and conclude by shifting the focus to *l'homme capable*" (Kearney, 2004: 167). Human weakness, frailty and failure co-exist with human capability, power and possibility, and Ricoeur's analysis may be construed as a commitment to strive towards the possible in full cognizance of its obstacles; thus it provides a relevant framework for the exploration of love's possibility.

Ricoeur justifies his insistence on the hermeneutical nature of human existence because, he argues, "language is the only complete, exhaustive, and objectively intelligible expression of human interiority" (Ricoeur, 1970: 545). This view of language, as "the only...intelligible expression of human interiority", acknowledges the limitations of language,[2] and leads Ricoeur to work towards the possibility of a restorative hermeneutics wherein meaning is retrieved/restored/recovered through open and comprehensive attempts at interpretation. This may appear to conflict with a hermeneutics of suspicion which Ricoeur associates with Freudian psychoanalysis as the latter discerns a hidden meaning concealed or distorted in the conscious expression of language. However, as Kearney explains, for Ricoeur, the hermeneutics of suspicion is necessary for a hermeneutics of affirmation (Kearney, 2004: 7):

> Suspicion takes the form of a critique of false consciousness by the three 'masters of suspicion' – Freud, Marx and Nietzsche...All three recognized that meaning, far from being transparent to itself, is an enigmatic process which conceals at the same time as it reveals. Ricoeur insists therefore on the need for a hermeneutics of suspicion which demystifies our illusions (Kearney, 2004: 7, 8).

---

[2] The limitations of language in expressing the innermost depths of human being is a key issue explored by Lacan in the next section.

Both hermeneutical practices endeavour, albeit through different methods and directions, to disclose truth and meaning, and to confront the ambiguities of self-knowledge and self-deception. Kearney, in his introduction to Ricoeur's short thesis, *On Translation*, explains that for Ricoeur, translation "indicates the everyday act of speaking as a way not only of translating oneself to another...but also and more explicitly of translating oneself to oneself", and he supports this view with a quotation from Dominico Jervolino: "To speak is already to translate (even when one is speaking to oneself); further, one has to take into account the plurality of languages, which demand a more exacting encounter with the different Other" (qtd. in Ricoeur, 2006: xv). The titles of some of Ricoeur's works, for example, *The Course of Recognition, Fallible Man,* and *Oneself as Another*, suggest an outline of some of the obstacles to the fulfilment of human potential, the complexities inherent in encountering the alterity of the other, and hence an analysis of the barriers to the experience of love.

Ricoeur's work involves an acknowledgement of opposition and conflict as an inescapable dimension of human living. He notes the oppositional nature of diverse political ambitions, of different national aspirations, of contrasting ideological convictions, and of myriad philosophical and historical interpretations of human experience. Without cynicism, and without despair, Ricoeur acknowledges human failure to realize genuine human community as recounted throughout history. Underlying these failures, Ricoeur recognizes the conflicting nature of many inter-personal relationships, as the human subject strives to discover, and to maintain, his or her identity in a world which is already interpreted before the individual's entry to it: "In being born I enter into the world of language that precedes me and envelops me" (Ricoeur, 2002: 27). This point is also made by Lacan who notes that before language is acquired, the subject is already in the symbolic dimension. Ricoeur's response to the acknowledgement of difference and incompatibility is not merely to seek conciliation and agreement; he extends the proposition of the other great philosopher of hermeneutics, Hans Georg Gadamer, who suggests an open-minded meeting of different perspectives, with a view to reaching a new perspective, "a fusion of horizons" (Gadamer, 2004: 367). Ricoeur argues for an acceptance of difference, for a living-with diversity, and for a respect which honours the multiplicity of human thought and interpretation. According to David Kaplan, this is "one of Ricoeur's many strengths as a philosopher...He tends to think in terms of opposites, pairs, and contrasts juxtaposed in such a way that highlights and preserves differences, while resisting the temptation to synthesize a new unity"

(Kaplan, 2003: 1). Thus, Ricoeur advocates a focus on bridge-building and mediation between diverse positions and interpretations rather than an unrealistic attempt to integrate difference.

When Ricoeur defines the "ethical intention" as "*aiming at the 'good life' with and for others, in just institutions*" (Ricoeur, 1992: 172), he is firmly asserting the existential bond between the self and the other, and he is also insisting on a philosophy of action, the practical expression of his philosophical thought. Ricoeur is using the phrase, "the good life" in the Aristotelian sense of "living well" or the Proustean concept of the "true life"; he explains that "the 'good life' is, for each of us, the nebulous of ideals and dreams of achievement with regard to which a life is held to be more or less fulfilled or unfulfilled", and he stresses the practical manifestation of this aim: "we would say that it is the unending work of interpretation applied to action and to oneself that we pursue the search for adequation between what seems to us to be best with regard to our life as a whole and the preferential choices that govern our practice" (Ricoeur, 1992: 179). The living of "the good life" entails living "with others" and resounds with Buber's definition of "community". The difficulties involved in the open embrace of the other, in interpersonal and institutional realms, are aptly chronicled in various interpretations of human history, and continue to challenge contemporary ideals of peaceful co-existence between nations, groups, and individuals. These difficulties and challenges inevitably pose obstacles to the experience of love in human living, and are confronted and analysed creatively in the philosophy of Ricoeur.

The Fragmented Multiplicity of the Subject

> We do not mistake ourselves without also being mistaken about others and our relations with them (Ricoeur, 2005: 257).

Illusions pertaining to concepts of subjectivity, distorted assumptions regarding human nature, and mistaken perceptions of self and other, diminish the potential of human relationships and pose obstacles to the possible experience of love. Ricoeur's analysis of the human subject examines and critiques diverse interpretations and descriptions which have been offered throughout the history of philosophy. He questions the concept of the self as a fixed unity which underlies the Cartesian cogito, and he notes "the humiliation of the cogito reduced to sheer illusion following the Nietzschean critique" (Ricoeur, 1992: 299); he rejects the contention of thinkers such as Michel Foucault that the subject is merely a construct of particular cultures; and he dismisses the description of subjectivity as a biochemical entity endorsed by some analytic philosophers. Instead, Ricoeur proposes a narrative understanding of subjectivity that takes into account the open-ended and fluid nature of one's life description, and which, as Kearney points out, cannot be restricted to dogmatic formulations: "The narrative model of identity suggests that the age-old virtue of self-knowledge...involves not some self-enclosed ego but a hermeneutically examined life freed from naïve archaisms and dogmatisms" (Kearney, 2004: 199). According to this narrative understanding of identity, the temporal dimension of selfhood precludes fixed definitions, unchangeable certainties, and necessitates an acceptance of fragility, vulnerability and fallibility: "the Self is aimed at rather than experienced...the person is primarily a project which I represent to myself, which I set before me and entertain" (Ricoeur, 2002: 69). Thus, Ricoeur explains the "mobile" nature of identity:

> narrative identity is not that of an immutable substance or of a fixed structure, but rather the mobile identity issuing from the combination of the concordance of the story, taken as a structured totality, and the discordance imposed by the encountered events...it is possible to revise a recounted story which takes account of other events, or even which organizes the recounted events differently (Ricoeur, 1996: 6).

Morny Joy refers to this aspect of Ricoeur's work in her introduction to *Paul Ricoeur and Narrative*:

> Ricoeur's approach is hermeneutical in that it accepts that we are constantly part of a process of interpretation and reinterpretation. We are involved in a constant evolution whereby the past is being integrated into the present, and the present refining its perceptions of the past and of its own definitions (Joy: 1977: xxvi).

Thus, Ricoeur asserts that the temporal unfolding of life may be understood as the unfolding of a narrative, an open-ended life-story which is constantly re-narrated in the light of reflection and experience: "Learning to narrate oneself is also learning how to narrate oneself in other ways" (Ricoeur, 2005: 101). This resounds with Nietzsche's words. "I tell myself to myself", while also concurring with his concept of "becoming" as a continual process (Nietzsche, 2003a: 214). This Ricoeuerian concept is aptly captured in the title given to one of Ricoeur's essays on the theme, "Life: A Story in Search of a Narrator", and he opens the essay with the

following words: "That life has to do with narration has always been
known and said; we speak of the story of a life to characterize the interval
between birth and death". However, Ricoeur adds a warning note: "And
yet this assimilation of a life to a history should not be automatic; it is a
commonplace that should first be subjected to critical doubt" (Ricoeur,
1991: 425). Story-telling, personal as well as fictional, helps one to make
sense of one's life, and the importance of narration, especially in the light
of insight gained through interpretation, memory and integration, is an
essential characteristic of the psychoanalytic process as outlined by Freud
and Lacan. Judith Butler refers to this experience as *Giving an Account of
Oneself*, and stresses that narration always implies a listening and
receiving other: "An account of oneself is always given to an-other,
whether conjured or existing" (Butler, 2005: 21). Hence, narration, as
integral to human understanding, evinces the relational essence of human
living as asserted by Buber. According to Freud, the unconscious also
emerges as a narrative in dreams; Lacan expands on this theme, famously
stating that "the unconscious is structured like a language" (Lacan, 1999:
15); thus, through the medium of language in the psychoanalytic
encounter, an integration of the past with the present is enabled in a re-
narration of the subject's life-story. This process, inside or outside the
psychoanalytic setting, requires a radical shift from illusions of self-
knowledge, self-transparency, and self-righteous possession of the truth of
oneself and of others; it requires a different interpretation of the subject, a
renunciation of "the ideal of the perfect translation" (Ricoeur, 2006: 8).
Accordingly, meaning can only ever be temporary, as the openness to
ongoing interpretation precludes completion and fixity. This aspect of
Ricoeur's thought raises the question of authority, or authorship, regarding
the narration of a life. Does this authority rest with the individual, or can
other narrators of that life also be valid? This is central to Derrida's
critique of psychoanalysis, as he argues that the process of analysis
inevitably involves the imposition of another's truth on the subject
(Derrida, 1998: 9). Derrida extends his argument to question the validity
of biography, whereby a person's story is restricted to the perspective of
the biographer, with its inevitable prejudices and selective emphasis. The
analogy between biography and history is obvious – history is essentially
constructed through whole or partial biographies, and hence is susceptible
to similar arguments.[3]

---

[3] Ricoeur provides a comprehensive exploration of the challenges posed by
concepts relating to history, giving witness, remembering, forgiving, forgetting,
etc. in his work *Memory, History, Forgetting*.

Ricoeur explores the complicated nature of selfhood in *Oneself as Another,* and his conclusion is summarized by Kaplan, in *Ricoeur's Critical Theory*, as the assertion that "the many different ways of posing the question of selfhood suggests that there is no single, unitary conception of the self but multiple aspects of selfhood that are illuminated by posing different questions" (Kaplan, 2003: 83). Ricoeur refers to the influence of society on the conditions of our adjustment and consequently on our understanding of the self, echoing Freud's discussion of the conflict between individual happiness and the demands of civilization: "most often we treat ourselves as objects. Working and social life require this objectification" (Ricoeur, 2002: 101), but he suggests that the individual personality also plays a part in imposing these requirements, and thus he describes "a level of pretension that is determined jointly by society and the subject's personality" (Ricoeur, 2002: 101). Irigaray expands on this reference to the demands of society by stating that the consequence is the diminishment of love: "Besides the fact that love in our culture has been poorly cultivated…individual feeling and the approach of the other harmonize with difficulty to collective imperatives coming from the outside" (Irigaray, 2002: 57).

Unquestioned acceptance of illusory theories of selfhood which profess ideals of self-knowledge, self-sufficiency, and self-unity, entails a rejection of the essential multiplicity of the self, with its diverse and often discordant pluralities and variations. This is achieved only by a masking of one's vulnerabilities and mutability. The necessary mask is that of unity and coherence, suggestive of a fixed subjectivity which is closed and secure from the permeations of encounter with experience, since this experiential encounter necessarily demands an openness to change and revision. The mask of self-unity and self-completion also, either consciously or unconsciously, imposes a veil of *a priori* judgements and expectations on the other, whether this other is an event, a text or a person, and it therefore precludes and prevents a recognition and reception of difference or alterity, in oneself and in the other; if the self is fixed, the other is also fixed. The inherent danger and limitation of illusory unity is asserted by Kearney; "Narrative concordance can mask discordance; its drive for order and unity displacing difference…it can degenerate into oppressive grand narratives"[4] (Kearney, 2004: 110). The desire for unity and the corresponding denial of difference and complexity necessitates the oppression of that which does not correspond to this ideal, and the

---

[4] The critique of grand narratives as valid representations of reality and experience is a central characteristic of postmodern thought.

repression of one's awareness of such ambiguity and plurality diminishes the possibility of mediation within oneself and with others:

> Man is not intermediate because he is between angel and animal; he is intermediate within himself, within his selves. He is intermediate because he is a mixture, and a mixture because he brings about mediations. His ontological characteristic of being-intermediate consists precisely in that his act of existing is the very act of bringing about mediations between all the modalities and all the levels of reality within him and outside him (Ricoeur, 2002: 3).

Ricoeur suggests that the self is therefore a mediation between constancy and change, between innate characteristics and the transformations which result from the ongoing character of lived experience, between what he describes as *idem*-identity and *ipse*-identity:

> ipse-identity involves a dialectic complementary to that of selfhood and sameness, namely the dialectic of self and the other than self. As long as one remains within the circle of sameness-identity, the otherness of the other than self remains within the circle of sameness-identity, the otherness of the other than self offers nothing original (Ricoeur, 1992: 3).

This is very close to the thought of Derrida, as he also maintains that acknowledgement of "the radical otherness of the other…is the condition of my relation to the other". For Derrida, the inability to know the other "from the inside" is integral to human relationships and so also to love: "I cannot reach the other…This is not an obstacle but the condition of love" (Derrida, 2004a: 14).[5] The attraction of remaining within this closed circle of illusory self-knowledge and transparency also restricts access to the otherness of the self, and consequently limits the capacity for self-love because it denies an essential part of that self. It restricts the creation of a narrative identity whereby one's life-story, one's understanding of oneself, is enriched by the attempted synthesis of past, present and future, and by the willingness to revise and reinterpret one's identity in the light of new experiences and new translations of previous stories one has told about oneself and others. In this way, as is argued by Kearney, "story-telling can also be a breeding ground of illusions, distortions and ideological

---

[5] The desire to know the other "from the inside", rather than being an emanation of love, may perhaps be seen as a pathological desire to obliterate the otherness of the other or to bolster the illusion that one can interpret anything or anyone perfectly or completely.

falsehoods...narrative emplotment can easily serve as a cover up" (Kearney, 2004: 199). The self is never a completed possession, it is never a fixed entity, it is never a self-sufficient cogito; rather it is a living, and therefore a growing, changing, and responding "becoming" which is in the process of interpreting and reinterpreting itself and its world. It implies an exposure to life's unceasing questions and challenges, a plurality of interpretations and answers, and an on-going tension between what it is and what it is becoming: "It seems, then, that conflict is a function of man's most primordial constitution; the object is synthesis; the self is conflict" (Ricoeur, 2002: 132). In his introduction to Ricoeur's work, *Figuring the Sacred*, Mark Wallace summarises Ricoeur's thesis of selfhood as "a task to be performed, not a given that awaits passive reception by the subject" (Ricoeur, 1995: 3). Without acknowledgement of one's complex and often contradictory nature, the self imposes a self-captivity to narrowness, disproportion, and alienation from itself and from others. Rejection of one's multiplicity and mutability is a rejection of Nietzsche's call for a more realistic appraisal of the subject as "Human, All Too Human", and it is also a denial of human frailty and fallibility. The resulting self-righteousness, coupled with a pseudo-self-constancy, inevitably fosters an alienation from the full spectrum of being human, an estrangement from the diverse potentialities of self and other, and erects a barrier against the openness and mutuality inherent in any approach to the possibility of love.

Narrowness of Vision

> Habit *fixes* our tastes and aptitudes and thus shrinks our field of availability; the range of the possible narrows down; my life has taken shape (Ricoeur, 2002: 57).

The quest for certainty and security, for control and solution, and for fixity and permanence, is often sourced in a perceived need for acceptable self-image; this self-image, whether individual or collective, personal or national, entails a confining restriction of boundaries, a selective portrayal of human nature, and the imposition of constricting limitations in the possibilities of human relationship. The experience of love is blocked in this narrowing of perception, as the self withdraws behind illusions of self-sufficiency, self-knowledge and self-acceptance. Vulnerability, fallibility, and change are rejected in favour of insurance against risk, but this insurance is maintained only through a refusal to encounter the possibilities of life in their fullness and ambivalence.

Ricoeur's hermeneutics of the self, his description of identity as narrative, and his emphasis on interpretation as essential to understanding, cohere in his insistence that mediation is integral to selfhood and being. Mediation is intrinsic to the individual's relationship with himself or herself and the diverse complexities within the self; it is inherent in the individual's encounter with the world; and it is prerequisite to the mutuality and reciprocity of genuine relationship between self and others. Ricoeur's thesis of mediation resounds with Buber's contention that life is essentially relational, and also echoes Buber's acceptance of the individual's incapacity to consistently maintain the vision of the other as a Thou in all areas of inter-relationships. Like Buber and Nietzsche, Ricoeur argues for a recognition of human fallibility and error, he calls for the embrace of plurality and tension within the human condition, and he warns against the consequences of a one-sided and narrow vision of human nature which denies its ambiguities and contradictions. As Irigaray states, "consciousness of the difficulty opens the way to new strategies" (Irigaray, 2002: 61), while blindness and denial ensure that difficulties are ignored and neglected. Narrowness of vision can centre on one side of the polarities which Ricoeur sees as framing human existence; polarities of freedom and finitude, of responsibility and fallibility, of good and evil, and of self and other. Restriction of vision, and consequently of understanding, is "endemic to all of human thought, the tendency to avoid the risk of openness and otherness by seeking refuge 'within the circle which I form for myself'" (Ricoeur, 2002: xv). This results in a diminishment of perception, a narrowing of vision, and a closing off of possibility and understanding. The romantic poet, William Blake describes this phenomenon of self-created limitation and imprisonment: "For man has closed himself up, till he sees all things thro' / narrow chinks of his cavern" (Blake, 2004: 142). The closed circle of a one-sided interpretation of reality and of human nature is linked, but not synonymous, with Nietzsche's perspectivism. Ricoeur echoes Nietzsche saying that "All perception is perspectival", but he suggests the possibility of transcending this limitation "by situating my perspective in relation to other possible perspectives that deny mine as the zero-origin" (Ricoeur, 2002: 26). A refusal to consider other possible perspectives leads to a diminishment of life, a stagnation of growth, and a dismissal of the possibilities of the other.

The selective disavowal of one side of the apparent polarities inherent in the human condition is tempting in its illusory power to enhance one's self-image. Nussbaum, in her expansive work on philosophy and literature, refers to this understandable attraction to a distorted vision: "When we examine our own lives, we have so many obstacles to correct vision, so many motives to blindness and stupidity. The 'vulgar heat' of jealousy and personal interest comes between us and the loving perception of each particular" (Nussbaum, 1992: 162). Restricted vision, with its limited focus on selected aspects of human nature, can result in a veil of ignorance and illusion, distortion and denial. Concentration on human freedom, "the voluntary", to the exclusion of human finitude, "the involuntary", and a similar selection along the spectrum of good/evil, power/domination, responsibility/fallibility, intellect/emotion, and patient/agent, results in a distortion of individuality, as the other cannot be perceived as being like oneself, and one cannot see oneself as another. Instead, unacceptable, uncomfortable, unfamiliar aspects of human nature are projected elsewhere to one's own situation, and the commonality of a shared human existence is denied. Denial of weakness and fault, of "fallibility; the constitutional weakness that makes evil possible" (Ricoeur, 2002: xliii), and of any aspects of humanity which are deemed unacceptable, prevents the necessary confrontation with and resolution of the difficulties and conflicts which ensue in spite of their repression and denial, and thwarts the "opportunity for a much more extensive study of the structures of human reality" (Ricoeur, 2002: xliii). A one-sided vision of oneself, of others, and of reality is mistaken in taking the part for the whole.

Ricoeur argues that this denial is a denial of the essence of human nature: "the idea that man is by nature fragile and liable to err…designates a characteristic of man's being" (Ricoeur, 2002: 1). Denial of an essential aspect of human being within the self diminishes an approach to the humanity of the other. Ricoeur asserts that "My humanity is my essential community with all that is human outside myself; that community makes every man my like", and he supports his argument by quoting Alain Badiou:

> In every human body all passions and errors are possible…There are as many ways of being wicked as there are men in the world. But there is also a salvation peculiar to each man, of the same complexion, of the same turn as he (qtd. in Ricoeur, 2002: 61).

Ricoeur explains that "all values are accessible to all men, but in a way that is peculiar to each one. It is in this sense that "each" man is "man"" (Ricoeur, 2002: 61.) Denial of this essential interrelationship of self and other, refusal to see oneself, in all one's weakness and glory, in the other, and restricting one's horizon to that of illusory self-containment and self-righteousness, while superficially creating a sense of self-satisfaction and security, inevitably results in one's alienation from the reality of oneself.

Ricoeur consistently asserts the relational and dialogical nature of human existence, he rejects the fantasy of individual self-sufficiency in an acknowledgement of the realities of human interdependence; however, he does not equate interrelationship with the negation of one's existential solitude:

> the feeling of the primal difference between I and all others; to find oneself in a certain mood is to feel one's individuality as inexpressible and incommunicable. Just as one's position cannot be shared with another, so also the affective situation in which I find myself and feel myself cannot be exchanged (Ricoeur, 2002: 55).

Rather, Ricoeur suggests a respect for and an accommodation of both solitude and solicitude, a mediation between the incommensurable aloneness of the individual and the undeniable human striving for community and connection. Solitude, aloneness, is both challenging and inevitable, but the entrenchment of self-protection and projection results in alienation and loneliness. Erich Fromm asserts that in the absence of this mediation "our civilization offers many palliatives which help people to be consciously unaware of this loneliness" (Fromm, 1995: 67). The palliatives range from "beneficial" categories of work, group membership, material compensation, to "destructive" obsessions of drug and alcohol addiction, crime and psychosis. The obsessive character of these palliatives suggests their failure in satiating the desire which propels them. Ricoeur refers to the resulting "oblivion and dissimulation of the ontological destination of human desire…Crafts or professions, in fact, present themselves as careers more or less 'open' or 'blocked' in which we raise our level of pretension" (Ricoeur, 2002: 100).[6] The numbing or "blocking" effect of immersion in professional roles is also argued by Nietzsche: "A profession makes us thoughtless; therein lies its greatest blessing. For it is a bulwark, behind which we are allowed to withdraw when qualms and worries of a general kind attack us" (Nietzsche, 1984: 241). The denial of one's essential aloneness ironically diminishes the level of connection with others which could make one's aloneness

---

[6] The philosophy of Ricoeur explores the ambiguous concept of identity, for example in his work, *The Course of Recognition*; his reference to "pretension", with regard to "careers" and other "roles" which are used to describe the self, suggests that identity is something integral to human being and is therefore not dependent on anything external to it.

bearable and fruitful. This point is supported strongly by Ilham Dilham in his analysis of love, *Love: Its Forms, Dimensions and Paradoxes.* He states: "I argue that it is in accepting this separateness that we find our individuality and that it is only as such that we can establish a genuine reciprocity in our personal relationships" (Dilman, 1998: 1). However, the difficulties involved in finding our individuality are often sourced in the quest for relationships, especially when relationships are seen as potentially providing identity, esteem and recognition.

The Fragility of Identity

> Nothing is more fragile, nothing is
> easier to wound than an existence that
> is at the mercy of a belief (Ricoeur,
> 2002: 125).

The human need for recognition, reflection, affirmation and acknowledgement is a phenomenon explored and debated in many areas of philosophy and psychoanalysis. Many theorists look to the earliest experiences of infantile life to analyze and describe the development of this need in the human subject.[7] Ricoeur examines the quest for recognition in its diverse manifestations, and outlines the fragility of a personal identity which is solely dependent on its provision by an other. He sees the quest for recognition and esteem as a basic human need; however, he suggests that if/when it resides solely in the convictions and opinions of others, it is constantly threatened. This understandable fragility can confine the subject to a fear-driven concentration on protection and performance, thereby precluding the possibility of open encounter with self and other which is prerequisite to the experience of love.

The concept of identity is the subject of much philosophical debate, particularly in postmodern literature where cognizance of the dissolution of hitherto established sources of identity and meaning is central. Ricoeur situates identity in close proximity to recognition, and therefore as influenced by the perception of the other: "the demand for recognition expresses an expectation that can be satisfied only by mutual recognition" (Ricoeur, 2005: 19). Self-recognition and self-identity require reflection, acceptance and support of others; hence, the "dialectic of identity confronted by otherness" (Ricoeur, 2005: 103). According to Kearney,

---

[7] Freud firmly asserted the lasting influence of childhood experience on adult life, and this has been further explored by psychoanalysts like Donald Winnicott, Wilfred Bion, and Karen Horney and Melanie Klein.

Ricoeur's dictum is that "the shortest route from self to self is through the other...the self is never enough, is never sufficient unto itself, but constantly seeks out signs and signals of meaning in the other" (Kearney, 1996: 1). Identifying the self through the other is a common thread in the philosophy of Hegel, Levinas and Lacan, although these three philosophers diverge in their analysis of the dialectic of self and other. Hegel's analysis centres on the master-slave dialectic which is only resolved when both master and slave recognize the need for recognition by an other which is the same as itself; otherwise the proffered recognition is valueless. Levinas posits the other – its existence, its demands, its needs and its enhancement, as the basis of selfhood; accordingly, the self can only exist in a meaningful way when it "answers" to the call of the other. Lacan points to the mirror-stage as the moment when the subject begins to identify itself with the reflection emanating from the other, but he insists that this other, this "subject supposed to know" is merely the symbolization of a "fundamental fantasy" (Lacan, 1999: 67). Nietzsche expresses his understanding of this human need whereby "the individual wants to confirm the opinion he has of himself through the opinion of others and strengthen it in his own eyes", but he warns of the danger of "habituation to authority which...leads many to base their own belief in themselves upon authority, to accept it only from the hand of others" (Nietzsche, 1984: 63). Ricoeur explores the interplay between identity and recognition stating that "I actively recognize things, persons, myself; I ask, even demand, to be recognized by others" (Ricoeur, 2005: x), and suggests that this is the demand for recognition of "my genuine identity" (Ricoeur, 2005: xi). However, the need for recognition by another as essential to our sense of identity coexists with a perception of the other, because different, as a possible threat to our fragile identity:

> It is a fact that the other...comes to be perceived as a danger for one's identity...is our identity so fragile that we are unable to bear, unable to endure the fact that others have different ways of leading their lives, of understanding themselves, of inscribing their own identity in the web of living together? (Ricoeur, 2004: 81).

This is part of the tension between selfhood and alterity, the dialectic of the self and the other than self, whereby the fragility of personal as well as national, racial, cultural and institutional identity is commonly perceived to be threatened by difference, unfamiliarity and discordance.

Ricoeur's analysis of narrative identity entails an accommodation of all aspects of one's self, of one's life-story, with the integration of past, present and future as essential to a genuine narrative. This resounds with

Nietzsche's thought experiment of the eternal recurrence, whereby one must be willing to accept all of one's life, even to the point of accepting the possibility of its recurrence over and over again, in order to take responsibility and autonomy for one's self. However, there are difficulties inherent in this attempted integration. Memory is the door to the past, but it is susceptible to selective remembering and forgetting; action in the present is the action of the agent/subject, but it is correlative to its impact on the patient/other; the future is the focus of intentionality based on a trust in self-constancy and self-fulfilment, but it is vulnerable to the vicissitudes of personal feeling and commitment, as well as to the unpredictable nature of the external world. Wordsworth acknowledges the difficulties encountered in the attempted creation of a life-story: "I cannot say what portion is in truth / The naked recollection of that time / And what may rather have been called to life / By after-meditation" (Wordsworth, 2000: 420,421). Hence narrative is fragile, uncertain, and unfinished, and this fragility is coupled with the always present potential to self-deception.[8] The apparent paradox inherent in the concept of self-deception – how is it possible to deceive ourselves? – is given at least partial resolution in the inevitable gap between the unconscious dimension of the psyche and its manifest translation in conscious speech. Nietzsche sees it as the victory of pride over memory: "'I have done that', says my memory. 'I cannot have done that' – says my pride, and remains adamant. At last – memory yields" (Nietzsche, 2003: 91). Freud agrees, stating that "there's no guarantee whatever for what our memory tells us" (Freud, 2006: 553), and explains the phenomenon from an individual and social perspective: "it is inherent in human nature to have an inclination to consider a thing untrue if one does not like it...society makes what is disagreeable into what is untrue" (Freud, 1991: 48). The stories we tell ourselves about ourselves are not always truthful or comprehensive; the stories we tell to others about ourselves are sometimes coloured by our quest for recognition and approval. In the light of the analyses and insights developed through Freud and Nietzsche, the possibility of complete self-knowledge remains an unattainable ideal; self-deception is a phenomenon which must be acknowledged. According to Lacan, personal truth is often evaded, because "Truth does in effect seem to be foreign to us, I mean our own truth. It is no doubt with us, but without concerning us to the point that one really wants to speak it" (Lacan, 2007: 58). In varying degrees, self-deception entails a disavowal of certain aspects of the self, and in the

---

[8] For an exploration of the phenomenon of self-deception see Herbert Fingarette's classic study, *Self-Deception*.

ensuing diminishment of the self, the possibility of love is weakened; it is
thwarted in that parts of the self are withheld from awareness and
recognition, and the experience of communication, mutuality and intimacy
is distorted and restricted. In an essay on Ricoeur's philosophy of the self,
Joseph Dunne outlines this possibility of self-deception: "This is the
province of self-deception, which might be defined as a significant
discrepancy between the story one lives and the story one tells", and this
reflects "a deeper conflict *within who one is*, when one part is lived out
only at the cost of disowning another part which, though disowned,
continues to find disguised expression in one's life" (Dunne, 1996: 153).
This concurs with Freud's theories of repression and neuroses. As a result,
"there is thus the whole margin hidden by censorship, prohibition, the
margin of what is unspoken, criss-crossed by all the figures of the hidden"
(Ricoeur, 2006: 26). The "unspoken", "the hidden", the unconscious
fantasies and motivations of human thought and action, are often beyond
the power of speech to elucidate. Echoing Lacan's concept of "empty
speech" Ricoeur refers to "the uses of speech where one aims at something
other than the true, other than the real…namely, the lie", and goes on to
argue that this is not the greatest misrepresentation which speech is
capable of, but rather that "it is language's propensity for the enigma, for
artifice, for abstruseness, for the secret, in fact for non-communication"
that curtails and diminishes the narrative identity of the subject. Kearney
explains that "for narrative identity to be ethically responsible it must
ensure that self-constancy is always informed by self-questioning"
(Kearney, 2004: 112). The opposition between self-knowledge and self-
deception is deconstructed in this acceptance of the spectrum between
them, a spectrum which may be diminished in an openness to self-
questioning, and to the integration of the often uncomfortable answers
which may ensue.

    Another difficulty encountered in the construction of a narrative of the
self is the reality of entanglement between one's life history and that of
others; Dunne attests to this aspect of narrative identity in Ricoeur's
philosophy: "The self…is historical through and through, and is enfolded
ab initio within a web of relationships" (Dunne, 1996: 144). From birth,
one's history is linked to the histories of others, and as these histories
unfold and reveal themselves one's own narrative has to be continually
revised. It has to be revised and refigured in an attempt to mediate one's
own identity with the radically different and changing worlds of others,
and in the attempt to produce new meaning which integrates this
difference. Failure to do this results in deception regarding identity of the
self, and confinement of the other to the status of the foreigner, the alien.

The difficulties inherent in the construction of narratives extend to collective narrative relating the stories of nations, groups and institutions. Kaplan outlines Ricoeur's analysis of ideology in this respect:

> The danger of the stories groups tell about themselves is that they often become frozen oversimplifications, expressed in slogans and caricature, serving only the interests of power and authority. Ideology functions through this kind of collective memory, as well as through ritualization, stereotype, and rhetoric, all of which prevent us from interpreting and recalling things differently (Kaplan, 2003: 96).

However, while Ricoeur insists on the necessity of exposing the dangers of ideological interpretations of reality, he also warns of the propensity of the critique to become another ideology.[9]

Ricoeur suggests a "triple quest" in the constitution of the self (Ricoeur, 2002: 126); this order "is built on the themes of having, power, and worth", and these quests are intricately linked (Ricoeur, 2002: 113). The quest for having, for possession, is fuelled by a desire for control through appropriation of objects, and a dependence on this possession and ownership as a protection against loss. The loss which is feared is that of self-affirmation, and the mode of having as a bulwark against this threat can range from "a just possession which would distinguish among men without mutually excluding them", to "unjust having" which sees appropriation by the other as loss for oneself. In this sense "the category of having designates a vast domain in which the wrong done to others wears innumerable guises" (Ricoeur, 1992: 221). A second root of self-affirmation follows from the relation of the quest for having, because having implies the power of man over man. The world of work, especially, posits the individual as a force dominating other forces. Ricoeur argues that almost all human actions entail the exertion of one will over another. This coheres with the philosophy of Nietzsche, where he argues that the exertion of one's will, over everything that confronts it, is the 'will-to-power' which underlines all human drive and life. Ricoeur differentiates

---

[9]The relevance of Ricoeur's warning may be discerned in the historical examples of the phenomenon whereby personalities and groups inspired by opposition and rebellion against established orders are transformed into protectors of newly-established orders. Kennelly refers to this phenomenon in Irish history where the achievement of freedom and independence from a colonial power coincided with the establishment, explicit or implicit, of another set of restrictions and ideologies. Žižek offers an ironical discourse on such reversals in his discussion of the paradoxical injunction "to enjoy" which he discerns in the "liberal", "rule-free" experience of contemporary society.

between *power-in-common* whereby a community shares the exercise of power in order to live together, and *power-over* which can easily become violence towards the other.

> The descending slope is easy to mark off, from influence, the gentle form of holding power-over, all the way to torture, the extreme form of abuse…from the simple use of threats, passing through all the degrees of constraint, and ending in murder. In all these diverse forms, violence is equivalent to the diminishment or the destruction of the power-to-do of others. But there is something even worse…humiliation – a horrible caricature of humility (Ricoeur, 1992: 220).

Ricoeur's observation that the problem of power and the problem evil are intertwined is solidified by his experience of the atrocities of the concentration camps, the terror of totalitarian regimes, and the peril of nuclear power, (Ricoeur, 2002: xiv), and also by his personal response to cruelty and betrayal between man and man, man and woman, adult and child, and the myriad forms of suffering which are inflicted physically and verbally by one human being upon another: "the possibility of moral evil is inherent in man's constitution" (Ricoeur, 2002: 133); Evil is a reality of human life: "it is manifest only in the way it *affects* human existence…In all hypotheses, evil manifests itself in man's humanity" (Ricoeur, 2002: xlvi). In his analysis of the ethical dimension in Ricoeur's thought, John Wall reminds us that "violence remains ultimately our own free choice, [and that if] we refuse to acknowledge our responsibility for violence…we deny our own freedom to re-create our own moral world" (Wall, 2005: 109). This reference to our individual responsibility for and involvement in the reality of conflict is asserted by Ricoeur:

> Even if it is true that the real conflicts that stake out affective history are accidents, in the literal sense of the word, random encounters between our effort, our power of affirmation, and the forces of nature, or the familial, social, and cultural environment, the fact remains that all these external conflicts could not be interiorized if a latent conflict within ourselves did not precede them (Ricoeur, 2002: 132).

This statement is echoed in the words of Lacan: "it's never, in any way whatever, by another person's excesses that one turns out, in appearance at least, to be overwhelmed. It is always because their excesses happen to coincide with your own" (Lacan, 2007: 12). Nietzsche anticipates this sentiment: "whatever may yet come to me as fate and experience…in the final analysis one experiences only oneself" (Nietzsche, 2003a: 173).

What Ricoeur terms "something even worse...humiliation - a horrible caricature of humility" (Ricoeur, 1992: 220), is the utmost assault upon the integrity of the other because it attempts to obliterate that which is deemed indispensable to human survival, one's sense of worth or self-esteem. The desire for esteem as reflected in the eyes of another "is a desire to exist, not through a vital affirmation of oneself, but through the favour of another's recognition" (Ricoeur, 2002: 120). The ambiguity of this desire is noted by Nietzsche: "One man runs to his neighbour because he is looking for himself, and another because he wants to lose himself" (Nietzsche, 2003: 87). It is in the realm of interpersonal relations that one desires acceptance, approval and recognition. As Kaplan asserts, "recognition is something we owe to others not merely as a courtesy but because it is a necessary human need" (Kaplan, 2003: 156). The fragility of this esteem, dependent as it is on the opinion of the other, is open to deception, neglect, scorn and humiliation: "Here there is a threat of existing in a quasi-phantasmal manner, of being a reflection...the possibility of being no more than the word of another, the dependence on fragile opinion" (Ricoeur, 2002: 121). Thus the quest for recognition by another cannot permanently answer the need for self-worth and self-esteem. The identity of the self is not dependent on opinion, judgement or description; it is integral to human being. Unless this is acknowledged within the self there is a constant hunger for affirmation and recognition, and this takes precedence over any attempted genuine connection with the other which is essential to the experience of love.

Solicitude

> Talking about love may be too easy, or rather too difficult. How can we avoid simply praising it or falling into sentimental platitudes? (Ricoeur, 1996: 23).

Ricoeur's exploration of love ranges over concepts of friendship, agape, self-love and sexual love, and he discerns the desire for possession, power and worth as potentially motivating various manifestations of these experiences. Human fallibility, frailty and need can diminish the possibility of love in human living; the quest for recognition and affirmation can impose conformity to the demands and expectations of others; and the fear of one's existential aloneness can propel a flight from the self towards the potential safeguard of belonging and acceptance. Ricoeur accepts these constraints on human capability: "self-recognition requires, at each step, the help of others" (Ricoeur, 2005: 69), but he suggests a dialectic of self and other which acknowledges human solitude, understands the need for self-esteem, and strives for the co-existence of personal solitude and intersubjective solicitude: "my thesis is that solicitude is not something added on to self-esteem from outside but that it unfolds the dialogic dimension of self-esteem" (Ricoeur, 1992: 180). Within this comprehensive and ambivalent framework, the possibility of love is enabled:

> My own self-esteem that I search for by means of the esteem of others is of the same nature as the esteem I experience for others. If humanity is what I esteem in another and in myself, I esteem myself as a thou for another. I esteem myself in the second person…I love myself as if what I loved were another (Ricoeur, 2002: 124).

Freud says something similar when he refutes the precept of universal love: "I love another…if…he so much resembles me that in him I can love myself" (Freud, 2002: 46). The dialectic between self-esteem and solicitude for others suggests that they are intrinsically linked. Lacan echoes this sentiment when he suggests the link between the experience of love and the acknowledgement by the subject of the ego-ideal: "It's one's own ego that one loves in love, one's own ego made real on the imaginary level" (Lacan, 1991: 142). This is also the argument of Fromm in his discussion of love:

> The love for my own self is inseparably connected with the love for any other being…love of others and love of ourselves are not alternatives. On the contrary, an attitude of love towards themselves will be found in all those who are capable of loving others. *Love,* in principle, *is indivisible as far as the connection between 'objects' and one's own self is concerned* (Fromm, 1995: 46).

Esteem for oneself implies the esteem for the other, because the self is an other and the other is a self. One-sided esteem is not genuine; it is distorted in some way, as it infers a splintered and selective understanding of humanity. Žižek rejects the opposition of self-love and altruism, supporting the arguments outlined above: "the true opposite of egotistic self-love is not altruism, concern for the common Good, but envy, ressentiment, which makes me act 'against' my own interests" (Žižek, 2007: 312).

The lure of escape from one's essential aloneness is often focused on a desired fusion with the other, but Ricoeur insists that this fusion is illusory and deceptive: "The one is not the other. We exchange gifts, but not places...the benefit of this admission is that it protects mutuality against the pitfalls of a fusional union...a just distance is maintained at the heart of mutuality, a just distance that integrates respect into intimacy" (Ricoeur, 2005: 263). Kearney explains the attraction and impossibility of this desired union as "the lure of fusion, that is, for the illusion that some ecstasy or addiction might make us 'one with the other'. But it cannot. The other will never 'be' me, nor even 'like' me" (Kearney, 2001: 13), and he urges "an awareness that no amount of intimacy can ever grasp the other" (Kearney, 2001: 14). In Ricoeur's words "the lived experience of the other always remains inaccessible to me" (Ricoeur, 2005: 157) Acceptance of this reality is not synonymous with failure or defeat in the realm of human relationships: "Is reality simply necessity offered to my resignation? Is it not also possibility opened to the power of loving?" (Ricoeur, 1970: 550). Acknowledgement of human solitude and a respect for the alterity of the other enables the emergence of a dialectical esteem wherein self and other are recognized in their unique humanity. In this dialectic, "the voice of solicitude" is heard, "the voice which asked that the plurality of persons and their otherness not be obliterated by the globalizing idea of humanity" (Ricoeur, 1992: 227).

Freedom from the constraints of identity and recognition sought exclusively in the affirmation of the other enables the attainment of personal autonomy and responsibility: "it is not a fate that governs my life from the outside but the inimitable way in which I exercise my freedom as a man" (Ricoeur, 2002: 61). However, Ricoeur distinguishes between an illusory self-sufficiency and an autonomy which recognizes, and indeed celebrates, the need for otherness: "the selfhood of oneself implies otherness to such an intimate degree that one cannot be thought without the other" (Ricoeur, 1992: 3). This need is not reducible to quests for assimilation, absorption, or control, but is intrinsically linked to esteem for the self and for the other than self: "The autonomy of the self will appear then to be tightly bound up with solicitude for one's neighbour and with justice for each individual" (Ricoeur, 1992: 18). This concurs with Fromm's description of love: "*Love is union under the condition of preserving one's integrity*, one's individuality" (Fromm, 1995: 16). As Kennelly notes, "the self knows that self is not enough" (Kennelly, 2004: 425), and the possibility of love exists within a welcoming acknowledgement of this insufficiency. Solicitude embraces the need for love, the need for others, without obliterating autonomy, responsibility, or self-esteem: "To self-esteem, understood as a reflexive moment of the wish for the 'good life', solicitude adds essentially the dimension of *lack*, the fact that we *need* friends; as a reaction to the effect of solicitude on self-esteem, the self perceives itself as another among others" (Ricoeur, 1992: 192). Love is transitive; it needs an object; "to love" means "to love someone or something".

Ricoeur differentiates between solicitude and "obedience to duty",[10] and he argues that "its status is that of benevolent spontaneity, intimately related to self-esteem within the framework of the aim of the 'good' life" (Ricoeur, 1992: 190). Esteem, recognition, and the experience of love imply a mutuality which embraces self and others in their autonomy, frailty, capability and vulnerability. Ricoeur explains this mutuality with reference to Aristotle's thesis on *Philia*: "the good man's own being is desirable to him; given this, the being of his friend is then equally desirable to him" (Ricoeur, 1992: 186). Faith in human goodness, in oneself and in others, co-existing with an acknowledgement of human frailty, fallibility and evil, enables the possibility of love. This is Ricoeur's thesis, according to Wall: "for Ricoeur, love is given to the other from the self, originating in a prior faith in the self's own human created goodness that is then applied to the other as another such self" (Wall, 2005: 121).[11]

---

[10] This differentiation between solicitude and "obedience to duty" echoes Lacan's critique of "philanthropy", altruism and the many instances of relationships based on obligation of some kind; from this perspective, such relationships lack dignity and mutuality.

[11] In response to the thesis question, John Wall offers the following reflections:
In brief, Ricoeur's view seems to be that love is what helps drive the self toward the other in the other's irreducible singularity. It functions, he says, as a corrective to golden rule justice ("do to others as you'd have them do to you") by refusing to let it become reduced to mere reciprocity ("do to others *so that* they do to you") but instead includes an element of genuine concern for the other as other. Love in this sense is never, therefore, completed; nor does it stand alone; rather, it functions as a "hyperethical corrective" drawing us always beyond ourselves. At the same time, Ricoeur describes love as the second moment in a three-part "economy of the gift" that first starts in "faith" in the ultimate goodness of oneself within the universe, passes through "love" as the affirmation therefore of the humanity of the other, despite their difference, and thereby aims ultimately toward "hope" for a fully reconciled humanity. So, love in Ricoeur's view is not a stable ethic. It has the dual function of driving ordinary views of justice to their own wider implications and animating a movement toward the reconciliation of all. In my view Ricoeur also speaks to your term "possibility"—indeed, as my book's subtitle puts it, "the poetics of possibility." My view is that Ricoeur's notion of love represents a helpful way to speak of ethical life, not as applying fixed principles, but as opening the self up to wider possibilities—in this case, meaningful relations to others. So, love for Ricoeur is never merely self-sacrifice but

Self-esteem and self-appreciation simultaneously open to appreciation and respect for others, and this mutuality is enhanced rather than hindered by the embrace of solitude and distance: "must one not, in order to make oneself open, available, belong to oneself in a certain sense?" (Ricoeur, 1992: 138). As Kearney explains, "By deepening solitude, the self discovers that it receives from others all that it appreciates in its own being, and consequently it is not alone" (Kearney, 1996: 44).

Ricoeur's acknowledgement of human frailty, fallibility and evil does not belie a belief in the potential goodness of the human subject and the possibility of love and happiness within his appraisal. He situates this possibility in the concrete experiences of action and relation, and concurs with Buber when he states that "It is for the other who is in my charge that I am responsible" (Ricoeur, 2005: 108), rather than some illusory and distant other of theoretical pronouncements. In the immediate, individual and unique encounters with reality, of self and other, choices are made, judgements are considered, and the possibility of love presents itself: "The events that bespeak happiness are those which remove obstacles and uncover a vast landscape of existence" (Ricoeur, 2002: 68). Ricoeur accepts the human desire for happiness, but sees its attainment as experienced in the encounters and "events" through which life is directed; it is a by-product of action and response, decision and choice: "happiness is not given in any experience; it is only adumbrated in a consciousness of direction. No act gives happiness, but the encounters of our life that are most worthy of being called 'events' indicate the direction of happiness" (Ricoeur, 2002: 68). Deception, denial, projection and blindness pose obstacles to love, but these may be overcome in an on-going openness to "the vast landscape of existence" (Ricoeur, 2002: 136). Ricoeur sees this as the "function" of the human subject:

> This essential openness or accessibility to...the 'function' or the 'project' of man as such, grounds the person in giving him a horizon of humanity that is neither I nor you but the task of treating the person, in me and in you, as an end and not as a means (Ricoeur, 2002: 136).

Within this "horizon of humanity", love is enabled, both as an attainable possibility and as the way of being which fulfils itself: "It is Eros, it is Love that shows that this aim, which is immanent to the function of man,

---

rather the poetic effort to stretch or expand oneself into wider imaginative relation to others. It takes poetics to imagine love for the other (2006: email).

is happiness anticipated in a consciousness of direction and of belonging"
(Ricoeur, 2002: 137).

While Ricoeur acknowledges the fallibility and frailty of human
nature, and while he insists on an acceptance of the reality of evil as a
creation of humanity, he nevertheless maintains a belief in the primordial
goodness of the human being, he confirms the possibility of hope even
amid impossible constraints, and he expresses a love of life in spite of its
brokenness: "Man is the Joy of Yes in the sadness of the finite" (Ricoeur,
2002: 140). Thus he articulates the possibility of love as integral to human
living, but, echoing Nietzsche and Buber, he sees the obstacles to this
possibility as resulting from misinterpretation, deception, fear and
distortion. His emphasis on language as the medium of understanding, his
argument that hermeneutical interpretation is essential to understanding,
and his call for "the reappraisal of narratives" (Ricoeur, 1996: 8) as an
ongoing integration of self and other, of past and present, and of the
known and the not-yet-known, suggest many of the principles of
psychoanalysis as developed by Freud. Ricoeur's exploration of Freudian
thought, in his work *Freud and Philosophy: An Essay on Interpretation*, is
prompted by his commitment to undergo a personal search for meaning
and understanding. Thus, Ricoeur asserts the potential insight and
interpretation which psychoanalysis offers when faced with the dilemmas
of human experience. This discipline is the subject of the following
section.

SECTION II:

PSYCHOANALYSIS

CHAPTER FOUR

SIGMUND FREUD

The birth of psychoanalysis at the close of the nineteenth century coincided with a questioning of philosophical traditions and methods epitomized by Nietzsche's assault on the cherished assumptions of metaphysics and rationalism hitherto deemed to be the legacy of the Enlightenment. The Enlightenment had seen the questioning of religion as an explanation and a revelation of reality and of human life within that reality; science had been instigated as a more "enlightened" and a more rational provider of truth and knowledge; but the ongoing nature of philosophical thought continued to encounter new challenges and the re-phrasing of old questions. Attempting to combine the exactness of scientific method with the openness of philosophical inquiry, psychoanalysis broached the terrain of the human mind, and attempted to explore the perennial questions of meaning, truth and life with an understanding enhanced by the discoveries of its founder, Sigmund Freud. In an essay titled "Freud's Philosophical Roots", the Irish philosopher, John Hayes, firmly states that "there are profound and inextricable links between psychoanalysis and philosophy" (Hayes, 1988: 47), and these links continue to be the subject of exploration in contemporary analyses of Freudian thought.[1]

The theories of psychoanalysis as developed, outlined, and revised by Freud are the subject of debate in almost every area of the human sciences, and continue to provoke praise and criticism, adulation and disdain, interpretation and re-interpretation, to the present day. In his writings, Freud often acknowledged the possibility of fallibility; echoing Nietzsche's perspectivism, he prefaced many of his remarks as being his own speculations, "I therefore dare not set myself up as a prophet *vis-à-vis* my fellow men" (Freud, 2002: 81), and he expressed the hope that what he had merely initiated would profit from the thought and experience of future reflection and insight:

---

[1] I refer to writers such as Richard Boothby and Jonathan Lear who, like Ricoeur, offer a philosophical interpretation of Freud's work.

> You will not find me inaccessible to your criticism. I know how difficult it
> is to avoid illusions; perhaps the hopes I have confessed to are of an
> illusory nature…If experience should show…that we have been mistaken,
> we will give up our expectations (Freud, 1995: 719).

A poetic expression of these sentiments is offered by W. H. Auden in his
poem, "In Memory of Sigmund Freud": "For every day they die / among
us, those who were doing us some good, / who knew it was never enough
but / hoped to improve a little by living" (Auden, 1994: 273). It is not the
purpose of this study to offer a critique of Freud's thought; the
questionable nature of the scientific basis of his pronouncements and
techniques, his limited and distorted representation of female sexuality and
psychology, and the prejudices and limitations inherent in his historical
and geographical position, are subjects explored competently and
comprehensively by many writers;[2] the focus here is on a reading of Freud
from the point of view of his contribution to our understanding of human
nature, the limits to that understanding, and the obstacles which stand in
the way of understanding, happiness and love within the experience of the
human condition.[3] This is the view of Jonathan Lear as he outlines Freud's
legacy: "He listened to ordinary people, and, on the basis of what he heard,
he transformed our conception of the human" (Lear, 2005: 9). This
contribution is summarized with hope and humility in the closing words of
Freud's short essay, "An Autobiographical Study", where he reflects:

> Looking back, then, over the patchwork of my life's labours, I can say that
> I have made many beginnings and thrown out many suggestions.
> Something will come of them in the future, though I cannot myself tell
> whether it will be much or little. I can, however, express a hope that I have
> opened up a pathway for an important advance in our knowledge (Freud,
> 1995: 41).

---

[2] Walter Kaufmann, Jonathan Lear and Adam Phillips provide commentaries on
the issues which are sympathetic to Freud's position; Philip Rieff is less
enthusiastic in his appraisal and sees in Freud's thought a conservative moralism;
Richard Webster finds much to condemn and ridicule in his reading of Freud.
Carol Gilligan, among other feminists, offers a feminist critique of Freud's work
and the gender bias underlying psychoanalysis in general.
[3] Perhaps the words of Anthony Storr, with reference to the thought of Carl Jung,
may be applicable here: "Jung's valuable contributions to psychotherapy and to the
understanding of individuals can be appreciated without subscribing to the whole
of his system of belief" (Storr, 1998: 27).

The "pathway" which Freud "opened up" evolved from his theories of the unconscious, the structure of the mind, the influences of past experiences, and the interpretation of dreams as "the *via regia* to a knowledge of the unconscious element in our psychic life" (Freud, 1997: 441). It has led to an acknowledgement of the indeterminacy of knowledge, especially self-knowledge, an awareness of unconscious forces motivating and directing human behaviour, and an attempt to understand and alleviate human distress through an innovative approach to language and interpretation.

The development of psychoanalysis centres on the relationship between two human beings, the analyst and the analysand, and within this relationship the neuroses, sufferings and conflicts of the individual are explored through expression/narration, interpretation/hermeneutics, and understanding/integration. The revolutionary nature of this approach lies in the proposition that human suffering can be understood and alleviated by the presence of an understanding, listening and attentive other, rather than through the diagnosis-prescription model. The enriching power of dialogue, the cathartic liberation of narrating one's life-story, and the potential for healing in an encounter with a non- judgemental, accepting and interpretive reflection of an other, not only heralds a radical innovation in the treatment of mental diseases but also suggests a new framework for an understanding of the human condition, and particularly the sourcing of that understanding in the realm of language. This resounds with Buber's analysis of human life as essentially relational, and with Ricoeur's description of the narrative identity of the self. In his analysis of Freud's influence, Adam Phillips emphasises the role of language as the medium of psychoanalysis. He suggests that the work of listening and talking in a psychotherapeutic encounter aims at a re-description of the individual's life story, a re-interpretation of what he finds unacceptable or unbearable, in such a way that it becomes tolerable, sensible, and hopefully pleasurable; "that suffering can sometimes be transformed by applying words to wounds...the appeal to another person to listen and reply is fraught with hope" (Phillips, 2006: 19). The goal of psychoanalysis for Freud is the amelioration of mental suffering, the release of the individual from unnecessary psychic conflict and constraint, and the liberation of the human subject to live, work and love in the world. He believes that bringing to consciousness the memories, desires, unfulfilled wishes and forgotten traumas which have been repressed, enables the subject to attain a more realistic and a more honest understanding of motivation, feeling and behaviour, and ultimately empowers the individual to make an autonomous decision regarding a response to this increase in self-knowledge. The psychoanalytic aim is "to uncover repressions and replace them by acts of judgement which might result either in the accepting or in the condemning of what had formerly been repudiated" (Freud, 1995: 18). However, these goals can only be pursued through self-honesty, self-acceptance, and self-integration. Thus, Freud's psychoanalysis inevitably examines the obstacles to such an achievement, and contributes to an exploration of the potential obstacles to love.

The Unconscious

> The decisive rules of logic don't apply in the unconscious; we could call it the Empire of the Illogical (Freud, 2006: 23).[4]

Freud's development of psychoanalysis centres on his close observation of human behaviour including an on-going analysis of his own psyche, dreams and motivations. This observation leads to a growing conviction that in many life situations unconscious influences impact on human thought, feeling and action, and from this insight Freud discerns many of the obstacles to love, health and optimum living. Misconceptions, disavowals and transferred feelings from one situation to another diminish the possibility of genuine relationship, with self and other, and according to Freud, distort and thwart the experience of love. Exploration of the unconscious, the retrieval of repressed material, and the assumption of personal responsibility, would, according to Freud's theories, enhance self-knowledge and self-acceptance, and free the subject to make life-enhancing choices unrestricted by developmental arrest or traumatic fixation.[4]

Through his studies, writings, clinical practice and self-analysis, Freud develops a new and broader picture of psychic life than had hitherto been considered. Examining the symptoms of malaise and unhappiness, Freud

---

[4] The positing of the unconscious as a propellant of human behaviour and motivation is rejected by Sartre's critique of Freudian psychoanalysis; he develops the concept of "bad faith" to account for the phenomenon of self-deception. (Sartre's argument is outlined in his philosophical work *Being and Nothingness,* and is also explored in novelistic form in works such as *Nausea* and *The Reprieve*) However, his assertion that choice is an inescapable component of human living may cohere with Freud's commitment to creating conditions favourable to informed and open decisions and choices freed from the limitations of disavowal and repression.

discerns that one's conscious awareness of oneself is only one part of the mind's structure: "mental processes are in themselves unconscious and …of all mental life it is only certain individual acts and portions that are conscious" (Freud, 1991: 46). The original inspiration for the term is literary, as Lacan reminds us: "Freud called the locus of the unconscious *ein anderer Schauplatz,* another scene, borrowing a term that had struck him in a text by Fechner" (Lacan, 2006: 183). Hence, Freud develops a model of the mind which takes account of the existence of the unconscious. His model breaks with the Cartesian cogito with its emphasis on direct introspection and transparency, and rational thought as the guarantor of ontology, and it overturns the pretension of consciousness to truth and meaning as an illusion masking its propensity to be inadequate, capable of mistakes and self-deception. On rare occasions, Freud makes reference to his debt to Nietzschean philosophy, and he credits him with some of his insights into the unconscious: "Nietzsche…whose guesses and intuitions often agree in the most astonishing way with the laborious findings of psychoanalysis" (Freud, 1989: 67). Many Freudian concepts resound with those of Nietzsche, such as dreams, memory, and motivation, but Freud insists that he has "carefully avoided any contact with philosophy proper…I was less concerned with the question of priority than with keeping my mind unembarrassed" (Freud, 1995: 38).[5] Freud asserts that behind one's conscious awareness of oneself lurks a powerful influence on one's behaviour and health. This part of the mind's structure Freud terms "the unconscious", suggesting that what is conscious to the self is but a mere layer of awareness, and that the greater part of mental life lies hidden in this unconscious state: "Psychoanalysis…defines what is mental as processes such as feeling, thinking and willing, and it is obliged to maintain that there is unconscious thinking and unapprehended willing" (Freud, 1991: 46). The reality of the unconscious, and its role in psychic life, demands a recognition of what the individual tries to hide from himself or herself. Repressed in the unconscious are the hidden, unacknowledged conflicts of the individual, disguised truths and buried memories that strive to be revealed.

Freud believes that human behaviour is determined unconsciously by these primitive drives and impulses, but without our awareness of their influence. According to Lear, "this goes to the heart of Freud's insight: that humans tend toward certain forms of motivated irrationality of which they have little or no awareness" (Lear, 2005: 4). Human suffering can be

---

[5] For an exploration of the "conjunction" between Freud and Nietzsche and an interrogation of "the interface between philosophy and psychoanalysis", see Paul-Laurent Assoun's work, *Freud and Nietzsche.*

understood and alleviated only through a recognition of hidden and denied wishes, frustrations, and desires: "Interpreting means finding a hidden sense in something" (Freud, 1991: 115). This definition of interpretation later leads to Freud being described, along with Nietzsche and Marx, as one of "the masters of suspicion". In his *Essay on Interpretation: Freud and Philosophy*, Ricoeur differentiates between interpretation as restoration of meaning and the hermeneutics of suspicion as exemplified by psychoanalysis: "Psychoanalysis…has uncovered a variety of processes of elaboration that are operative between the apparent and the latent meaning", and he describes this hermeneutics as "a tearing off of masks, and interpretation that reduces disguises" (Ricoeur, 1970: 17, 30). Among the masks to be uncovered through the insights of psychoanalysis is the mask of self-deception and its illusion of self-knowledge. Freud understands the popular opposition to this analysis, and he likens it to the difficulty in accepting the historical blows to naïve vanity produced by the discoveries of Copernicus and Darwin. Lacan explains that by comparing his discovery to "the so-called Copernican revolution" Freud is "emphasizing that what was at stake was once again the place man assigns himself at the centre of a universe" (Lacan, 2006: 156). With the insights of psychoanalysis, the centrality of the human subject is again questioned:

> But human megalomania will have suffered its third and most wounding blow from the psychological research of the present time which seeks to prove to the ego that it is not even master in its own house, but must content itself with scanty information of what is going on unconsciously in its mind (Freud, 1991: 326).

The assertion that the ego is "not even master in its own house" infers that it lacks a full awareness of its motivations and expectations, that it is curtailed and directed by unconscious desires and fears, and that its claim to self-knowledge is illusory and mistaken. The difficulty in accepting the limitations of human knowledge, and the simultaneous challenge to our illusory and distorted view of human nature, lie, according to Freud, at the root of human suffering and unhappiness, and he urges a more honest appraisal of human nature which takes cognizance of its contradictions and conflicts. This involves an acceptance of the ambiguity pervading much of human emotion and thought; this ambiguity is evident in the motivation of human behaviour, and possibly is nowhere more influential than in the human striving for love.

   Freud presents us with case histories in order to highlight the obstacles to love which arise when desire and motivation are camouflaged; idealization of the love-object, rescue-fantasies, the search for parent-surrogates, and the prohibition of sexual activity under certain conditions, all point to a reluctance to acknowledge the complexity of human experience. In the words of Auden, "Nothing can be loved too much, / but all things can be loved / in the wrong way" (Auden, 1994: 885). Rejecting the validity of the Christian dictum of neighbourly love, Freud points to various historical manifestations of its incongruence: "After St Paul had made universal brotherly love the foundation of his Christian community, the extreme intolerance of Christianity towards those left outside it was an inevitable consequence" (Freud, 2002: 51). Freud's argument against this dictum resounds with Buber's avowal that one cannot love everyone one meets, and stresses the concrete and practical nature of love over universal theories: "My love is something I value and must not throw away irresponsibly. It imposes duties on me, and in performing these duties I must be prepared to make sacrifices" (Freud, 2002: 46).

The case histories outlined and analyzed in Freud's texts are instructive, because, he asserts, they illustrate the contradictions inherent in all human behaviour: "we who laugh at other people's failings are not always free from them ourselves",[6] and he concludes that the mystery of love eludes systematization and tidy formulae: "things that have to do with love are incommensurable with everything else; they are, as it were, written on a special page on which no other writing is tolerated" (Freud, 1995: 379). The "special page" on which love is written, the "madness" of love, is a perennial theme of literature and philosophy, and is central to Lacan's essay, "A Love Letter", where he suggests that being in love is akin to madness! (Lacan, 1999: 81). However, Lacan stresses that this interpretation reflects the limitations of the symbolic order: "when you're in love, you are mad, as ordinary language puts it"; he suggests that love is a phenomenon that somehow transcends this constraint: "Love is a phenomenon which takes place on the imaginary level, and which provokes a veritable subduction of the symbolic, a sort of annihilation, of perturbation of the function of the ego-ideal'; and he asserts the thrust of this phenomenon: "Love opens the door...to perfection" (Lacan, 1991: 142). Nietzsche also addresses the ambiguity of this "madness": "There is always a certain madness in love. But also there is always a certain method in madness" (Nietzsche, 2003a: 68). Freud agrees, stating that "departures from the norm constitute precisely what is essential about being in love" (Freud, 1995: 385).

---

[6] In light of Freud's persistent atheism, it is interesting to note in this quote the echo of the biblical story of the prostitute and the words of Christ: "He who is without sin among you, let him cast the first stone at her" (John 8:7).

Psychic Conflict

> It is a conflict, then, between what the
> drive demands and what reality forbids
> (Freud, 2006: 64).

The ambivalence of love is perhaps relative to its essentially subjective character which militates against theoretical formulations and definitions, and which suggests some explanation regarding the diverse interpretations and explorations of the concept. As a subjective experience, whether loving or being loved, it is susceptible to the often conflicting and contradictory demands and needs of the individual, whereby juxtapositions such as desire and duty, fear and fortitude, self-preservation and self-giving, and the myriad manifestations of the complexity of the human condition, jostle with each other towards the attainment of satisfaction. Peter Gay refers to "instinctual dualism…[such as]…the great antagonists, love and hate, [which] wrestle for control in man's social life quite as much as in his unconscious" (Gay, 1998: 366). The ensuing conflicts of psychic life seek resolution in diverse forms and behaviours, including disavowal of "unacceptable" sources of motivation, projection of "negative" aspects of human nature onto convenient containers, or, in line with psychoanalytic aims, the attempted integration of the full spectrum of instinctual, emotional and mental experience.

Freud's study of the phenomenon of the unconscious leads him to conclude that it contains no sort of unity or organisation, but rather uncoordinated impulses seeking satisfaction, often in opposition with each other. Perhaps foreshadowing Ricoeur's assertion that "the self is conflict" (Ricoeur, 2002: 132), Freud understands the mind as potentially in conflict with itself, and he sees this conflict as the primary cause of human anxiety and unhappiness. According to Boothby,

> the genuine Freudian insight places the most important site of conflict not between our wishes and the world that limits their fulfilment, but between our wishes and ourselves. The problem is not [only] that we are prevented by reality from fulfilling our desire but that we are prevented from knowing that desire in the first place (Boothby, 2001: 278).

The significance of desire, and the consequences accruing from its denial or its dismissal, is central to Lacan's thought. Elucidating the reality of psychic conflict, Freud puts forward a tripartite division of the mind, whereby different mental functions operate at different levels. His description of three conflicting or competing internal tendencies, the id, ego, and superego, which are not physical structures, but rather aspects and elements of a theoretical model, helps to explain the link between early childhood experiences and the mature adult personality. Here, Freud points to the inherent wisdom of poetic vision, stating that: "What poets and students of human nature had always asserted turned out to be true: the impressions of that early period of life, though they were for the most part buried in amnesia, left in-eradicable traces upon the individual's growth" (Freud, 1995: 20). Thus, he encouraged a re-visiting of the past, "he merely told / the unhappy Present to recite the Past / like a poetry lesson", with a view to enabling a more hopeful and a more autonomous encounter with the future, "to approach the Future as a friend / without a wardrobe of excuses, without / a set mask of rectitude" (Auden, 1994: 274). Freud's reference to poets as "students of human nature", and his acknowledgement that his own insights, developed through arduous reflection and observation, are often intuitively and creatively known and felt by artists such as poets, makes the co-analysis of psychoanalysis and poetry in this study particularly appropriate from a Freudian perspective.

According to Freud's description of the tripartite division of the mind, the uncoordinated instinctual trends of psychic life form the id. As a primitive motivational force, the id is ruled by the "pleasure principle", demanding satisfaction now, regardless of circumstances and possibly undesirable consequences; "it contains everything that is inherited, everything present at birth, everything constitutionally determined"[7] (Freud, 2003:176). The desires of the id, to be centre-stage, to be omnipotent, and to be permanently satisfied, are driven by the instincts, which are the innate needs of psychic life. These desires are based on the demand for love, for total union and mergence with "the beloved", symbolized by the mother, and for the protection of that love, by the symbolic father. Ambivalence pervades the direction of these desires as the protective role of the father is alternated with his challenging position as the mother's lover and thus as a threatening rival for her affections; love and hate are ambiguously and simultaneously experienced. Hence, there is an ongoing attraction of the mirage of the perfect love and the prototypes which embody it, replicating this state which is later "forgotten" but never fully abandoned.

---

[7] A major critique of Freud's thought centres on the perception/interpretation that his theories confine the human subject to restrictions imposed by the determinism of biography and biology, thus limiting the possibilities of autonomy, responsibility and "free will". This analysis, the apparent conflict between determinism and autonomy, is explored in my MA thesis, 2006.

In his analysis of the subject, Freud argues against the notion of a *tabula rasa,* a clean slate upon which the individual freely constructs his/her identity and sketches the outline of his/her life. According to Freud, the infant arrives into a world which is already created, already interpreted, already expectant. This thesis that the subject enters a world which is already interpreted, a world of language, is central to the thought of Ricoeur and Lacan. The interpreted world and its subsequent expectations and demands are reflected in the familial and societal mores and values which are directly or indirectly imposed on the child, and which continue to potentially shape its understanding of and relation to, itself and the world in which it finds itself.

As the child moves from a narcissist conception of himself or herself as embodying the universe, and comes to a mature realisation of the existence of the "other", there is a grudging acceptance of the necessity of object-relations; this is experienced in the attempted accommodation of solitude and connection, self-preservation and self-giving: "the two strivings – for individual happiness and for human fellowship – have to contend with each other in every individual" (Freud, 2002: 77). The reality of social and communal life entails a restriction of instinctual desires and primitive drives: "Men cannot remain children forever. They must in the end go out into 'hostile life'. We may call this 'education to reality'" (Freud, 1995: 717). Hence, there is the emergence of "the reality principle" which must be accommodated in frequent contradiction to "the pleasure principle". Pleasure/satisfaction must be pursued within an acknowledgement of the constraints of reality.

The eventual understanding that immediate gratification is usually impossible and often unwise, and that "a child's desires are incompatible with reality" (Freud, 2006: 147), comes with the formation of the ego. The ego develops as the child forms an image of itself in relation to its environment; it is the gradual emergence of the persona or social self, the public presentation of the self. This developmental phase is later described by Lacan as the mirror stage, and the "moment in which the mirror-stage comes to an end", is the moment when the self is propelled into desire:

> It is this moment that decisively tips the whole of human knowledge into mediatization through the desire of the other, constitutes its objects in an abstract equivalence by the co-operation of others, and turns the I into that apparatus for which every instinctual thrust constitutes a danger (Lacan, 1977: 5).

The ego mediates between the conflicting internal demands of the id and the demands and constraints of the social world: "It has the task of self-assertion, and fulfils it with respect to the outside world…and with respect to the inner world…the id" (Freud, 2003: 176). In its attempted accommodation to the public and social environment, the ego is governed by the "reality principle", and in subordinating the demands of the id, it serves as a "modifier" of the "pleasure principle", as it seeks more realistic and attainable goals. Freud explains:

> Thanks to the influence of the ego's self-preservation drive it is displaced by the *reality principle*, which, without abandoning the aim of ultimately achieving pleasure, none the less demands and procures the postponement of gratification, the rejection of sundry opportunities for such gratification, and the temporary toleration of unpleasure on the long and circuitous road to pleasure (Freud, 2006: 135).

The child learns that his/her needs are met in proportion to the supply by others, and this learning is inevitably followed by an acknowledgement of the power differentials at work in his/her surroundings. Satisfaction of one's needs is dependent on the good-will of one's carers, and their good-will becomes a prerequisite of desire fulfilment: "the Freudian child suffers, so to speak, from an intensity of desire and an excess of vulnerability" (Phillips, 2002: 151). The intersubjective context of desire is reiterated by Ricoeur, in his interpretation of Freud's theory; the desire of the self is confronted by the desire of the other:

> if desire were not located within an interhuman situation, there would be no such thing as repression, censorship, or wish-fulfilment through fantasies; that the other and others are primarily bearers of prohibitions is simply another way of saying that desire encounters another desire – an opposed desire (Ricoeur, 1970: 387).

The "interhuman situation" resounds with Buber's analysis of human-being as essentially intersubjective, with all the possibilities for growth and withdrawal which this entails. The potential for camouflage and subterfuge has been created; the experience, imaginary or real, of total, unconditional, unlimited love by another person becomes a distant dream of the past or an insatiable thirst in the present. The possibility of love seems to recede.

The fulfilment of desire is frustrated by the tensions between what is sought and what is possible. Freud turns to the paradigm of the nuclear family and the mythology of Oedipus to portray these tensions: "the Oedipus fable should probably be understood as the poetic treatment of what is typical about such relationships" (Freud, 2006: 476). He refers to "the profound and universal validity of the old legends" and tells us that the fate of Oedipus "moves us only because it might have been our own" (Freud, 1997: 156). Lear refers to the cathartic effect of this experience:

> It is the essence of Freud's account of the appeal of great literature that we can in some way, dimly, recognize ourselves in it. And yet, it is only because the spectator remains aware of the gulf that separates his own life from that of the dramatic hero that he can enjoy indulging in imaginative identification. It is in this fine balance of sympathy and distance that a catharsis can occur (Lear, 1998: 54).

Kennelly makes a similar point with reference to his "contemporary versions of three Greek tragedies": "There's an element of healing present pain when one converses with the mythic world" (Kennelly, 2006: 7). The legend enables an acknowledgement, within the safe distance of a fictional/literary container, of our hidden desires and fears. This is a particular function of creative writing according to Phillips: "What distinguishes the creative writer is that – like the dreamer and the playing child – he has found a way of rendering unacceptable desires into sharable form" (Phillips, 2001: 7). Referring to the imaginative uncovering of forbidden and denied desires, Freud explains the impact of literary portrayals: "Like Oedipus, we live in ignorance of the desires that offend morality, the desires that nature has forced upon us, and after their unveiling we may well prefer to avert our gaze from the scenes of our childhood" (Freud, 1997: 157). Freud corroborates this argument with a reference to *Hamlet*, and suggests that Hamlet's hesitation in fulfilling his late father's injunction to avenge his death is due to the repressed realisation that the murderer, his uncle, has in fact achieved what he himself desired, the death of his father and the possession of his mother. This interpretation of the dynamics of childhood and family life subverts the sentimental view of innocence and harmony idealized in the romantic tradition. "The desires that nature has forced upon us" are complex and ambiguous, but ultimately centre on the desire for love, its offering and its reception. Morality, social demands, and the intricacies of human relationships can often frustrate and distort this desire.

In his critique of morality, and of religion as an aspect of that morality, Freud agrees with Nietzsche's thesis that all moral values are pragmatic in nature and that their effect is often the creation of a herd-mentality and the diminishment of individual autonomy. Freud urges a rejection of the illusory consolations of religion in favour of a more realistic acknowledgement and appreciation of life as it is: "Of what use to them is the mirage of wide acres in the moon, whose harvest no one has ever seen? As honest small-holders on this earth they will know how to cultivate their plot in such a way that it supports them" (Freud, 1995: 717). Freud acknowledges "the value and importance of religion", but he argues that "it has no right in any way to restrict thought"; herein lies the danger of compliance to unquestioned conviction and formulation: "The prohibition against thought issued by religion to assist in its self-preservation is also far from being free from danger either for the individual or for human society" (Freud, 1995: 789).

Freud reveals, in his depiction of human relations, in mythology, literature, and case histories, as well as in his discussion of his own dreams and experiences, the rivalries, deceptions, envies and jealousies – the love-hate triangles permeating the psychic life of the individual – and he sees the resolution of these conflicts through a tolerance for ambiguity, in contrast to their denial, as the key to optimum living. His reinterpretation of family life acknowledges the competitive nature of the child's environment, and portrays the role of the family as constricting as well as protecting. The child gradually realises that desire is limited and thwarted by the unconsciously understood values and taboos of his community. Certain wishes and dreams are necessarily dismissed and "forgotten", but as Freud explains in his description of this "process of *repression*, which we must stress is not to be equated with abolition" (Freud, 2006a: 215), the unfulfilled wishes are never completely eradicated, but rather are buried in the unconscious of the ego from where they continue to exert an influence over our lives. Lacan concurs with this interpretation of repression: "This is what is essential in repression. It's not that the affect is suppressed, it's that it is displaced and unrecognizable" (Lacan, 2007: 144).

Repression

> If the meaning of our dreams usually
> remains obscure to us…it is because of
> the circumstances that at night there
> also arise in us wishes of which we are
> ashamed; these we must conceal from
> ourselves, and they have consequently
> been repressed, pushed into the
> unconscious (Freud, 1995: 440).

The ideal of self-acceptance remains a mirage of clichéd agreement unless it translates into acknowledgement and ownership of the vast complexity and ambiguity of human being. Disavowal, rejection and denial of selected aspects of the self in pursuit of a more ideal image, and the alternating affirmation and negation, are accomplished through selective amnesia, self-deception, or the projection of what is disowned onto a convenient other. Through this phenomenon, part of the self is deemed unacceptable and unwelcome; the self is not loved in its full and changing complexity. A corollary to this self-rejection is a simultaneous dismissal of the full possibility of the other. Incomplete versions of self and other, while seemingly convenient and pleasing, restrict the possibility of relationship, including that of love, to experiences which are partial and conditional. Thus, Freud's description of the role of repression in individual and communal experience is pivotal to an exploration of the possibilities of love.

Freud's discovery that unconscious forces permeate and influence our desires, emotions, thoughts and actions, and that often there is an unconscious rejection and disavowal of uncomfortable and unacceptable drives and impulses, leads to his formulation of repression as the activity whereby what is feared and unwelcome is kept from consciousness. The reasons for this repression are, in Freud's analysis, to be found in early childhood experiences, when unpalatable realities, portrayed in private thought or public behaviour, in oneself or in one's carers, overwhelmed the subject's ability to assimilate them. According to Freud, these repressed memories had their roots in sexual wishes or fantasies which could not be given expression in the face of adult codes of morality and reality. Thus the authentic experience of the child/adult did not fit the picture of reality which one was expected to embody, survival depended on acceptance of another reality, and these early experiences were denied and split off from consciousness. According to Freudian psychoanalysis, maturity entails coming to terms with these split-off aspects of the self, a withdrawal of projections, and integration of all that one is.

Adam Phillips, in his comprehensive study of Freudian thought, sees the attempt at unselective self-acceptance as one of the key roles of psychoanalysis: "Psychoanalysis is, among other things, a redescription of the question: what would it be to accept ourselves and others" (Phillips, 2006: xiv). In this sense, self-acceptance would entail a recognition and acknowledgement of aspects of humanity which are otherwise denied, or at least projected onto some monstrous other;[8] passion, sexuality, aggression, envy and many other components of human nature which are rejected and denied in the quest for a superior image of who we are.

---

[8] The dangers inherent in this projection of evil, aggression, cruelty and terror, and any human characteristics which are deemed uncomfortable or unacceptable, are explored by Richard Kearney in his work *Strangers, Gods and Monsters*; the title is suggestive of the scapegoats which are constructed to facilitate this projection.

Kearney points to this deception as a threatening obstacle to human relations: "The threat to a genuine relation to others comes in fetishizing the Other as much as it does in glorifying the Ego" (Kearney, 2003: 229). In the absence of acceptance, of self, of others, and of reality, denial and deception are inevitable, and the potential for love, of self and of others, is thwarted.

In his realistic appraisal of the individual's life in society – family, community, culture – and the inevitable constraints that such relational living entails, Freud acknowledges the necessity of some degree of repression as one progresses from the narcissist preoccupation and infantile sense of omniscience of childhood to a more mature awareness of one's place in the interconnectedness of human beings and their relation to the world: "Just as the planet still circles round its sun, yet at the same time rotates on its own axis, so the individual partakes in the development of humanity while making his own way through life" (Freud, 2002: 77). As the child moves through a growing awareness of prohibitions and restrictions, expressed through the family and the larger community, it gradually develops a super-ego, an internalisation of the rules and judgements of the authority figures in its life, and the transition from an "objective fear to a conscience-based fear" (Freud, 2003: 57). The critical and moralising function of the super-ego develops as external sources of judgement and punishment are internalised: "As the child was once under a compulsion to obey its parents, so the ego submits to the categorical imperative of its super-ego" (Freud, 1995: 651). The super-ego uses guilt, fear, and self-reproach as its primary means of enforcing these internalized rules; it functions as a voice of conscience, repressing the desires of the id, and forcing the ego to inhibit pleasure-seeking impulses in pursuit of morally acceptable goals. It sets up an image of ideals to be worked towards, and it acts as judge and censor in the inevitable conflict between desire and morality. The unavoidable tension between the ego and this prohibiting super-ego can result in profound feelings of melancholy and guilt: "The *Uber-Ich* imposes the strictest moral standards on its helpless victim, the *Ich;* indeed it represents the claims of morality as a whole, and we see at a glance that our moral feeling of guilt is the expression of the tension between the *Ich* and the *Uber-Ich*" (Freud, 2003: 56). Depending on the nature of what has been internalised, this super-ego will be compassionate, understanding and realistic, or punitive, unforgiving and idealistic, and most commonly operating on a continuum between the two. The characteristics of this internal authority will dictate the degree and the nature of the repression, while it will also be decisive in determining the influence of cultural and societal values and expectations on the individual. In a healthy developmental maturation the super-ego is internalized with awareness and flexibility, it is recreated in accordance with one's own judgements and ongoing experience. In Ricoeurian terms, it coincides with re-interpretation and re-narration in an on-going embrace of experience and knowledge, and in this scenario it becomes a constructive and instructive force in the living of a satisfactory life; it becomes the ego-ideal, which enables the sublimation of one's desires and passions in a way which facilitates a satisfactory compromise between individual satisfaction and the demands of civilization. In other cases however, the super-ego becomes a tormenting, critical and insatiable voice of condemnation and shame resulting in denial and repression.

The repressive role of the internal super-ego is reflected in the power of "the cultural super-ego" (Freud, 2002: 79). The analogy between the superego and the superstructure of the state is outlined in Freud's critique of civilization, *Civilization and Its Discontents*, where he explores the inevitable conflict between the freedom and the drives of the individual and the repression and curtailment imposed by civilized society: "it is a conflict, then, between what the drive demands and what reality forbids" (Freud, 2006: 64). According to Gay, in his biography of Freud, "Freud found the predicament of civilized humanity easy to state: men cannot live without civilization, but they cannot live happily within it...at best, sensible human beings may merge a truce between desire and control" (Gay, 1998: 363). Freud describes civilization as "the sum total of those achievements and institutions that distinguish our life from that of our animal ancestors and serve the dual purpose of protecting human beings against nature and regulating their mutual relations" (Freud, 2002: 27). The protective and regulating authority of society places the well-being of the community above the instinctual strivings of the individual; therefore, according to Freud, "individual liberty is not an asset of civilization" (Freud, 2002: 32). Freud sees that society creates mechanisms to ensure social control of human instincts, and that consequently life in society necessarily frustrates some of our fundamental desires: "In this way civilization overcomes the dangerous aggressivity of the individual, by weakening him, disarming him and setting up an internal authority to watch over him, like a garrison in a conquered town" (Freud, 2002: 61). While stressing the incompatibility of civilization and human happiness, Freud does not deny the necessary protective role of regulation and consensus: "Civilized man has traded in a portion of his chances of happiness for a certain measure of security" (Freud, 2002: 51). Freud argues that adaptation to social and cultural life necessitates the control of primitive instincts, especially sexuality and aggression: "We recognize that it is easy for the barbarian to be healthy, whereas it is a difficult task for the civilized human" (Freud, 2006: 40). Thus, the development of personality is an ongoing accommodation of one's deepest drives to the demands and laws of social living. This accommodation exacts a toll: "the restrictions imposed on our drives mean that a serious psychological burden is laid upon us" (Freud, 1997: 101). Repression, denial, and subjugation characterized Western society in general, according to Freud, and the resulting breakdown and disaster were only too evident in the events of the twentieth century. Linking "civilized sexual morality and modern nervous illness", Freud refers to the "double standards" imposed by society: "a society that entertains such a double standard cannot carry 'love of truth, honesty, and humanity' beyond a certain narrow limit; it cannot help teaching its members to cloak the truth, to gloss over things, and to deceive themselves and others" (Freud, 2002: 86). His critique of Western society was particularly directed against American culture, and its obsession with success and money. In a letter to Ernest Jones in 1921, Freud stated that for the Americans "competition is more pungent with them, not succeeding means civil death to every one, and they have no private resources apart from their profession, no hobby, games, love, or other interests...and success means money" (Gay, 1998: 383). Thus, in his biography of Freud, Gay notes that "his earliest comments on Americans had centred on their inability – as he saw it – to feel, or express, love" (Gay, 1998: 386). One wonders if these comments are applicable to most Western nations. Indeed, Freud noted, in a letter to Wilhelm Fliess in March 1902, that both Europe and America were in thrall to some rule: "I have learned that the old world is ruled by authority, as the new is ruled by the dollar" (Freud, 1985: 457). This analysis has led some commentators to view Freud's vision as essentially pessimistic. In words which resound with Eliot's observation that "Man cannot bear too much reality" (Eliot, 2004: 172), Freud poignantly reflects that "life, as we find it, is too hard for us; it brings us too many pains, disappointments and impossible tasks. In order to bear it we cannot dispense with palliative measures" (Freud, 1995: 728). These palliatives measures range over dedication to career or some other worthwhile project, various forms of intoxication, artistic sublimation, and the compensatory promises of religion.

The pessimistic nature of Freud's vision of human nature is central to Philip Rieff's understanding of Freudianism. On a note of resigned disillusionment, he states that "psychoanalysis is yet another method of learning how to endure the loneliness produced by culture" and he refers to "the normality of disillusion and a controlling sense of resignation, which was the most for which Freud had hoped" (Rieff, 1979: 43). He credits Freud with ripping away the facades of conventional notions of self-understanding, freedom and honesty. He discerns in Freudian anthropology the idea of psychological man as essentially a contradiction, a creature of not finally satiable instincts, impulses, and desires, in endless tensions with himself or herself and society; he is tragically doomed:

> Freud maintains a sober vision of man in the middle, a go-between, aware of the fact the he had little strength of his own, forever mediating between culture and instinct in an effort to gain some room to manoeuvre between these two hostile forces. Maturity, according to Freud, lay in the capacity to keep the negotiations from breaking down (Rieff, 1966: 31).

Certainly, Freud's analysis is that human life is inevitably conflict-ridden, but in accepting this reality Freud enables us to deal with it; as Lear states, "For Freud discovered in the heart of these battles at least the potential for human growth" (Lear, 1998: 27). Nussbaum concurs with this ambiguity as it applies to love: "We deceive ourselves about love – about who, and how, and when, and whether. We also discover and correct our self-deceptions" (Nussbaum, 1992: 261). By acknowledging the reality of conflict in human nature Freud enables the possibility of its accommodation and resolution.

The Art of Living Based on Love

> Our inborn instincts and the world
> around us being what they are, I could
> not but regard that love is no less
> essential for the survival of the human
> race than such things as technology
> (Freud, qtd. in Erikson, 1998: 20).

In the practical situation of clinical work, Freud attempted to free his patients from the tyranny of repression, guilt and anxiety. However, the development of his thought led Freud to believe that as well as attempting to ease the pain of those who are mentally distressed, "psychoanalysis was also the starting-point of a new and deeper science of the mind which would be equally indispensable for the understanding of the normal" (Freud, 1997: 30). The techniques of psychoanalysis were developed with the aim of bringing to consciousness that which had been repressed; these techniques were, the interpretation of dreams – the uncovering of their latent meaning as distinct from the distortions and displacements of their manifest expression, the rule of "free association" – the demand for uncensored expression of one's innermost thoughts, "a withdrawal of the watchers from the gates of the intellect" (Freud, 1997: 17), and the provision of a non-judgemental, understanding and "neutral" listener – the unprejudiced attention to the concerns of the individual. Buber also situates the domain of sleep, and the reduction of inhibiting forces in the experience of dreams therein, as a possible source of connection with "the undivided primal world that precedes form"; entry into the world, "into personal life", entails a separation from this "cosmic connexion, with its true *Thou*", and in sleep/dream there is a "slipping free in the dark hours to be close to her again; night by night this happens to the healthy man" (Buber, 2004a: 26). Ricoeur concludes that "Indeed, dreams supply Freud with his ultimate proof of the unconscious" (Ricoeur, 1970: 119). Through these techniques, according to Freudian psychoanalysis, repressed wishes are revealed, traumatic events are recalled, and the lingering influence of past experiences is acknowledged. Nietzsche's plea for understanding is answered: "Listen to the dream which I dreamed, friends, and help me to read its meaning" (Nietzsche, 2003a: 156). Ricoeur echoes this sentiment: "narrating, like saying, calls for an ear, a power to hear, a reception" (Ricoeur, 2005: 253).

At the core of much of the neuroses which presented themselves in the consulting rooms, Freud identifies love, its distortions, its loss, its necessity, and the obstacles to its experience, as a central factor, leading him to contemplate "this recognition of love as one of the foundations of civilization" (Freud, 1995: 743). The universal need for love is often not gratified, and Freud suggests that the psychoanalyst attempts to replicate what has been neglected and lacking:

> the doctor, in his educative work, makes use of one of the components of love…side by side with the exigencies of life, love is the great educator; and it is by the love of those nearest him that the incomplete human being is induced to respect the decrees of necessity and to spare himself the punishment that follows any infringement of them (Freud, 1995: 591).

The desire for happiness epitomised in the recollected infantile pleasures of being loved, cared for, attended to and responded to, and the unhappiness experienced when these desires are denied and unspoken, form the basis of the analytic encounter. In this practical application of Freud's theories self-knowledge is facilitated by the encounter with another. The relationship between self and other, between analyst and analysand, enables an enlargement of consciousness, as conflicts and neuroses are interpreted and experienced with greater awareness. As Freud states in a letter to Jung in December 1906, "Essentially, one might say, the cure is effected by love" (Freud, 1974: 10). Julia Kristeva concurs with this understanding as she asks: "For what is psychoanalysis if not an infinite quest for rebirths through the experience of love?" (Kristeva, 1987: 2). The absence of love and the obstacles to its experience result in alienation from reality: "neurotics turn away from reality because they find it unbearable – either the whole or parts of it" (Freud, 1995: 301). The need to love and to be loved is portrayed in the psychoanalytic setting by the development of "transference love", whereby the analysand transfers feelings and wishes onto the analyst which actually belong to an earlier experience and an earlier relationship. As Ricoeur states, "the therapeutic relation acts as a mirror image in reviving a whole series of situations all of which were already intersubjective" (Ricoeur, 1970: 474). In this transference relationship, what is "forgotten" is acted out in a repetition of earlier relationships and responses: "the compulsion to repeat…takes the place of the impulse to remember" (Freud, 2006: 395). The links between memory, forgetfulness and dreams, and the phenomenon of transference, is suggested by Nietzsche: "What we do in dreams we also do when we are awake; we invent and fabricate the person with whom we associate – and immediately forget that we have done so" (Nietzsche, 2003: 101).

With these techniques of psychoanalysis, Freud ascertains that most adult neuroses or mental suffering originate in childhood experiences, but, echoing Nietzsche's assertion above, he also claims that transference is a universal phenomenon in human experience. In exploring these childhood experiences which resulted in "the tangled roots of adult love" (Gay, 1998: 291), Freud develops a theory of sexuality which states that most problems in living have their source in sexual or "erotic" experiences. This theory of infantile sexuality was greeted with horror and disgust in Freud's time, and today is still shunned by many. It is argued by some commentators, such as Lear, that Freud's concept of sexuality was broader than its more common connotations, and is closer to our idea of "sensuality", sensual life in all its forms (Lear, 2005: 55). Freud elaborates on his theory in one of his later essays: "the sexual impulses are regarded as including all of those merely affectionate and friendly impulses to which usage applies the exceedingly ambiguous word 'love'" (Freud, 1995: 23). Indeed, Freud describes "two currents whose union is necessary to ensure a completely normal attitude in love…as the affectionate and the sensual current. The affectionate is the older of the two" (Freud, 1995: 395). According to Freud's theory, the present predicament of the individual is seen to be determined by the experiences, traumatic or otherwise, of the past; the symptoms of illness are interpreted as the translation of repressed material; and the restoration of psychic harmony and equilibrium is attained through the integration of conflicted and disowned aspects of the self. However, Freud frequently reminds us that the difficulties, in living and in loving, which are observed in the neurotic, are prevalent universally: "we have since found good reason to suppose that our patients tell us nothing that we might not also hear from healthy people" (Freud, 1995: 439), and he postulates that transference "is the essential character of every state of being in love" (Freud, 1995: 385). It is the rejection of reality, one's own and that of others, that poses the obstacle to love and happiness, and thus Freud insists that it is only in embracing the conflicting, ambiguous nature of life in its ugliness and beauty, its pain and joy, that one can be free to live and love: "psychoanalytic treatment is founded on truthfulness" (Freud, 1995: 382).

Lacan refers to this quest for truth as central to Freud's work: "Freud was taken up in the quest for a truth which engaged him totally, including there in his own self", and he interprets the scientific domain of this endeavour: "Freud progressed on a course of research which is not characterized by the same style as other scientific research. Its domain is that of the truth of the subject. The quest for truth is not entirely reducible to the objective, and objectifying, quest of ordinary scientific methods. What is at stake is the realization of the truth of the subject" (Lacan, 1991: 20, 21). Phillips asserts that psychoanalysis strives to overcome the projection, idealization, and fantasy whereby we hide from the reality of ourselves: "Psychoanalysis asks us to reconsider the unacceptable, in ourselves and in others, in our personal and cultural histories, in our desires and thoughts and feelings and beliefs" (Phillips, 2006: xv). The difficulties at the heart of love are not proof of its impossibility, but rather the denial of its complexities and ambiguities pose obstacles which are insurmountable while they remained denied" "we are never so defenceless against suffering as when we love, never so helplessly unhappy as when we have lost our loved object or its love. But this does not dispose of the technique of living based on the value of love as a means to happiness" (Freud, 1995: 733). Freud lists this technique as one of "the methods that human beings employ in trying to gain happiness", and the following outline suggests his admiration for an "art of living" based on love:

> this particular technique in the art of living…does not turn away from the external world: on the contrary, it clings to the things of this world and obtains happiness through an emotional attachment to them. Nor is it content with the avoidance of unpleasurable experience, a goal that derives, as it were, from tired resignation; indeed, it bypasses this goal, pays no attention to it, and adheres to the original, passionate striving for the positive achievement of happiness. Perhaps it gets closer to this goal

than any other method. I am referring of course to the way of life that places love at the centre of everything and expects all satisfaction to come from loving and being loved' (Freud, 2002: 19).

The insights of Freud into the workings of the human mind demand a renunciation of unrealistic portrayals of human nature, an acceptance of vulnerability and fallibility, and a rejection of mirages of omniscience and invincibility; they propose a realistic awareness and acceptance of one's limitations in order to grapple with the vicissitudes of life as it is, and they urge a confrontation with the obstacles to love and happiness as the only route to overcoming them. These insights and their consequent demand for a comprehensive acknowledgement of the ambiguous and conflictual nature of the human subject, resound with much of Nietzsche's philosophy. Freud's writings, academic and personal, assert that the concepts of "human" and "perfection" are incompatible; for him this is an inescapable truth of the human condition. However, the imperfectability of the human being, echoed in Nietzsche's *Human, All Too Human,* and Ricoeur's *Fallible Man,* is not an insurmountable obstacle to love and happiness, but rather an integral and often enriching component of their experience. Echoing Ricoeur's description of "the good life", Bettelheim outlines Freud's comprehensive vision of a meaningful life where loving relationships are enabled through an acknowledgement of all aspects of human nature:

> The good life, in Freud's view, is one that is full of meaning through the lasting, sustaining, mutually gratifying relations we are able to establish with those we love, and the satisfaction we derive from knowing that we are engaged in work that helps us and others to have a better life. A good life denies neither its real and often painful difficulties nor the dark aspects of our psyche (Bettelheim, 1984: 108).

Freud's thought explores and permeates areas of human being previously uncharted; his insights into human nature are the culmination of his self-observation as well as his clinical work, his attempts to understand the motivations, needs and potentialities of the human subject, and his ongoing openness to revision and re-interpretation. Freud was passionate about the subject of his life's work, and this passion accommodated the possibility of correction: "a person in love is humble" (Freud, 1995: 560). His view of the human condition dispels with untenable glorifications and super-human depictions; but in embracing the reality of the human subject as imperfect, ambivalent, and not fully knowable to self or to others, Freud remains convinced of the power of love to answer many human needs, and to enhance the experience of human living: "but he would have us remember most of all / to be enthusiastic over the night, / not only for the sense of wonder / it alone has to offer, but also / because it needs our love" (Auden, 1994: 276).

CHAPTER FIVE

JACQUES LACAN

The theories of psychoanalysis developed by Freud have been, and continue to be, interpreted and reinterpreted in diverse and often controversial ways by different personalities, different disciplines, and different cultures. Interpretation and commentary on Freud's ideas range over the spectrum of rejection and ridicule, selective adoption and acquiescence, revision and re-reading. As Lacan's biographer, Elisabeth Roudinesco explains, "psychoanalysis might well bring healing to every kind of society and the discovery of the unconscious might indeed have universal relevance; but that didn't stop every country interpreting Freud in its own particular way" (Roudinesco, 1997: 16). The French psychoanalyst, Jacques Lacan, undertook to "return to Freud" with the professed intention of pursuing a meticulous re-reading of Freudian texts, an exposition of what he considered the misreading and misunderstanding of psychoanalysis, and a determination to remain loyal to "the letter" of Freud's thought: "We...are trying to articulate Freud's thought and experience so as to give them their due weight and importance" (Lacan, 1997: 181). Lacan sought to re-situate psychoanalysis in a strict and comprehensive adherence to Freud's work, and to shun any deviation from the text. According to Slavoj Žižek's stated defence of Lacan, this has been admirably achieved: "Seen through the eyes of Lacan...Freud's key insights finally emerge in their true dimension" (Žižek, 2006: 2). Richard Boothby refers to Lacan as "arguably the most theoretically ambitious and sophisticated of all Freud's interpreters", and claims that "through Lacan's rereading, Freud emerges as a philosophical thinker of the first order, whose contribution is to be ranked with that of Heidegger or Hegel" (Boothby, 2001: 9).[1]

Over the course of a long career, Lacan produced ideas which had their source in Freudian texts, but which were also formulated in the light of his own reading of philosophy and linguistics, and which inevitably bore the

---

[1] Ricoeur, as another French interpreter of Freud, offers his own philosophical understanding of the work.

hallmark of his own response. Lacan credits Freud with developing the most revolutionary insights into the human mind. He examines in detail the particular textual expressions of Freudian concepts, and by relating them to philosophical developments as diverse as Plato and Hegel, Aristotle and Kant, St. Augustine and Nietzsche, he provides a unique interpretation of psychoanalysis.[2]

> Anyone capable of glimpsing the changes we have lived through in our own lives can see that Freudianism, however misunderstood it has been and however nebulous its consequences have been, constitutes an intangible but radical revolution...everything...has been affected by it (Lacan, 2006: 165).

Lacan's thesis is that Freud's discoveries are revolutionary and that their significance applies universally: "The meaning of what Freud said may be conveyed to anyone because, while addressed to everyone, it concerns each person...Freud's discovery calls truth into question, and there is no one who is not personally concerned by truth" (Lacan, 2006: 111). The questioning of "truth" is also central to Nietzsche's philosophy, and concepts such as universalism and relativism are henceforth central to ongoing description and debate pertaining to this issue. Postmodern thought, in particular Derrida's deconstruction, simultaneously mourns the apparent demise of absolute "truth" and celebrates the diverse possibilities which ensue from this "loss". Lacan argues that the meaning of Freud's thought has not been fully embraced or understood: "Freud didn't finish at a stroke the trail he blazed for us" (Lacan, 1997: 88), and he assigns to himself the task of continuing this "trail".

Lacan's writing style is notoriously difficult to read and to understand; this is seen by some commentators as illustrative of Lacan's objective in postulating the difficulties inherent in all understanding,[3] while for others it is symptomatic of unnecessary obscurity and feigned profundity.[4] The argument centres on whether the basic truth, the essential message of any writer, is best expressed in simple language, or whether simplicity and directness permit an "easy" understanding which misreads the message. Lacan, referring to his use of terminology, points out that "the things I say

---

[2] Lacan's work incorporates various critiques of philosophy and philosophical endeavours; however, when confronted with the accusation that he is "attacking philosophy", his response is: "That's greatly exaggerated" (Lacan, 2007: 146).
[3] See Charles Sheperdson's essay "Lacan and Philosophy", in *The Cambridge Companion to Lacan*, and the many commentaries of J.A. Miller.
[4] This is the contention of writers such as N. Chomsky and R. Webster.

are calculated to emphasize a certain mirage" (Lacan, 1997: 253). Apart
from the potential difficulties involved in striving for a "perfect
translation" of any work,[5] and the added difficulty of translating an oral
deliverance of ideas,[6] Lacan's work is strewn with philosophical,
scientific, and linguistic references which he uses to foreground his own
arguments. An added impediment results from the relatively recent
chronological situation of his work, and the correlative issues of
ownership and copyright, whereby much of his ideas, insights, and
revisions await publication, translation, and general circulation. Much of
the difficulty and obscurity experienced in approaching his work lies in
Lacan's preference for the exactness and clarity of mathematical science,
and the resulting graphs, schema, and algorithms through which he
delivers his thought. This chapter explores a reading of selected Lacanian
texts with an acknowledgement of the potential involved in opening up a
new way of thinking which appears to be at variance with accepted and
familiar experiences of reading, writing, and expression. The material
selected is limited to that which most obviously relates to the concept of
love and concentrates on aspects of his work which are deemed relevant to
Lacan's thoughts on the possibility of love.

In his exploration of various aspects of the human condition and
particularly the concept of subjectivity, Lacan questions and analyses the
way the human subject is structured by language, as he designates this
structuring as central to human existence. The significance of language to
an understanding of subjectivity is central to the philosophy of
hermeneutics, and is the focus of thinkers such as Ricoeur and Gadamer.
This description of the subject's experience focuses on the meaning of
subjectivity, the experiential stages determined in the development of the
human subject, and the ambiguities and conflicts inherent in the living of a
human life. According to the interpretation of Lorenzo Chiesa, "Lacan
outlines a revolutionary theory of the subject and, despite his relentless
attacks against philosophy, repeatedly invites it to collaborate with
psychoanalysis in order to build on his groundbreaking investigations"
(Chiesa, 2007: 5). One Lacanian translator and interpreter, Juliet Mitchell,
thus summarises Lacan's objective: "Lacan dedicated himself to
reorienting psychoanalysis to its task of deciphering the ways in which the
human subject is constructed" (Mitchell, 1982: 5). Lacan's work is

[5] See chapter three for reference to Ricoeur's reflections on "the perfect
translation".
[6] Lacan's preferred mode of communicating his ideas was the spoken word,
lectures, seminars and radio and television interviews, rather than the written form
of standard publication.

essentially an exploration of the following questions: What is a human being? What does it mean to be human? What does a human being need? How is a human being to live? And especially, what does a human being desire? Such questions have exercised the minds of philosophers from Plato and Aristotle, to Derrida and Kristeva, and have also inspired the world of literature, especially in its poetic offering; most, if not all, human beings grapple with these issues at some point in lives, however diversely the questions are encountered and expressed. Integral to these questions is the concept of love. The central importance of this concept for Lacanian thought can be verified by Lacan's statement that the question of love has always been pivotal to his work: "I've been doing nothing but that since I was twenty, exploring the philosophers on the subject of love" (Lacan, 1999: 75). According to Lacan, psychoanalytic theory, as evidenced in Freudian texts, inevitably impinges on our understanding of love, and firmly positions this understanding within an ethical framework: "Analysis has brought a very important change of perspective on love by placing it at the centre of ethical experience" (Lacan, 1997: 8). Nussbaum's work on Hellenistic ethics may suggest that this is not altogether a "change of perspective" as she explores Platonic, Aristotelian and Stoic philosophers and the literature of poetic tragedy in a search for "a practical and compassionate philosophy", (Nussbaum, 1994: 3); her reading in these realms deals with human life in its complexity and ambivalence, and particularly with the place of love in ethical behaviour, and she suggests that this topic was central to the philosophy and literature of ancient Greece, and therefore was not an innovation of psychoanalysis.[7] According to Alain Badiou, in his essay "Lacan and the Pre-Socratics", two major themes of Lacan's thought are "the primacy of discourse and the function of love in the truth-process", and he reminds us that for Lacan "love…is what brings being face to face with itself" (Badiou, 2006: 8,10). The possibility of love, in sexual and non-sexual forms, is therefore questioned throughout Lacan's work, and in suggesting that it is often apparently impossible, he engages with the obstacles to its experience.

The Paradox of Language

> In everything that approaches it,
> language merely manifests its
> inadequacy (Lacan, 1999: 45).

---

[7] I refer here to Nussbaum's works, *The Therapy of Desire, The Fragility of Goodness*, and *Love's Knowledge*.

The centrality of language to human being pervades the disciplines of philosophy and psychoanalysis, and is creatively manifested in the experience of the poetic word. The human condition, in its manifold and ambivalent components, is explored, analyzed and defined through the medium of language. This applies consequently to the human experience of love. However, love is essentially a subjective experience, and while language is the vehicle of its communication and its description, the intrinsic limitations and constraints of the written or spoken word, particularly its inability to articulate fully the private, inner landscape of thought, emotion, desire and motivation, impact on the quality and range of intersubjectivity, and consequently on the possibility of love as a significant propellant of human relationship.

Lacan's formulation of his philosophy was informed by the radical developments in linguistics and anthropology, particularly evident in the works of Ferdinand de Saussure and Claude Levi-Strauss. The influence of these writers extended to psychoanalysis, which at that time was embroiled in controversy and questioning regarding the Freudian legacy and its legitimacy. As an avid reader and conversationalist across many disciplines, Lacan was aware of the potential insights of Saussure and Levi-Strauss as applied to psychoanalysis, and the development of his thought reflected this influence. Lacan's philosophy explores perennial questions pertaining to our understanding of concepts such as the subject, identity, recognition, desire, the good, and happiness. In tacit agreement with the philosophies of Buber and Ricoeur, and in adherence to the analysis of human nature proffered by Nietzsche and Freud, Lacan emphasises the inter-subjective constitution of human desire and motivation, stating that desire is always desire for the other (Lacan, 2004: 300). However, in contrast to Buber's contention that authentic relationship involves a perception of the other as a Thou rather than an object, and Ricoeur's proposition of relationship as seeing oneself as another, Lacan's view of human relationships places the subject as always at a distance from the object, the other. It is in this complex interrelationship between subject and object, self and other, that Lacan situates his anthropology of the subject. He reformulates and expands on the dialogical and linguistic exigencies of human nature which are central to the above-mentioned philosophies, and in rendering the subject as essentially a speaking being, a *parle-être*, he outlines the potential obstacles to love, knowledge, truth and happiness which originate in the alienation of the subject from the real, from desire, from the self; an alienation that is congruent with the individual's inescapable dependence on the distancing effect of language: "And the subject, while he may appear to be the slave of language, is still more the slave of a discourse in the universal movement of which his place is already inscribed at his birth, if only in the form of his proper name" (Lacan, 2006: 140). Thus, Lacan raises questions regarding the conception of the subject, the approach of the other, and the possibility or impossibility of a relationship between the two. He suggests that all of our understanding is susceptible to the illusions, mirages, and distortions which are often implied by the unquestioned supremacy which is allocated to the signifiers that define our experience – words which name and translate both our inner and outer perceptions. The power of signifiers to label our experience and define our actions entails a threat to individual interpretation of one's personal reality, and an attraction to the safety of conformity and adaptation, regardless of whether the object of adaptation is beneficial or destructive, life-enhancing or dysfunctional.

The paradox of language, in Lacan's exposition, emerges from the conflict between the subject's dependence on the apparatus of language as the only recourse available for expression, discourse, and relationship, "the world of interhuman relations, the world of language" (Lacan, 1997: 121), and the failure of language to say it all: "The whole truth is what cannot be told. It is what can only be told on the condition that one doesn't push it to the edge, that one only half-tells (*mi-dire*) it" (Lacan, 2006: 92). As Nietzsche states, "not everything may be spoken in the presence of day" (Nietzsche, 2003a: 187). Lacan repeatedly returns to his argument that the truth can only be half-said: "half-saying is the internal law of any kind of enunciation of the truth" (Lacan, 1997: 126), but he nevertheless considers the attempt essential and worthwhile. Auden echoes the paradox: "At lucky moments we seem on the brink / Of really saying what we think we think: / But, even then, an honest eye should wink" (Auden, 1994: 695). Another poetic expression of this paradox is given by Philip Larkin, in his poignant portrayal of the commonly experienced conflict between honesty and kindness, the intensity of which appears to expand according to the degree of intimacy being experienced, and which is therefore relevant to the possibility of love: "Nothing shows why / At this unique distance from isolation / It becomes still more difficult to find / Words at once true and kind / Or not untrue and not unkind" (Larkin, 1988: 129). The paradox of language, as both a means and an obstacle to communication, inevitably impacts on the communication, the experience, and the possibility of love, as it is constitutive of love that it is somehow communicable. However, attention may be directed to the *somehow*. Lacan's emphasis on the failure of language to fully express the real, suggests that love cannot be communicated solely through words, but this is not an insurmountable obstacle: acknowledgement of the limitation of language opens the way for an understanding of what cannot be verbalized, and leaves a space for the potential significance of silence and action to be expressed and heard: "Truth hollows out its way into the real thanks to the dimension of speech. There is neither true nor false prior to speech" (Lacan, 1991: 228). Lacan insists that "speech is in its essence ambiguous" Lacan, 1991: 228), and it is sometimes within these ambiguous realms, which often resist symbolization and systematic analysis, that love finds its expression and its communication.

In his outline of the development of individuality and personality, Lacan formulates the mirror stage as the developmental moment in the subject's life when recognition of itself is assumed. The reflection in the mirror, in the gaze of the other, is taken as representing the identity of the subject. Roudinesco describes it thus: "The mirror stage... [is] a psychic or ontological operation through which a human being is made by means of identification with his fellow-beings" (Roudinesco, 2003: 29). The child is captivated by its own image and misrecognizes this "image" as its "self". Entry into what Lacan terms the imaginary realm is accomplished. Henceforth, the child is aware of a rupture, a separation, between itself and the other; the pre-mirror stage of complete mergence with the source of need satisfaction is fractured, and thus a gap, a lack, is created. This lack is the birth of desire, the desire to return to the state of unspoken and unconscious equilibrium where there is no demand because every need is capable of satisfaction. Now the lack necessitates the communication of need and demand, and hence the development of the subject within language. Perhaps anticipating Lacan's reflections on the limits of language, Nietzsche asks, "are words and music not rainbows and seeming bridges between things eternally separate?" (Nietzsche, 2003a: 234). Here, the bridge-building/mediating/communicating role of language is questioned through the insertion of the adjective "seeming". (Nietzsche, 2003a: 234). The child's entry into language is an entry into the symbolic mode of identification and representation which precedes the subject; "language, with its structures, exists prior to each subject's entry into it at a certain moment in his mental development" (Lacan, 2006: 139). From this moment in development, this entanglement of individual and collective meaning, there are two forces which distance the subject from the real; the imaginary realm wherein one's identity, one's sense of self and one's sense of the world, is constructed through the image, the reflection, the recognition, of the other: "The transformation that takes place in the subject when he assumes an image" (Lacan, 2006: 4), and the symbolic realm wherein one abides by the laws, the structures, and the incompleteness of language in order to attain and maintain one's identity as a human subject in the world: "Because the law of man has been the law of language since the first words of recognition presided over the first gifts" (Lacan, 2006: 61). The irrevocable link between self and other, between the individual and the social world, establishes the potential dilemma between contradictory desires of autonomy and relationship, identity and recognition, solitude and connection.

The paradox of language is its effect in distancing the subject from the real, the impossible to say, while simultaneously providing the only pathway to the reality of one's experience, of oneself and of others: "The function of the mirror stage thus turns out, in my view, to be a particular case of the function of imagos, which is to establish a relationship between an organism and its reality" (Lacan, 2006: 6). Lacan's reference to "the function of imagos" resounds with concepts such as "the false self", "persona", and "the mask" as signifiers of the public image of the subject which is variously close to or distant from the inner, private self.[8] The necessity of establishing a relationship between the organism and its reality is central to Freud's analysis of the conflict between individual happiness and collective security, outlined in his essay *Civilization and its Discontents*, and this title is echoed by Lacan when he refers to "the malaise of civilization" (Lacan, 2006: 29). According to Roudinesco, there is a continuity in Lacan's ideas in that he is always "concerned with the relationship between the individual and society", and she points to his confrontation with the political reality of his day as an impetus to this concern: "he needed to find out how fascism managed to harness human aspiration in the service of evil"[9] (Roudinesco, 1997: 171). Lacan's study of the subject in tension with the socio-cultural environment, the essence of the social bond, and the ensuing relationship between autonomy and constraint, leads him to the conclusion that repression is inevitable: "From the moment he begins to speak, from that exact moment onward and not before, I can understand that there is such a thing as repression" (Lacan, 2006: 56). Repression is necessitated by an awareness that one's position, as relative to the law, the law of others and their signifiers, implies a splitting off and a denial of that which is deemed unacceptable to that law. Boothby asserts that "Lacan's notion of alienation is absolutely

---

[8] This conflict between inner and outer realities, between the mask and the real, is creatively explored by W.B. Yeats, in his poetry, drama, and prose.
[9] The attempt to approach some understanding of evil, especially as manifested so blatantly and so shockingly in events of their lifetime, is evident in the works of many writers of this period, and inspired the title of one of Ricoeur's works, *The Symbolism of Evil*.

fundamental to his thought", and he relates this to the mirror stage: "The imaginary identification of the mirror stage is formative and enabling but also deeply alienating. Paradoxically, the subject is estranged from itself in the very moment in which it achieves a measure of self-representation" (Boothby, 2001: 141). The phenomenon of repression as the "forgetting" of the truth is highlighted by Lacan as he links, through their echoing sound, the words *Lethe*, the river of forgetfulness, and *aletheia*, the Greek word for truth: "In every entry of being into its habitation in words, there's a margin of forgetting, a *lethe* complementary to every *aletheia*" (Lacan, 1991: 192).

The alienation resulting from the child's entry into language, into the world signified by others, situates the search for identity, the quest for an answer to the question, "who am I?", in the response and reflection of the other. Deborah Luepnitz points to this self-estrangement in her feminist perspective on Lacan's notion of identity:

> Having recognized ourselves in the mirror, we are bound to go through life looking outward for evidence of who we are...identity, for Lacan, is necessarily an alienated state, something crucial for functioning in the world, but also radically unstable...because in answer to the question "who am I?" there is no truth that can be given by an agency outside the subject (Luepnitz, 2003: 225).

These sentiments resound with Ricoeur's explorations of the concepts of recognition and identity. Lacan argues that the images we have of ourselves are always filtered through language, through the signifiers of others, as experienced through family, community and culture. Alienation from the real, from the true, entails a repression or a displacement of one's constitutive drives, and hence an incommensurability of the reality of oneself and that of others. In his clinical work, Lacan, like Freud before him, witnessed the suffering and confusion resulting from this alienation, and he stressed repeatedly that the aim of psychoanalysis was not the adaptation of the individual to a system of perceived normality: "There's absolutely no reason why we should make ourselves the guarantors of the bourgeois dream. A little more rigor and firmness are required in our confrontation with the human condition" (Lacan, 1997: 303). The absence of this confrontation results in "empty chatter about maturity, love, joy, peace" according to Laing's exploration of the dichotomy between sanity and madness: "What we call 'normal' is a product of repression, denial, splitting, projection, introjection and other forms of destructive action on experience. It is radically estranged from the structure of being" (Laing, 1967: 27). Chiesa claims that "Lacan progressively questions the very existence of a "normal" subject. The borderline between 'normality' and 'abnormality' is gradually blurred" (Chiesa, 2007: 7). The failure to confront the reality of the human condition results in a diminishment of love, of self and of others, because what is in question is merely a mask, a disguise, a fiction: "Distance creates mirages" (Lacan, 1997: 316). Mark Patrick Hederman, in his brief essay on love, *Manikon Eros*, opposes this argument, and describes it as "the depressing suggestion of Lacan…that we never have access to others as they are" (Hederman, 2000: 26). He refers to Lacan's famous statement regarding the impossibility of a sexual relationship:

> even though we can be enthralled by sexual desire, there is no such thing as a sexual relationship because our libidinal mechanisms are not involved with another person as such. So, as lovers we are like ships passing each other in the night…we are submerged in a solipsistic psychic miasma, and the periscope, which is just about able to pierce through, has distorted and restricted vision (Hederman, 2000: 26).

Hederman accordingly interprets Lacan's analysis of subjectivity as the confinement of a private world which can never grasp or gain access to the real of the other.

The quest for recognition through the reflection and the signifier of the other resounds with Hegel's master-slave dialectic, but Lacan is sceptical of the possibility of a resolution to this dialectic, suggesting that lived experience rarely remains fixated within this binary opposition but vacillates between the two, and often combines elements of both master and slave. In Lacan's constitution of the subject, whereby there is a demand for recognition from the other, as he says, "man's…first objective is to be recognized by the other" (Lacan, 2006: 58), there seems little place for Buber's ideal of emphatic understanding and mediation integral to the "I-Thou" relationship: Lacan asserts that "Between two, whatever they may be, there is always the One and the Other" (Lacan, 1999: 49). Lacan, therefore, rejects the popular notion of the unifying power of love, sexual or otherwise, to merge two into one. This craving to merge with the other is a human experience explored from the philosophy of Plato to the present day. Fromm states categorically that "the deepest need of man…is the need to overcome his separateness, to leave the prison of his aloneness" (Fromm, 1995: 8).[10] Similarly, in the light of Lacan's reference to the

---

[10] Philip Roth, in his most recent novel, *Exit Ghost*, offers an interesting and contemporary depiction of the urge to escape solitude and aloneness; he suggests that the preponderance of cell phones is an example of this craving, and he

artifice of language, "language always involves artifice relative to anything intuitive, material or lived" (Lacan, 1997: 136), its capacity to hide as much as it reveals, Ricoeur's thesis of narrative identity appears to be susceptible to the distorting and limiting constraints of the law of language. Chiesa refers to this problem as "the mistaken equation between intentionality and consciousness", and explains that "the subject is alienated in language because he never manages to say exactly what he really wants to say…words do not suffice to convey the subject's desire appropriately, and consequently fail to satisfy it" (Chiesa, 2007: 38). This analysis appears to be close to Nietzsche's depiction of herd-mentality, where the desire for love, for acceptance, for recognition, results in a variable level of conformity to the symbolic law and a resentful acquiescence to the social imposition of distortion and repression. The loss of the real, integral to the subject's entry into the symbolic domain of language, results in a gap, a lack, which henceforth separates the subject from his/her desire.

The Mystery of the Unconscious

> In fact, to a certain degree, at a certain
> level, fantasms cannot bear the
> revelation of speech (Lacan, 1997: 80).

Human desire and motivation is often ambiguous, conflicting, and transient, and in the light of Nietzschean and Freudian insights, is sometimes expressed in distorted and concealing modes. The desire and motivation of love, the urge, decision, and need to love and to be loved, is susceptible to these exigencies, and may be thwarted by the voluntary or involuntary denial and deception which commonly accompanies the translation of human desire and need into socially acceptable mediums of language and behaviour. Hence, the possibility of love is diminished to a variety of disguises and pretences, as the subject strives to attain a compromise between authentic being and interpersonal and social expectations.

However, there is another dimension to the subject which is not limited and defined by an external imposition - the law of language, of society, of the other – and it is the revelation and description of this dimension that Lacan interprets as the greatest Freudian contribution to an understanding of the human subject: "It all began with a particular truth, an unveiling, the

---

suggests that "to eradicate the experience of separation must inevitably have a dramatic effect" (Roth, 2007: 64).

effect of which is that reality is no longer the same for us as it was before" (Lacan, 2006: 113). This is the dimension of the unconscious, that aspect of the mind which is outside of one's awareness and understanding, and which resists systematization, measurement, and adaptation. In Nietzsche's words, "Here there is much hidden misery that wants to speak out" (Nietzsche, 2003a: 314). It is the seat of all that is deemed unacceptable to one's private and public image, all that is too frightening, incomprehensible, and "dangerous" to confront, all that is repressed in order for the subject to survive in a world that designates, through language, the conditions and expectations of human being: "The fundamental situation of repression is organized around a relation of the subject to the signifier" (Lacan, 1997: 44). The universality of this phenomenon is attested by Freud: "No human individual is spared traumatic experiences...none is absolved from the repressions that they give rise to" (Freud, 2006: 39). Aversion towards certain aspects of humanity – evil, aggression, duplicity, greed, and much more – leads to a disavowal of unwanted parts of the self, and finds the solution in repression and selective amnesia: "Man deals with selected bits of reality" (Lacan, 1997: 47).[11] This resounds with Nietzsche's assertion that the denial of our animal instincts is demanded by a morality which rejects and distorts the true nature of human life.

The distorted image of human nature is attractive in its idealized picture of wisdom, goodness and kindness: "Those who like fairy stories turn a deaf ear to talk of man's innate tendencies to evil, aggression, destruction, and thus to cruelty" (Lacan, 1997: 185). In this fairy-land, human experience is diminished to a pseudo-existence where passions of love and hate, compassion and destruction, are replaced by more "comfortable" and "polite" representations. Here, Lacan is in agreement with Ricoeur's thesis that evil is a reality of human nature, and that recognition of this reality entails the only possibility of confronting it.[12] As Freud states, "one cannot destroy an enemy if he is absent or out of reach" (Freud, 2006: 397). Rather than the embrace of delusions pertaining to idealistic and unreal ideologies of human nature, Lacan, like Nietzsche and Freud before him, urges a more honest and realistic appraisal. Žižek explains:

---

[11] This quote has strong echoes of Eliot's observation, "man cannot bear too much reality" (Eliot, 2004: 172). Lacan's familiarity with Eliot's work is obvious in his use of extracts as elucidation of his own work; for example, see *Écrits*, pp.70 and 103-104.

[12] This is a central argument in Ricoeur's work, especially as outlined in *Fallible Man* and *Memory, History and Forgetting*.

Lacan advocates that we recognize practical anti-humanism, an ethics that
goes beyond the dimension of what Nietzsche called 'human, all too
human', and confronts the inhuman core of humanity. This means an ethics
that fearlessly stands up to the latent monstrosity of being human, the
diabolic dimension that erupted in the phenomena broadly covered by the
label 'Auschwitz' (Žižek, 2006, 46).

Adhering to Freudian doctrine, Lacan asserts that denial and repression is
a futile attempt to eliminate what is "unbearable", whether this is
considered "evil", "trauma", or any concept which is deemed excluded
from human nature; repression is counterpoised with the "return of the
repressed".

Lacan looks to Freud's exploration of the unconscious and finds there
several pathways to the truth which is concealed therein: "The
unconscious evinces knowledge that, for the most part, escapes the
speaking being" (Lacan, 1999: 139), but paradoxically, Lacan states that
"the unconscious is only accessible through the artifice of the spoken
word" (Lacan, 1997: 48). What is repressed in the unconscious is not
obliterated, but is expressed through various detours: "The true...is never
reached except by twisted pathways" (Lacan, 1999: 95). The difficulty
attendant on any attempt to reach or to express "the true" is humbly stated
by the Irish novelist, John McGahern: "I believe that it is a great
achievement for any man to state, even once, a measure of his experience
truthfully" (McGahern, qtd. in *The Irish Times* 2006). From his clinical
practice and general observation of human nature, Lacan observed that the
unconscious is transmitted through dreams, fantasies, symptoms, slips of
the tongue, jokes, and myriad hidden messages lurking behind speech and
behaviour, by which "the path of truth is suggested in a masked form"
(Lacan, 1997: 74), and that the interpretation of these transmissions,
through psychoanalytic insight, can provide access to the real: "The real, I
will say, is the mystery of the speaking body, the mystery of the
unconscious" (Lacan, 1999: 131). As Žižek asserts in his interpretation of
Lacan's formulation of the Freudian unconscious, "The unconscious
is...the site where a traumatic truth speaks out" (Žižek, 2006: 3). The
masked forms in which the unconscious is manifested, the dream, the
symptom, the fantasy, can only be deciphered when they are expressed in
language, in words which try to both reveal and conceal their latent
content:

We can only grasp the unconscious finally when it is explicated, in that
part of it which is articulated by passing into word. It is for this reason that

> we have the right…to recognize that the unconscious itself has in the end
> no other structure than the structure of language (Lacan, 1997: 32).

It is here that the insights and techniques of psychoanalysis are used to enable the emergence of truth in human reality, and in so doing, to testify to the obstacles which hinder such truth; these are also the obstacles to the possibility of love. Freudian and Lacanian psychoanalysis posits truth as its ultimate purpose, characterized by Rieff as an ethic of honesty, while he also makes reference to the potential of literature to articulate truth: "Psychoanalysis…demands a special capacity for candour which not only distinguishes it as a healing movement, but also connects it with a drive toward disenchantment characteristic of modern literature" (Rieff, 1959: 315). Freud states clearly "that psychoanalytic treatment is founded on truthfulness. In this fact lies a great part of its educative effect and its ethical value" (Freud, 1995: 382). It is not suggested here that truth and love are synonymous, but it is argued that truth is essential to love, in the sense of a recognition of its motivation, desire, and experience, and an acknowledgement of the many guises which masquerade as love. The relationship between truth and love is explored by Badiou in an article titled "What Is Love?" in which he claims that "love does not take the place of anything. It *supplements,* which is completely different. It is a *production of truth*" (Badiou, 2000: 266). This relationship between love and truth inevitably posits the question of access to truth; is it ever possible, given Lacan's exposition of the barriers to truth inherent in the subject's constitutive position within the symbolic and the imaginary realms of human existence, and accepting the Freudian assertion of the powers of the unconscious, that truth can be accessed? Žižek bases his answer to this question on Lacan's insight into the real: "truth itself can function in the mode of the Real" (Žižek, 2006: 63). Thus, love, truth, and the real are intrinsically related, perennially questioned, and continue to elude fixed systematization and ultimate definition. Žižek's interventions into the investigation of love will be explored in the next chapter.

In the clinical setting, which can be used as a microcosm of the wider reality of love, its experience, its communication, its desire and need, its attempt and its failure, its indomitable recurrence and repetition, and which mirrors the interaction between subject and object, between self and other, the analysand approaches the analyst initially with a symptom, an experience, a behaviour, which is causing suffering and distress. From this initial encounter to the end of the analysis, everything that takes place is grounded in language, in some sort of discourse: "psychoanalysis has but one medium: the patient's speech" (Lacan, 2006: 40). An encounter is initiated and develops through dialogical action, an action which takes place through language, dialogue, the spoken word. As Lacan states, "psychoanalytic action develops in and through verbal communication, that is, in a dialectical grasping of meaning. Thus it presupposes a subject who manifests himself verbally in addressing another subject" (Lacan, 2006: 11). According to Lacan, this approach is in fact a demand; a demand perhaps disguised in the request that the symptom be alleviated or eliminated altogether, and that the analyst fulfil the function of "the subject supposed to know" (Lacan, 1999: 67), the embodiment of the prototypical omniscience which variously takes form as God, Buddha, The Father, or in more contemporary categories of "the expert", "the guru". According to Lacan, his "formula of the subject supposed to know [is] the mainspring of the transference" (Lacan, 2007: 186). The subject/patient transfers the possibility of insight, understanding and truth onto the analyst as the figure empowered to guide, explain or dictate the terms whereby the symptoms and discomfort may be removed, and wherein vague, often unnameable desires such as meaning, purpose, authenticity and happiness may be attained. In psychoanalytic practice, this response is denied. Lacan claims that speech always implies a demand, that "all speech calls for a response" (Lacan, 2006: 40), even if this response is silence. The analyst's response is to listen, to what is said and unsaid, whether in the symbol of the word or the symptom: "we must be attentive to the unsaid that dwells in the holes of discourse" (Lacan, 2006: 91), and listen "in order to detect what is to be understood" (Lacan, 2006: 46). This kind of listening accepts that the meaning which is striving to be articulated, and which is sourced in the deepest recesses of the struggling speaker, is prohibited or censored in the subject's ego and so is often "impossible knowledge", but Lacan claims that this impossibility can be overcome by listening to what "is said between the words, between the lines" (Lacan, 1999: 119), what he terms the "*inter-dit*".

In contrast to the initial demand of the analysand, the aim of Lacanian psychoanalysis is therefore not the removal of the symptom, nor the directive pronouncements of "an expert in human living", but rather the revelation of the symptom's meaning for the subject, its attempted expression of the subject's desire, so that "a certain real may be reached" (Lacan, 1999: 22); it is to enable the revelation of an answer to the question, "what does the subject want?". As Žižek explains, "for Lacan, the goal of psychoanalytic treatment is not the patient's well-being, successful social life or personal fulfilment, but to bring the patient to confront the elementary coordinates and dead-lock of his or her desire" (Žižek, 2006, 4). According to Lacan, this meaning exists within the subject and is not to be discovered or imposed in the mirage of the other as possessing the truth; it exists in the unconscious of the subject and manifests itself in myriad forms which are often outside the scope of signification. It is above all a desire which has been denied and excluded from awareness, but which strives for acknowledgement through the detours of symptom and fantasy: "The unconscious is the chapter of my history that is marked by a blank or occupied by a lie; it is the censored chapter. But the truth can be refound; most often it has already been written elsewhere" (Lacan, 2006: 50). Lacan explains that this chapter, the unconscious, is written in bodily symptoms, childhood memories, life-style and vocabulary, and distortions of truth which its repression necessitates. It is in fact the subject's history, "a page of shame that one forgets or undoes, or a page of glory that obliges"[13] (Lacan, 2006: 52). The meaning which is sought, demanded, by the subject, does not however emanate from "the subject supposed to know"; the analyst merely "frees the subject's speech" (Lacan, 2006: 80), by "suspending the subject's certainties until their final mirages have been consumed" (Lacan, 2006: 44); only thus is the desired meaning interpreted and understood. The relinquishment of the fantasy of a knowing, guiding, wise "other", and the consequent acknowledgement that personal truth exists within the individual subject, is also urged in Nietzsche's thought as expressed in the words of Zarasthustra: "You had not yet sought yourselves when you found me...now I bid you lose me and find yourselves" (Nietzsche, 2003a: 103). The subject's certainties are fixed in certain words, scripts and stories wherein one explains oneself to oneself, but the process of the psychoanalytic experience is a new reading of the script: "You give a different reading to the signifiers that are enunciated than what they signify" (Lacan, 1999: 37). Thence, the subject recognizes his/her own truth, he/she allows it to come to awareness. Echoing Nietzsche's perspectivism, "these are my truths", Lacan states that "truth has more than one face" (Lacan, 2007: 172). The analyst is not the "one supposed to know", he or she merely enables the subject to arrive at his/her own meaning, because "true speech already contains its own response" (Lacan, 2006: 93).

This interpretation of the resolution of analysis is disputed by Derrida when he argues that in analysis a truth is imposed, no matter how this imposition is masked as interpretation, facilitation, or echoing of the subject's own truth: "To analyze anything whatsoever, anyone whatsoever, for anyone whatsoever, would mean saying to the other: choose my

---

[13] The co-existence of shame and glory, of gold and dross, in the repressed realms of the unconscious or the "shadow", resounds with the theories of Carl Jung.

solution, prefer my solution, take my solution, love my solution; you will be in truth if you do not resist my solution" (Derrida, 1998: 9). Reflecting the paradox inherent in the psychoanalytic "rule" of "free" association, and the psychoanalytic explanation of "resistance" to the analyst's interpretation, Derrida's argument poses questions of validity and ethics regarding the possible invasion of the private space of the individual and the forced acceptance of a new conformity, which may be a denied reality of psychoanalytic practice. Lacan's view repeatedly refutes this and sees the end of analysis as coinciding with the subject's relinquishment of the ideal of "the subject supposed to know", and a corresponding avowal of self-ownership and responsibility. In Freud's words, "people can only achieve insight through their own hurt and their own experience" (Freud, 2006: 398). In an open recognition and acknowledgement of what is contained in the unconscious the subject confronts his/her desire, an answer to the apparently simple but difficult question "what do I want?" and ultimately decides whether to pursue this desire or to endure its refusal. What has been achieved is at least the awareness and honesty whereby the choice can be made. According to Lacanian theory, through the insights and techniques of psychoanalysis the subject may approach the reality of desire, and discover, through experience, the truth therein: "Once one enters into the register of the true, one can no longer exit it" (Lacan, 1999: 108). For Lacan, this constitutes "the law of desire", the only proper ethical agency, an ethical agency which is far removed from philanthropy, pseudo-altruism and impossible selflessness, and as an authentic motivating force it resonates with Nietzsche's description of the will to power as the insatiable urge/desire to grow, to develop, and to overcome resistance.

From Demand to Desire

> I propose that...the only thing of which one can be guilty is of having given ground relative to desire (Lacan, 1997: 319).

What is this desire which Lacan insists is integral to the constitution of the subject? What is the desire revealed through psychoanalysis? Why is this desire repressed or denied in the assumption of a conventionally lived life? And where is the position of love in this ambiguity of desire? Lacan asserts that the answers to these questions are facilitated by access to the unconscious: "That is why the unconscious was invented – so that we could realize that man's desire is the Other's desire, and that love, while it is a passion that involves ignorance of desire, nevertheless leaves desire its whole import" (Lacan, 1999: 4). In questioning the popular portrayals of love as union and mergence, as a striving towards the One, as the release from the unbearable tenacity of separation, "Love…is but the desire to be One" (Lacan, 1999: 6), Lacan argues that it is in the gap between what is real – essential aloneness – and what is sought – complete connection, that desire dwells. It "leads us to aim at the gap" (Lacan, 1999: 5). However, the essence of desire is that it is not satisfied; a satisfied desire does not exist, and is automatically replaced by another version of itself. Ricoeur explains it thus: "the desire of desire has no end…non-saturated desirability…this allows us to go onward" (Ricoeur, 2002: 127). Nietzsche's doctrine of the "will to power" is suggested here as the persistent and ongoing striving in the human being to push against what stands in its way of fulfilment, the very essence of the life-force itself, the achievement and cessation of which only exists in death. Life is ongoing, a process striving towards but always out of reach of completion. So desire is what can never be accomplished, achieved, finished. As Buber reflects, "does there already stir, beneath all dissatisfactions that can be satisfied, an unknown and primal and deep dissatisfaction for which there is as yet no recipe of satisfaction anywhere?" (Buber, 2004: 43). It is the essence of desire that it is insatiable. This conflict between desire and attainment is often intricately connected with the experience of love, its need, its communication, its possibility. The gap remains because "Everyone knows, of course, that two have never become one" (Lacan, 1999: 47). Rejection of this truth understandably results from the demand that one gets what one wants, and from the reluctance to acknowledge that satisfaction of desire is the antithesis of living. Living is desire, or as Nietzsche says, "Life is will to power" (Nietzsche, 1968: 148). In Lacanian terms, the uncovering of desire, its revelation from the confines of symptom and displacement, metaphor and metonymy, is the work of psychoanalysis. Chiesa identifies this as the emergence of full speech: "In everyday life, human beings communicate through empty speech, [but] Lacan affirms that the subject's alienation in language can be superseded by full speech. The latter's emergence coincides with the subject's assumption of his unconscious desire" (Chiesa, 2007: 39). In a similar way, Nietzsche asks, "Are *your* desires under a thousand masks?" (Nietzsche, 2003a: 310).

   A corollary of desire is the quest for love, and so love is at the forefront of psychoanalytical discourse: "the linchpin of everything that has been instituted on the basis of analytic experience: Love" (Lacan,

1999: 39). Lacan credits Freud with unveiling many aspects of the phenomenon of love, in particular is narcissistic component:

> The beginning of wisdom should involve beginning to realize that it is in that respect that old father Freud broke new ground…to realize that love, while it is true that it has a relationship with the One, never makes anyone leave himself behind…everyone senses and sensed that the problem is how there can be love for another (Lacan, 1999: 47).

The paradox here is between the reality of narcissism which psychoanalysis witnesses in the various guises in which it attempts to disguise itself, and the urge to love, and/or the urge to be loved which propels the desire towards the other.[14] The apparent narcissistic nature of desire – it is rooted in the domain of the self – does not limit its aim. When desire is directed towards the other, it can have various goals, across a spectrum; this can range from the aim of control and power over the other, appropriation of the other, the desire to have one's own identity affirmed and recognized, to an acknowledgement of these potential aspect and attempts to transverse them. This enables a recognition of the other as not possessing that which one lacks, but rather as embodying vulnerability, incompleteness and disunity; the latter propels a desire to love, free of need, control, or assimilation. While the philosophies of Buber and Ricoeur situate the human condition as essentially relational, a mediation between self and other, Lacan, following Freud, and indeed Nietzsche, claims that relationship with the other is preconditioned with narcissist self-interest. The self is always involved. It is a reality of the human condition that it is self-centred. This appears to be an uncomfortable reality to embrace, so it is masked and sublimated through various images and personas, such as the Ideal I of the mirror stage: "a kind of mirage of the One you believe yourself to be" (Lacan, 1999: 47). Thus, interrelationships are based on semblances, negations of the truth, and are conducted within the framework of the mask: "It is only on the basis of the clothing of the self-image that envelops the object cause of desire that the object relationship is most often sustained" (Lacan, 1999: 92).

In his exploration of the concept of love, Lacan returns to Freud's rejection of the Christian dictum that one should "love one's neighbour as oneself", and agrees with Freud's assessment of love's capacity as being

---

[14] Idealistic notions and descriptions of love often discount the possibility of a real dilemma between the need/well-being/happiness of the subject and the simultaneous need of the loved other. It can be difficult to acknowledge the possibility of a conflict between the "needs" of self and other.

limited to a choice of beings considered worthy of one's love: "the energy that we put into all being brothers very clearly proves that we are not brothers" (Lacan, 2007: 114). Lacan differentiates between altruism and love, and reminds us that "in any encounter there's a big difference in reality between the response of philanthropy and that of love" (Lacan, 1997: 186). Mistaking one for the other is an obstacle to love, and for the recipient, is often felt to be insulting and manipulative. Highlighting the gap between the ideal of the good and the reality of human nature, Lacan warns that "only saints are sufficiently detached from the deepest of our shared passions to avoid the aggressive repercussions of charity" (Lacan, 2006: 15). The altruistic goal of working for the other's good begs the question as to the constitution of this good.[15] Lacan explains the appeal of this altruistic goal:

> It is a fact of experience that what I want is the good of others in the image of my own. That doesn't cost so much. What I want is the good of others provided that it remains in the image of my own...provided that it depends on my effort (Lacan, 1997: 187).

In a different context, Wordsworth makes a similar point: "the class that does the most harm consists of *well-intentioned* men, who, being ignorant of human nature, think that they may help" (Wordsworth, 2007: 218). Nietzsche also warns that "great obligations do not make a man grateful, they make him resentful; and if a small kindness is not forgotten it becomes a gnawing worm" (Nietzsche, 2003a: 113). One imagines the experiences, joys, sorrows, needs, of the other as being a mirror of one's own, and it is through one's own experience, one's own perception of the good, and one's own filtered reality that one assumes to know what is good for the other. Lacan describes it thus: "The benevolent fraud of wanting-to-do-one's-best-for-the-subject" (Lacan, 1997: 219). He outlines the complexities and ambiguities which are involved:

---

[15] At the time of writing the solitary incarceration of one human being in an Irish prison for twenty three hours a day for over a year, has been justified as being "for his own good". (See *The Irish Times*, May 19th, 2007). It is difficult to ascertain in this situation an interpretation of "good" or "inhuman". One is reminded of Nietzsche's observation: "let us not underestimate the extent to which precisely the sight of the judicial and executive procedures prevents the criminal from feeling his deed, the nature of his action, *as in itself* reprehensible, for he sees the very same kind of actions committed in the service of justice and then approved, committed with a good conscience" (Nietzsche, 1998: 54).

If one has to do things for the good, in practice one is always faced with
the question: for the good of whom? From that point on, things are no
longer obvious...Doing things in the name of the good, and even more in
the name of the good of the other, is something that is far from protecting
us not only from guilt but also from all kinds of inner catastrophes (Lacan,
1997: 319).

The subtle slide from the position of wanting the other's good to the more
sinister proclamation that one is acting "for the other's own good" implies
an assumption of knowledge that justifies one's power over another who is
deemed not to have such knowledge: "The domain of the good is the birth
of power" (Lacan, 1997: 229). This resounds with Ricoeur's analysis of
the relationship between the quests for possession, power, and worth.
Hence, the essence of group psychology, the demand for obedience, and
the suppressive power of tyranny emerges. The subtle nature of this slide
accounts for the manifold guises in which it masquerades; the "strong"
parent, the "controlling" or "dependent" partner, the "infallible" teacher,
the "civilizing" colonizer, the "patriarchal" president, and in Lacan's day,
the "protectors" of the national good in the personages of Hitler and
Mussolini. Hence, Lacan states, "a radical repudiation of a certain ideal of
the good is necessary" (Lacan, 1997: 230). The assumption of power in the
guise of altruistic action, or as the expression of pseudo-love, is an attempt
to obliterate the desire of the other: "The position of power of any kind in
all circumstances and in every case, whether historical or not, has always
been the same. Whether Alexander or Hitler: 'I have come to liberate you
from this or that...as far as desires are concerned, come back later, make
them wait'" (Lacan, 1997: 315). In Lacan's vision, the obliteration of
desire is the destruction of life itself; the repression of one's desire
necessitates duplicity and deception, betrayal of oneself and of others: "the
first effect of repression is that it speaks of something else" (Lacan, 1999:
62). Language can conceal as well as reveal, a point also made by
Nietzsche: "To talk about oneself a great deal can also be a means of
concealing oneself" (Nietzsche, 2003: 105).

The unfolding of desire resulting from an articulation of the
unconscious enables the decision to be made regarding its place in one's
life. According to Lacan, acknowledgement of one's desire is essential to
ethical living, and indeed to love: "desire...therein lies the mainspring of
love" (Lacan, 1999: 50). He asserts that desire is at the root of one's
destiny, and therefore to reject it is to say no to life, no to Nietzsche's
admonition of *amor fati*. The key question for Lacan in relation to love,
ethics, life, is: "Have you acted in accordance with the desire that is in
you?" (Lacan, 1997: 314). Lacan warns against the betrayal involved in

"giving ground relative to desire" because desire is integral to being: "The channel in which desire is located…what we are as well what we are not, our being, and our non-being" (Lacan, 1999: 321). This is also Nietzsche's conviction: " 'To live as I desire to live or not to live at all': that is what I want" (Nietzsche, 2003a: 285). Desire is central to who and what we are, it is unique and personal to the subject, and in Lacan's terms it insists on our response:

> Desire is nothing other than that which supports an unconscious theme, the very articulation of that which roots us in a particular destiny, and that destiny demands insistently that the debt be paid, and desire keeps coming back, keeps returning, and situates us once again in a given track, the track of something that is specifically our business (Lacan, 1999: 319).

On this point Hederman concurs with Lacan that "desire is an inescapable condition of humanity" and goes on to state that it is from an acceptance of this reality that love is born: "Such acceptance of reality is love. Love is the way we are in ourselves and amidst the others who surround us" (Hederman, 2000: 37). Desire and love as a way of being is central to Lacan's thesis: "In love what is aimed at is the subject…in something that is organized or can be organized on the basis of a whole life" (Lacan, 1999: 50), but he differentiates between desire and love stating that "Love is distinct from desire…because its aim is not satisfaction, but being" (Lacan, 1991: 276).[16] Here again, the co-existence of self-love and love for the other is asserted: "Love, the love of the person who desires to be loved, is essentially an attempt to capture the other in oneself, in oneself as object" (Lacan, 1991: 276).

Lacan's philosophical vision may appear to be pessimistic; he attempts to shatter illusions of relationship, goodness, and love. As Chiesa remarks,

---

[16] This is quite close to the view of an Irish philosopher, Felix O'Murchadha, given in response to the thesis question:

> My initial reaction is to say that love is its own possibility, by which I mean that there is no nature of things be that of the individual human being or be that of the collective of a society etc. which makes love possible. Rather, love is that which transforms the way in which the world appears to us. One must of course make distinctions… In Greek there are at least three words for love, eros, philia and agape. In each case there is more than simply the instrumental: sexual satisfaction, cooperation between equals and self-sacrifice are all possible without love and none of them make love necessary. But in each case love transforms the act and the other person for me (O'Murchadha, 2006: email).

"Commentators have often stated that Lacan's early work presents us with a uniquely pessimistic notion of love, which is easily reducible to imaginary narcissism", but he claims that "already in his first theory of the subject, love transcends the imaginary order due to its proximity to the emergence of the ego-ideal" (Chiesa, 2007: 23). The shattering of illusions enables the emergence of the real, and it is in the real that the possibility of love may be discovered. The difficulty in accessing the real, the obstacles outlined by Lacan as formulated in the constitution of the subject within the imaginary and the symbolic, and the complexity and ambiguity pertaining to any Lacanian definition of love, "love, in its essence is narcissistic" (Lacan, 1999: 6), or "true love gives way to hatred" (Lacan, 1999: 146)), suggests a cynical attitude to love in Lacan's thought, and a negative response to the thesis question "is love possible?". However, Lacan also points to the central role of love in human living, particularly as regards how it functions in relation to the cornerstone of humanness – desire, and he points out that "people have done nothing but speak of love in analytic discourse" (Lacan, 1999: 83). The pivotal role of love in releasing truth, desire, and freedom is stated clearly by Lacan when he urges recognition of "the imaginary servitude that love must always untie anew or sever'" (Lacan, 2006: 9).

Lacan rejects idealistic versions of human being and human relationship, and he argues that love becomes a possibility within an embrace of human imperfection: "One wants to be loved for everything... for one's idiosyncrasies, for one's weaknesses, for everything", and he suggests that love enables a different way of encountering and recognizing the other: "to love is to love a being beyond what he or she appears to be. The active gift of love is directed at the other, not in his specificity, but in his being" (Lacan, 1991: 276). The difficulties of love, the "impossibility" of its symbolization, and the obstacles to its experience, do not in themselves constitute love's impossibility, but rather point to its essential necessity, and the inescapable attempt to make possible the impossible.

CHAPTER SIX

SLAVOJ ŽIŽEK

Žižek enters the contemporary philosophical scene with the avowed intention to re-read Lacan in relation to Hegel, to revisit Hegelian thought in the light of Lacan's psychoanalytic insights, and to abolish the false dichotomies between high and low culture. His career in philosophy is punctuated and influenced by the political upheavals and changes which have characterized Eastern Europe in recent decades, the escalation of the threat of 'terrorism' in the West, and the ensuing confrontations between the diverse ideologies, religions and cultures, traditional and emergent, which strive for dominance or survival in various global partitions. Thus, his political views inevitably intertwine with his philosophical explorations.

Echoing Lacan's commitment to a "return to Freud", Žižek returns to Lacanian insights with a comprehensive examination of the development and progression of Lacan's thought. Commenting on the similar focus of direction in the work of both Lacan and Žižek, Sarah Kay explains the apparent paradox inherent in the drive to progress which is directed by an examination of the past: "Lacan presents his life's work as renewing psychoanalysis through a return to Freud. This paradoxical formula, whereby progress is secured by looking back, is central to psychoanalytical thinking. Žižek's work is dictated by this same temporal paradox". Kay argues that "the point of *après-coup* is that it does not seek to repeat the past, but to release its significance for the present"[1] (Kay, 2003: 19). Simultaneously, Žižek re-reads what he considers to be the tenets of Marxist philosophy, and consequently calls for a "return to Lenin" in order to explicate the message and value of Lenin's revolution. His work is characterized by an inter-disciplinary dimension as it draws from psychoanalytic, political, sociological, linguistic and cultural sources, and his method of presentation involves the use of film, literature and popular

---

[1] Kay appears to be using the term *après-coup* in its psychoanalytic context. It is a term relating to the interaction between past and present, especially in the recall of memories, where the memories are influenced and acted on by the present context.

culture as accessible portrayals of philosophical concepts. This leads Kay to assert that "Žižek is the most vital interdisciplinary thinker to emerge in recent years" (Kay, 2003: 123). Referring to his frequent resort "to examples from popular culture", Žižek explains the reason for his method: it is done "in order to avoid a kind of jargon, and to achieve the greatest possible clarity, not only for my readers but also for myself" (Žižek, 2006b: 56). Žižek is noted for his flamboyant style of address, his embrace of contradiction, and his often controversial exposure of dualities, deceptions and disavowals which characterize contemporary culture and subjectivity. Reflecting on these aspects of Žižek's work, Tony Myers states that "Slavoj Žižek is a philosopher. He is, however, no ordinary philosopher, for he thinks and writes in such a recklessly entertaining fashion, he constantly risks making philosophy enjoyable" (Myers, 2004: 1). What makes Žižek different from "ordinary philosophers", according to Myers, is his persistent sense of wonder and amazement which he expresses in a limitless questioning of everything: "With all the guile of a child asking his parents why the sky is blue, Žižek questions everything that passes for wisdom about who we are, what we are doing and why we do it" (Myers, 2004: 3). Žižek's vision of subjectivity is grounded in Freud's exposition of the unconscious as a permeating influence on behaviour, motivation and conflict; on Lacan's triad of the real, the imaginary, and the symbolic as the constitutive and often overlapping realms of human existence; and on his own examination of the role of ideology in the creation of unquestioned acceptance of portrayals of the human condition from pre-Socratic times to the "ideology-free" assumptions of contemporary postmodernism. As a keen analyst of the workings of power and the invisible shadow of ideology, Žižek provides an insightful and contentious account of the contemporary subject.

As an astute observer and commentator on historical and contemporary disasters and difficulties, Žižek examines political, social and individual issues with a combination of philosophical reflection and analysis of contemporary culture. His philosophical reading ranges over the pre-Socratics, Plato and Aristotle, Hegel and Heidegger, and Derrida and Kristeva, while his portrayal of postmodernity is facilitated by references to a wide range of literature, music, art and film. This expanse of engagement is reflected in the prolific nature of his work, which examines many of the dilemmas and conflicts confronting society in the third millennium; globalisation, poverty, war, terrorism, racism, and the myriad repercussions of scientific and technological advances. The rapidity of scientific and technological progress is seen by Žižek as a fourth humiliation to the illusions of superiority and vanity which is preceded by the reversals of Copernicus, Darwin and Freud: "the latest scientific breakthroughs seem to add a whole series of further 'humiliations' which radicalize the first three" (Žižek, 2006d: 163). Both Freud and Lacan assert that the acknowledgement of the unconscious as a powerful, and complex aspect of the human condition, is comparable to the radical effects of the Copernican revolution and Darwinian evolution; each has resulted in a decentring of the human subject, relegating it to a more fragile and unstable condition: "man loses his privileged place and is reduced to just another element of reality" (Žižek, 2006d: 164). Žižek posits a similar displacement emerging from the ever-new capacities of science and technology; he gives the example of the ongoing development of "virtual reality" where intersubjective communication takes place between computer screens, and the paradox of human creation and human annihilation ensuing from the possibilities of human cloning. Therefore, he claims that psychoanalysis, far from being outdated and irrelevant, is in fact a radical discipline essential to human understanding: "my aim is to demonstrate that it is only today that the time of psychoanalysis has come" (Žižek, 2006: 2).

Žižek's work is concerned with a vast array of questions and conflicts. He theorizes on politics, work, ideology, evil and culture, and thus he deals with issues which may be considered universal in their application. However, Žižek insists on the inescapable ambiguity, antagonism and falsity inherent in the particular/universal divide; he asks "how does the particular participate in the universal?" (Žižek, 1999: 137), and this question positions his work as an investigation of subjectivity, an examination of individuality, and an exploration of issues which focus on the personal as well as the universal. Žižek is clear in his assertion of this necessity:

> the Social, the field of social practices and socially held beliefs, is not simply on a different level from individual experience, but something to which the individual himself has to relate, which the individual himself has to experience as an order which is minimally "reified", externalized…the gap between the individual and the "impersonal" social dimension is to be inscribed back within the individual himself: this "objective" order of the social Substance exists only insofar as individuals treat it as such, relate to it as such (Žižek, 2006d: 6).

Hence, for the purposes of this study, Žižek's work is approached with an emphasis on his reflections on the individual, the human being, the person who is experiencing life in relation to self, others and the wider social world. With this emphasis, his work provides an exploration of perennial philosophical questions. What is a subject? What is human? What is truth? What is meaning? Žižek asserts the centrality of these questions in the contemporary world: "What we are witnessing today is a radical redefinition of what it means to be human" (Žižek, 2001a: etext), and he insists on the pivotal importance of the ethical in this redefinition. The emphasis on "a radical redefinition of what it means to be human" resounds firmly with Buber's similar reflections on the subject, and implicitly with the explorations of all the writers examined in this study. The centrality of ethics to Žižek's work is grounded in Lacan's assertion "that ethics belongs to the Real" (Žižek, 2006d: 49), and thus is often distorted and manipulated in the imaginary and the symbolic. However, Žižek asserts his conviction that the ensuing difficulties involved in approaching an ethical stance do not diminish its importance, and with a determined optimism, he looks to the Samuel Beckett play, *The Unnameable*, as a statement that "this simple persistence against all odds is ultimately the stuff ethics is made of" (Žižek, 2006: 119). Within the realm of ethics, Žižek discusses the relationship between determinism and autonomy, responsibility and freedom, emotion and rationalism, in human motivation and behaviour, and within this discussion he inevitably posits love, its impossibility and possibility, as a concept which is integral to the ethical question. In his discussion of ethics in his work, *On Belief*, Žižek refers to the "ethics of the Real", and in taking "the case of love", he suggests the Lacanian response:

> Lovers usually dream that in some mythical Otherness ('another time, another place'), their love would have found its true fulfillment, that it is only the present contingent circumstances which prevent this fulfillment; and is the Lacanian lesson here not that one should accept this obstacle as structurally necessary, that there is NO 'other place' of fulfillment, that this Otherness is the very Otherness of the fantasy? No: the 'real as impossible' means here that THE IMPOSSIBLE DOES HAPPEN, that 'miracles' like Love…DO occur (Žižek, 2006c: 84).

Hence, a selected reading of Žižek's work focuses on the question of love's possibility, and provides an exploration of the obstacles to its experience.

The New Big Other

I disavow what my eyes tell me and
choose to believe the symbolic fiction
(Žižek, 1997a: etext)

Explorations and analyses of subjectivity, personality and the self are central to philosophical and psychoanalytical inquiry, and within this framework the question of identity inevitably arises. The paradox of personal identity, as a construct of subjective experience and of objective appraisal, of private meaning and public acknowledgement, is an issue explored diversely by the writers outlined in previous chapters. The fragility of identity impinges on the possibility of love, as the motivation to seek recognition and acceptance may overwhelm or displace the openness and vulnerability inherent in the experience of loving and of being loved. Žižek approaches this concept with an astute reflection on the enduring power of the superego in spite of the demise of its more traditional and conventional forms. For Žižek, the superego expresses itself in the form of the big Other, and while it has disintegrated in some of its older guises, it still maintains its power to confer or annul personal identity. As Myers states, "For Žižek, it is the big Other which confers an identity upon the many decentred personalities of the contemporary subject" (Myers, 2004: 51).

As an unflinching commentator and interpreter of the contemporary world, Žižek challenges ideological presuppositions, familiar convictions, and illusions of freedom and goodness. In this sense, his analysis of the human condition as experienced in contemporary life can be compared to Nietzsche's call for a radical re-evaluation of values and morals, and a more honest acknowledgement of what it means to be human. Like Freud, he perceives the individual as having an ambiguous relationship with culture and civilization. In his persistent re-reading of philosophy and literature as explorations of being, truth, and subjectivity, he resounds with Ricoeur's hermeneutical analysis of experience and his acknowledgement of human frailty and fallibility.[2] Žižek examines the assumptions, grounded in the postmodern deconstruction of binary oppositions such as right and wrong, East and West, foreigner and native, whereby we convince ourselves that we are now free from the tyranny of ideology, patriarchy, and other forms of authoritarian mastery and domination. For Žižek, the question remains: "why, in spite of his 'liberation' from the constraints of traditional authority, is the subject not 'free'? Why does the retreat of traditional 'repressive' Prohibitions not only fail to relieve us of guilt, but even reinforce it?" (Žižek, 1997: 86). The demise of a society

---

[2] Žižek does not adhere fully to the conventional interpretations of hermeneutical philosophy; for example he is critical of what he considers "the fundamental thesis of Gadamer's hermeneutics…what we get in Gadamer is an 'urbanized' (domesticated, 'gentrified') Heidegger, a Heidegger purified of disagreeable excesses which do not fit the academic circuit" (Žižek, 2001: 169).

structured on authoritarian rules and values is seen by Žižek as a distorted
fiction. According to Myers, this involves a double-fiction:

> The big Other always was dead, in the sense that it never existed in the first
> place as a material thing. All it ever was (and is) is a purely symbolic or
> fictional order. What Žižek means by this is that we all engage in a
> minimum of idealization, disavowing the brute fact of the Real in favour of
> another Symbolic world behind it…If we wish to remain loyal subjects we
> act as if the emperor really is wearing new clothes and not parading
> through the street naked. The big Other is thus a kind of collective fib or lie
> to which we all individuality subscribe (Myers, 2004: 49).

Žižek examines the proposition that today "the big Other no longer exists",
but he asks "in WHAT sense" is this the case (Žižek, 1997a: etext).[3] Any
temptation to self-congratulatory stances is subverted by Žižek's exposé of
new, subtle, and often more sinister sources of control over thought and
behaviour: "Instead of bringing freedom, the fall of the oppressive
authority…gives rise to new and sterner prohibitions" (Žižek, 2006: 92).
This concurs with Lacan's reference to "what keeps appearing in the guise
of the superego", and his suggestion that what the subject has done is to
"change masters" (Lacan, 2007: 13, 32).

The present age is often characterized by an apparently all-pervading
permissiveness which seems to overturn the repression and constraint of
previous eras; sexuality, religion, education, and the concept of work, are
some areas which highlight changes of attitude and behaviour. However,
Žižek points to the erroneous nature of this picture, and suggests that in
many cases the subject is now constrained by subtler ideologies presented
in the guise of humane-sounding values such as "human rights", "freedom
of choice", and "equality": "You have a whole set of measures which
power uses, but [it] disavows them…that is for me the obscenity of
power" (Žižek, 1999a: etext). The Western world is presented as symbolic
of individual growth and advancement, but, in Žižek's view, there are
invisible codes of requirements which must be met in order to belong to
this world; there is a "subtle coercion under the guise of free choice"
(Žižek, 1997: 57). Žižek terms this "the forced choice", whereby
submission to the symbolic law is devoid of choice because there is no
alternative to the symbolic (Žižek, 2001: 77). Thus, Žižek points to the
double-sided nature of ideology; on the one hand it is visible in the openly

---

[3] The ironic co-existence of liberation from repressive authorities and ideologies
and private, involuntary adherence to the basic tenets of such values and rules is
poignantly portrayed in Ian McEwan's latest novel, *On Chesil Beach*, 2007.

proclaimed standards and values of the social and political domain, but on the other hand it is also sustained by the hidden, implicit, unspoken expectations and justifications underlying any social or political system. There is a trap which "makes us slide into ideology under the guise of stepping out of it" (Žižek, 1999: 70). Acquiescence to "universal" values and practices as constitutive of the social framework attempts to eradicate the existence of any divergence from the norm; it denies the reality of those who do not have a place within it: "a shared lie is an incomparably more effective bond for a group than the truth" (Žižek, 1999: 99). As in Nietzsche's description of herd-morality, adherence to popular opinion is easier and safer than risking any interrogation of "the way things are". Žižek claims that "only very few are ready to question this world" (Žižek, 2001a: etext).[4] The attraction of the "normal", the socially accepted forms of thought and behaviour, is understandable, according to Žižek, when opposed to its alternative: "how can one survive a direct confrontation with the Sun, the ultimate Real, without getting burned by the rays of its heat?...the risks of this confrontation, paying for it the highest price of madness" (Žižek, 2004a: etext). In the "post-ideological" fantasy of postmodernism, Žižek points to the paradox inherent in the gap between the awareness of the artificial/contingent construction of ideology, and the simultaneous acceptance of its power evinced in daily practice: "Our freedoms are increasingly reduced to the freedom to choose your lifestyle" (Žižek, 2001a: etext).

An example of the subtle, unspoken limitation of freedom in the postmodern world is, according to Žižek, the pervasive, unconditional injunction to enjoy, the command that the subject must experience pleasure in all aspects of experience, and must especially be seen to do so: it is "the official ideology of our postmodern society as bent on instant gratification and pleasure-seeking" (Žižek, 1997a: etext). Guilt accompanies any failure to fulfil this demand: "Superego is the reversal of the permissive 'You May!' into the prescriptive 'You Must!', the point in which permitted enjoyment turns into ordained enjoyment" (Žižek, 1999b: etext). The injunction to enjoy, and to be seen to enjoy, gives rise to obsessive concern with the appearances of enjoyment; the creation of "the

---

[4] On this point, Žižek credits Nietzsche with raising the topic of "cogito and madness" (Žižek, 1999: 189), and placing Nietzsche's question in a contemporary setting, he asks: "in what does this difference between the 'mad' (paranoid) construction and the 'normal' (social) construction of reality consist? Is 'normalcy' ultimately not merely a more 'mediated' form of madness?" (Žižek, 1999: 254). These sentiments resound firmly with the views of R.D. Laing as outlined in his works *The Divided Self* and *The Politics of Experience*.

beautiful body", the adherence to fitness regimes, and the myriad preparatory exercises which are deemed essential to the achievement of enjoyment in intellectual, sexual, individual and communal forms: "in a digitalised universe that is artificially constructed...we seem to live more and more with the thing deprived of its substance" (Žižek, 2001a: etext). Žižek offers a multitude of examples wherein the appearance of enjoyment is expressed in the popularity of the form without its substance: "meat without fat, coffee without caffeine...and even virtual sex without sex" (Žižek, 2001a: etext), and the myriad forms of interpassivity whereby even emotions are experienced indirectly as in canned laughter, mock horror, and the many adult variations on the Japanese toy, tamagochi, where feelings of love and care are delegated to inanimate objects: "tamagochi is a machine which allows you to satisfy your need to love your neighbour...without bothering your actual neighbours with your intrusive compassion" (Žižek, 1999:109). Thus, he believes that "in our 'society of the spectacle', in which what we experience as everyday reality more and more takes the form of the lie made real, Freud's insights show their true value" (Žižek, 2006f: etext). Injunctions from the superego abound in everyday life: "from direct enjoyment in sexual performance to enjoyment in professional achievement or spiritual awakening" (Žižek, 2005: 152). Fashion, food, life-style, and all the conscious and unconscious decisions and behaviours which project a presentation of the self, are regulated to endorse unspoken rules: "even the most intimate attitude towards one's body is used to make an ideological statement" (Žižek, 1999: 81). Enjoyment is now a duty, and fear of failure in performing this duty imposes a permanent anxiety; one must do one's duty and also be seen to enjoy doing so.[5] In this sense the obligation to do one's duty is doubled by the insistence that one freely chooses to do so. Žižek argues that the injunction to "enjoy!", rather than enabling the experience of pleasure, satisfaction, happiness or love, in fact, paradoxically hinders such a possibility: "the direct injunction 'Enjoy!' is a much more effective way to hinder the subject's access to enjoyment than the explicit Prohibition which sustains the space for its transgression" (Žižek,1997a: etext).[6]

The illusion of freedom ensuing from more "liberal" and more individualistic platitudes of personal freedom, free choice, equality, and self-creation, often belies its opposite. Freedom of choice is permitted "but

---

[5] The command to enjoy is also explored by another psychoanalytic cultural theorist, Todd McGowan, in his book *The End of Dissatisfaction? Jacques Lacan and the Emerging Society of Enjoyment.*

[6] McGowan concurs with this argument that enjoyment needs a barrier to be experienced fully.

with the explicit exclusion of the choices which may disturb the public" (Žižek, 2006c: 122). Žižek offers the analogy of a common childhood experience to portray the duplicity involved. The child in the traditional family situation was ordered/compelled to obey instructions such as behaving politely to relatives, respecting the elderly, and acknowledging his/her subservient position with regard to the adult world. Now, in contrast, the child is told that there are no rules, that one must make up one's own mind, and that one is free to choose. The reality of this situation is that the child intuitively knows what is expected of him/her, what behaviour is still being demanded, but there is now the added imposition that one must pretend that one chooses, and for that reason that one enjoys the "freely-chosen" behaviour:

> beneath the appearance of free choice there is an even more oppressive demand than the one formulated by the traditional authoritarian father...a false free choice is the obscene superego injunction: it deprives the child even of his inner freedom, instructing him not only what to do, but what to want to do (Žižek, 2006: 92).

Žižek looks to the literature of Kafka,[7] Kundera, James and others to highlight the subject's inscription within conscious and unconscious laws, and through a reading of William Styron's fictional account of Nazi brutality, *Sophie's Choice*, he outlines the traumatic experience of the forced choice (Žižek, 2001: 70). As a prisoner of the war camps, Sophie is given the choice to save the life of one of her two children; if she does not choose, they will both die. Hence she is given an impossible choice, but nevertheless she is forced to choose. The situation resounds with the failure of universally applicable ethical solutions or guidelines portrayed in mythology and literature throughout history; Sophocles' *Antigone*, Coetzee's *Disgrace*, McEwan's *Atonement*, and Greene's *The End of the Affair*, explore variations of a similar dilemma: "the paradox of the forced choice that marks our most fundamental relationship to the society to which we belong: at a certain point, society impels us to choose freely what is already necessarily imposed upon us" (Žižek, 2006a: 275).

The illusion of freedom, the feigned proclamation of free choice, and the refusal to acknowledge the impact of unspoken injunctions and expectations that constrain human behaviour, result in a diminishment of responsibility and autonomy: "We can go on making our small choices,

---

[7] The world of Kafka's fiction is that of guilt, alienation and impossibility, according to Žižek: "Kafka's universe is eminently that of the superego" (Žižek, 1999: 48).

'reinventing ourselves' thoroughly on condition that these choices do not seriously disturb the social and ideological balance" (Žižek, 2006c: 122). The unconscious imposition of expectations and codes of behaviour can result in the subject's alienation from the real kernel of desire and being as life is lived with the assumption of the symbolic gaze of the other: "I am only what I am for the other, in so far as I am inscribed into the network of the big Other. An insurmountable gap separates forever what I am 'in the real' from the symbolic mandate that procures my social identity" (Žižek, 1999: 135). Human experience is restrained and limited, and in the area of inter-relationships the experience of love is often distorted and thwarted.

Neighbourly Love

> In true love I hate the Beloved out of
> love. I hate the dimension of the
> beloved person's inscription into the
> socio-symbolic structure. I hate him or
> her on behalf of my very love for him
> as a unique person (Žižek, 1999a:
> etext).

Žižek revisits Freud and Lacan in their interrogative analysis of the Christian injunction "to love one's neighbour as oneself", and he outlines their rejection of its possibility and its expediency. Their argument centres on the assertion that the concept of universal love disavows that which is unlovable in human nature, and that love must in some sense be an autonomous decision. Simply, Žižek asserts that love cannot be commanded. In his analysis of this Christian dictum, Žižek poses the question: "who is the neighbour?" He turns to Lacan's answer that "the neighbour is the Real", and thereby concludes that the injunction to "love thy neighbour" and correlative preaching about equality, tolerance and universal love "are ultimately strategies to avoid encountering the neighbour" (Žižek, 2004: 72) in all his/her vulnerability, frailty, obscenity and fallibility – the traumatic Real of the neighbour. Derrida concurs with this argument when he states that "The measure is given by the act, by the capacity of loving in act…living is living with. But every time, it is only one person living with another", and he concludes with the assertion that "A finite being could not possibly be present in act to too great a number. There is no belonging or friendly community that is present, and first present to itself, in act, without election and without selection" (Derrida, 2005: 21). The universality of idealistic proclamations of love actually precludes the possibility of loving the neighbour as a Real, traumatic, inaccessible other; the popularity of humanitarian causes lies in their inherent paradox whereby one can "love" from a distance without getting involved:

> it is easy to love the idealized figure of a poor, helpless neighbour, the starving African or Indian, for example; in other words, it is easy to love one's neighbour as long as he stays far enough from us, as long as there is a proper distance separating us. The problem arises at the moment when he comes too near us, when we start to feel his suffocating proximity – at this moment when the neighbour exposes himself to us too much, love can suddenly turn into hatred (Žižek, 2001: 8).

Nietzsche states the case in his typically aphoristic style: "There is not enough love and kindness in the world to permit us to give any of it away to imaginary beings" (Nietzsche, 1984: 89). Love is something very different to sentimental reflection and arm-chair rhetoric.

The avoidance of the encounter with the actual, singular and concrete experience of the neighbour is propelled by an aversion to one's own vulnerability and lack which might be mirrored in the other. The proximity of love and hate, the imperceptible slippage from one to the other which characterizes so much of human existence, in personal, social and political experience, is explored and reflected throughout literature, and is a recurring theme in the works of all the writers examined in this study. As Lacan states, "not to know hatred in the least is not to know love in any way either...there is no love without hate" (Lacan, 1999: 89). In his depiction of the neighbour as a concretization of the Real, Žižek argues that access to the real is therefore not impossible, (it is to be found through the neighbour), but traumatic and threatening. Encountering the real via the neighbour confronts us with the raw, vulnerable, and conflicting nature of human being, and such an encounter is often avoided in favour of more acceptable and idealistic generalisations of humanity. In his analysis of human relationships, Žižek offers a careful critique of the ethics of Emmanuel Levinas, and particularly his insistence on the subject's responsibility to answer the other's call: "Levinas asserts the relation to my neighbour, my unconditional responsibility for him, as the true terrain of ethical activity" (Žižek, 2005: 146). Žižek asserts that the limitation of Levinasian ethics lies in its selective conceptualization of what it is to be human:

> The limitation of Levinas is not simply that of a Eurocentrist who relies on too narrow a definition of what is human, a definition that secretly excludes non-Europeans as 'not fully human'. What Levinas fails to include in the scope of 'human' is, rather, the inhuman itself, a dimension

which eludes the face-to-face relationship between human beings (Žižek, 2006d: 111).

He asks if Levinas, with his call for an ethical response to the other, is not reducing the concept of the other to "the 'gentrification' of the neighbour", and thereby excluding everything that is deemed "inhuman", and everything which does not fit into the already symbolized social world. Žižek's emphasis on the "inhuman" or the monstrous as inherently constitutive of being-human, is opposed by Richard Kearney as being "too alarmist": "The danger of Žižek's approach is the risk that our entire culture becomes little more than a symptom of an incurable postmodern pathology" (Kearney, 2003: 99).[8] Yet the exclusion of what is deemed inhuman monstrosity from a vision of human nature raises fundamental questions. By what and by whose criteria is such a distinction made? Has this distinction been changed and revised through different historical periods and in different cultural experiences? Where is the monstrosity in the juxtaposition of judicial, educative, or "rehabilitationary" actions which purportedly serve to "protect" society from "inhuman" evil through processes which are themselves susceptible to the label "inhuman"? These questions contain at least the seeds of their answers, in that they may elicit diverse and ambiguous responses, and so suggest a deconstruction of the universality presumed in the opposition of human/monstrous.

The search for the certainty of the ethical position denies the absence of external guarantees and evades the responsibility of ethical reflection, hence the popularity of empty catch-phrases preaching moralistic convictions such as "brotherhood of man", "universal peace", and "justice for all", and the co-existence of concrete situations which subvert the actuality of such clichés even in the midst of their proclamations. According to Myers, "For Žižek, the truth is always to be found in contradiction rather than the smooth effacement of differences" (Myers, 2004: 17). In his critique of the ideology of human rights, Žižek points to the duplicity involved in situations which disguise their motivation behind a veil of pseudo-love for the other: "charity is part of the game, a humanitarian mask hiding the underlying economic exploitation" (Žižek, 2006e: etext). Nietzsche's critique of morality, his exposition of the hypocrisy inherent in the disavowal of selected aspects of human nature, and his reversal of the false dualities descriptive of the human animal, are cited by Žižek in his argument that definitions of what it is to be human

---

[8] Thus, Kearney, in arguing for the acknowledgement of the stranger, the monster, within oneself, rather than its projection on to another, still insists on the necessity of discernment in distinguishing between some monsters and others.

often exclude that which is inhuman as belonging to a radically different other. In arguing the difference between the concepts "not human" and "inhuman" he echoes Nietzsche's assertion that we are "human, all too human":

> 'he is not human' means simply that he is external to humanity, animal or divine, while 'he is inhuman' means something thoroughly different, namely, that he is neither simply human nor simply inhuman, but marked by a terrifying excess which, although it negates what we understand as 'humanity', is inherent to being-human (Žižek, 2005: 160).

Throughout his work, Žižek looks to the experience of the holocaust as an inescapable confirmation of evil, deception and ideology, in the lived and recorded experience of human beings. The aggression, brutality, cruelty – the "inhuman" acts – which were performed by the Nazis and their supporters, make it impossible to deny the reality of evil in the world, and inevitably pose questions regarding what human beings are capable of: "the unbridgeable GAP between the horror of what went on and the 'human, all too human' character of its perpetrators" (Žižek, 2005c: 38). As Auden reflects, "we shan't, not since Stalin and Hitler, / trust ourselves ever again: / we know that, subjectively, / all is possible" (Auden, 1994: 692). The ideological framework which encompassed the atrocities of the holocaust was based on "love" of one's nation, defence against the enemy, and loyalty to ideals and aspirations. Žižek offers a psychoanalytic interpretation of this perplexing historical event. Accordingly, the ideology was based on the fantasy of "the one supposed to know", the ultimate expert, often represented in the master signifier of God, the analyst, the expert, and in this case, the Fuhrer. The success of this ideological illusion depended on the simultaneous depiction of a threatening other, in this case, the Jew, onto whom was projected everything that posed a threat to the realisation of the fantasy: "There is no ideology that does not come into being without asserting itself in the guise of one 'truth' against another" (Žižek, 1999: 54). Nietzsche explains it thus: "People whom we cannot tolerate, we try to make suspect" (Nietzsche, 1984: 243). Concurrently, the fantasy that the other held the key to truth and liberation necessitated a suspension of personal responsibility and autonomy. Thus, when confronted with the reality of their crimes, Nazi supporters had recourse to the excuse that they were merely following orders, doing their duty, and therefore not responsible; they did what they did out of love – love of country, cause, leader – and so they cannot be held accountable. Hindsight, historical perspective, and the safety of temporal distance enables a rejection of such contestable denials, and a demand for justice and retribution for what is deemed "inhuman" behaviour. The danger of complacent self-righteousness and moralistic superiority which might underlie this stance of authentic judgement is exposed by Žižek as he reminds us that the perpetrators of these inhuman acts were not a separate species or a category of "sub-human", but were in fact ordinary human beings, living their everyday lives within a historical context: "it is all too easy to dismiss the Nazis as inhuman and bestial – what if the problem with the Nazis was precisely that they remained 'human, all too human'?" (Žižek, 2006d: 42). They were not some monstrous other, radically different from us; they were the same as us in that they were human beings. Hence, the portrayal of the Nazis as monstrous bears at least some similarity to the Nazi's psychological projection of evil and threat onto the Jews.

The atrocity of the holocaust is commonly held to be the pinnacle of evil in the Western world, but it has its repetitions throughout history and throughout the world, as Buber reminds us: "I do not think any basic change took place in the human race when the Nazis came into power...it is a question of proportion, not of basic content...similar brutalities have occurred before in history" (Buber, quoted in Hobes, 1972: 146). Taking the example of colonial exploitation and degradation in South Africa, as experienced at first hand, the novelist Doris Lessing is at pains to point out the fallacy of smug disdain towards the evils of the past: "I do not think it can be said too often that it is a mistake to exclaim over past wrong-thinking before at least wondering how our present thinking will seem to posterity" (Lessing, 1995: 50). Nietzsche reminds us that "when we consider earlier periods, we must be careful not to fall into unjust abuse" as the events of these times "cannot be measured by our standards" (Nietzsche, 1984: 70). Contemporary events await the analysis of history, but inevitably portray similar dichotomies and contradictions.

The safety, survival of "the free world", as embodied by the West and especially by North America, is the ideal demanding and attaining loyalty and allegiance to leaders, parties, and nations, and finding its expression in selected codes pertaining to what it is to be human; what does not fit the norm is excluded, whether it is the East, the terrorist, or the Muslim, and this other is conveniently scapegoated as the threat to all that is held dear. Paradoxically, when the "free world" is confronted with incontestable evidence of its own brutality and terrorism, committed in the name of "fighting terrorism" – "rendition", the scenes at Guantanamo Bay and others – there is an aversion to the reality that this evil is perpetrated by ordinary, recognizable men and women of the Western world; but Žižek reminds us that "what shocks us in others we ourselves also do in a way"

(Žižek, 2001a: etext). The confrontation with evil understandably evinces a reaction of condemnation and rejection of this incomprehensible, monstrous other, but Žižek suggests that a more courageous response is necessary. In his reflections on the WTC bombing September 11th 2001, Žižek urges an acknowledgement of the political, economic, and ideological realities which preceded the event, and he warns against the dangers implicit in one-sided oppositions of right/wrong, good/evil, and crime/punishment. To support his plea, Žižek quotes from Derrida's speech in which he refer to the WTC attacks: "my unconditional compassion, addressed to the victims of September 11, does not prevent me from saying it loudly: With regard to this crime, I do not believe that anyone is politically guiltless"; Žižek concludes that "this self-relating, this inclusion of oneself in the picture, is the only true 'infinite justice'" (Žižek , 2007: 287).

Now the injunction to "love thy neighbour" is exposed in its unacceptable and repulsive command: " 'Love thy neighbour!' means 'Love the Muslims!' OR IT MEANS NOTHING AT ALL" (Žižek, 2001c: etext). In order to confront the true, the real dimensions of this and other traumatic events, the simple objectivization of the monstrous other must be subverted: "Whenever we encounter such a purely evil Outside, we should gather the courage to endorse the Hegelian lesson: in this pure Outside, we should recognize the distilled version of our own essence" (Žižek, 2001c: etext). Here, Žižek is restating the position of Nietzsche, Buber and Ricoeur, in their acknowledgement of the conflictual nature of subjectivity, their rejection of polarities of good and evil, and their call for a more comprehensive understanding of human nature. This is also an argument central to the work of Julia Kristeva explored in *Strangers to Ourselves* where she relates the drive to demonise the other back to an unconscious process whereby we externalise the "foreigner": "Strangely, the foreigner lives within us: he is the hidden face of our identity...by recognizing him within ourselves, we are spared detesting him in himself" (Kristeva, 1991: 1). Kristeva looks to psychoanalysis as an aid to transcending the projection of the foreigner/other/monster, and she recalls that Freud did not refer to foreigners but to the uncanny strangeness of ourselves:

> The foreigner is within me, hence we are all foreigners. If I am a foreigner, there are no foreigners. Therefore Freud does not talk about them. The ethics of psychoanalysis implies a politics: it would involve a cosmopolitanism of a new sort that, cutting across governments, economies, and markets, might work for a mankind whose solidarity is

founded on the consciousness of its unconscious – desiring, destructive,
fearful, empty, impossible (Kristeva, 1991: 192).

In highlighting the hypocrisy and contradiction which is sometimes
implicit in proclamations of neighbourly love, Žižek paradoxically does
not reject the value of the concept; like Kristeva,[9] he looks to the
psychoanalytic insights of Freud and Lacan, as he endeavours to approach
the complexities of object-relations, the obstacles to inter-subjectivity, and
the possibilities of love within these perplexities.

Traversing the Fantasy

> The only way to achieve this
> suspension, to break the chain of crime
> and punishment/retribution, is to
> assume the utter readiness of self-
> erasure. And LOVE, at its most
> elementary, is nothing but such a
> paradoxical gesture of breaking the
> chain of retribution (Žižek, 2004:
> etext).

Žižek's insistent exposé of duplicity and deception, in political,
sociological and personal realms, calls into question the motivation and
direction underlying many "virtuous", "humane", and "altruistic" behaviours
and convictions. The conclusion of his inquiries may initially suggest a
negative and a cynical vision of the possibilities of human living, and so
may point to a rejection of the possibility of love. However, Žižek
increasingly explores the concept of love within a realistic appraisal of
human being, and he continues to use psychoanalytic insights to support
this realism: "Psychoanalysis reintroduces notions of Evil and
responsibility into our ethical vocabulary" (Žižek, 2007: 313). The
centrality of love to Žižek's thought is asserted by Kay: "If, in his earliest
writings, Žižek was most interested in belief, he has always identified
psychoanalysis as a source of hope, and now, increasingly, he has turned
to love as the way of fulfilling that hope" (Kay, 2003: 123).

Freud discovered that behind much of the neurosis and suffering he
encountered in his clinical work lay a primordial fantasy of totality,

---

[9] Žižek is critical of Kristeva's *Strangers to Ourselves* because he states that "there
is a danger that issues of economic exploitation are converted into problems of
cultural tolerance…here we have a pure pseudo-psychoanalytic cultural
reductionism" (Žižek, 2001a: etext).

omniscience, completion and satisfaction, sometimes symbolized by the cocoon-like safety and need-free contentment of existence in the womb. The separation of the subject from this fantasmatic illusion creates, according to Lacanian theory, a lack, an incompleteness, and a wish to obliterate this gap. Žižek sees this thrust towards completion and harmony as being decisive in the motivation of inter-subjectivity. The subject is aware of a lack, an emptiness, and a discord, and the resolution of this discomfort is sometimes translated into a belief that the other is in possession of that which is most ardently desired: "This object is what is unconsciously believed will fill the void at the core of being" (Žižek, 1999: 3). This need is imagined and symbolized in many forms; recognition, acceptance, knowledge, and love are some of the signifiers of this demand: "Fantasy is a way for the subject to answer the question of what object they are for the Other, in the eyes of the Other, for the Other's desire" (Žižek, 2006b: 58). Žižek refers to Lacan's exposition of desire and offers the following interpretation: "The problem with human desire is that, as Lacan put it, it is always a 'desire of the Other'...desire for the Other, desire to be desired by the Other, and especially desire for what the Other desires" (Žižek, 2007: 313). Therefore, the approach to the other is propelled with a view to providing what is missing in the self, and the other is seen as either withholding this magical synthesis or as bestowing it conditionally. The acknowledgement of a lack in oneself, a deficit which may be filled by the other, is more bearable than the realisation that the lack is also in the other: "fantasy is precisely an attempt to fill out this lack in the Other" (Žižek, 2006b: 333). Hence the encounter between subject and object, and the ensuing relationship which is sometimes defined as love, raises the question: who or what do we love? Žižek argues that when love is impelled with a need to provide what is absent in the self, or in the other, it is based on illusion: "the other sees something in me and wants something from me, but I cannot give him what I do not possess" (Žižek, 1999: 163). The first illusion is that the other holds the magical key which will replace that which is missing; the second illusion is that the lack in the subject can ever be obliterated. Both of these fantasies must be traversed, the integral void must be accepted as constitutive of both subject and object, if the condition of authentic love is to be experienced. Kay explains the link between the real and the traversing of the fantasy: " 'traversing the fantasy' – a phrase referring to the outcome of Lacanian therapy, in which we glimpse that what we had taken for reality was all along an illusion masking the space of the real, and so have an opportunity to build 'reality' afresh" (Kay, 2003: 5). As with Žižek's identification of the neighbour with the Real, the other, if it is to be loved, must be recognized and embraced in all its limitation, emptiness and vulnerability. The raw, conflicting, ambiguous nature of the other is glimpsed in moments, gestures, or simply intuitions of the real; these momentary glimpses are enabled by the subject's acknowledgement of his/her own incompleteness, lack and disharmony. When both illusions are overturned there is an acceptance that the other does not possess what the subject lacks, and simultaneously an awareness that the subject does not possess what the other desires: "the subject gets proof that the agalma, the 'hidden treasure', is already wanting in the other" (Žižek, 2006b: 47).

There are many obstacles to traversing the fantasy, and according to Žižek these must be recognised if they are to be overcome. One such obstacle is the concept of subjectivity: "subjectivity must be reinvented" (Žižek, 2001a: etext). The illusion of a transparent, knowable, fixed subjectivity is renounced by Žižek, (as it is by Freud and Ricoeur), and he takes Nietzsche's definition of active and passive nihilism as a signpost towards his argument:

> Active nihilism, in the sense of wanting nothing itself, is this active self-destruction which would be precisely the passion of the real – the idea that, in order to love fully and authentically, you must engage in self-destruction. On the other hand, there is passive nihilism, what Nietzsche called 'The last man' – just living a stupid, self-satisfied life without great passions (Žižek, 2001a: etext).

The self which is to be destroyed in the assumption of active nihilism and authentic love is the illusory self seeking its completion, justification, and meaning in the desire of the other. This self-destruction is synonymous with the end of an analysis, according to Žižek, because the "effect of truth", the "self-understanding" which emerges at end of analysis means that "I am not the same subject as before" (Žižek, 2001: 33).[10] The ongoing creation and re-creation of the self resounds with Nietzsche's idea of "becoming" as opposed to being; the simultaneous renunciation of former self images which no longer hold validity is part of the process of narrative identity, as discussed by Ricoeur. The sentiment echoes the lines from Eliot's "Four Quartets": "You are not the same people who left that station / Or who will arrive at any terminus" (Eliot, 2004: 188). There are many barriers to such truth and understanding, and it is often more comfortable to maintain one's established sense of self than to risk the erasure of familiar roles, masks, and self-images, because the gaze of the

---

[10] Hederman echoes this sentiment in his exploration of love: "Unless my old self dies, it remains alone" (Hederman, 2000: 40).

big Other, albeit in less recognizable forms than hitherto experienced, is still imagined consequential to one's inclusion in the symbolic/social world. The persistence of the big Other in "post-ideological" times is evident in many guises; the expert, possessor of knowledge and understanding, who will tell one what to do, what to believe, what to desire. Žižek follows Lacan's depiction of desire as "the desire of the other", the desire for what the other wants. The world of media, and especially advertising, daily bombards us with images of what we should want, and the success of the enterprise lies in the belief that if others want something then it must be worth having. These never-satisfying entities, symbolized in material wealth and comfort, intellectual success and prestige, and the many characteristics of a desirable life-style, are mere substitutes for our real desire which remains hidden from us, and they are detours of avoidance whereby responsibility and freedom are inhibited. Žižek refers to these detours as gadget or fetish, and explains that "a fetish can play a very constructive role of allowing us to cope with the harsh reality" (Žižek, 2001b: etext). Therefore he asks: "What is your gadget, your favourite illusionary escape-hatch?" (Žižek, 2001b: etext). An array of possible answers abounds in the almost obsessive consumerism which characterizes postmodernity: "Post modernism is the cultural logic of late capitalism, or the response of culture to its colonization of the commodity' (Myers, 2004: 45).

Similarly, the growth of a victim-culture in recent times, where victimhood appears to be encouraged, glorified, or approached with a view to retaliation and reparation, is seen by Žižek as another phenomenon which maintains the fantasy of the other-supposed to know, the powerful other who will interpret one's story and redress the wrongs which have been endured. " 'The culture of complaint' thus calls on the big Other to intervene, and to set things straight" (Žižek, 1997a: etext). The necessity of testimony and accountability is not questioned here, but Žižek suggests that the proliferation of the status of victim often involves an underlying assumption of impotence and subjugation because it maintains the aura of helplessness and powerlessness of the victims and "is designed to prevent them turning into active agents" (Žižek, 2004: 143), while enhancing the notion of knowledge and capability residing in the powerful other; herein lies the paradox of victimization: "the ideological construction of the idea of subject-victim...an extremely violent gesture of reducing the other to the helpless victim" (Žižek, 1999a: etext). Examples abound; from revisionist readings of colonial suppression and exploitation to tribunals of justice, of truth, and of employment. Here, Žižek considers it important to differentiate between two levels of victimization:

> On the one hand we have the upper-middle-class discourse of victimization
> in our own societies. This is the narcissistic logic of whatever the other
> does to you is potentially a threat...we are all the time potentially victims
> of verbal harassment, sexual harassment, violence, smoking, obesity – an
> eternal threat...Then we have the third world catastrophes – or even with
> us the homeless and the excluded...there is an invisible distance here
> (Žižek, 2004: 143).

In either case, Žižek discerns a duplicity; in engaging in "humanitarian
exercises", the "benevolence" of the Western world maintains its distance
from third world victims, and in embracing the status of victimhood for
itself, the Western subject reaffirms the authority of the big Other as the
symbolic source of protection and retribution. On a personal,
intersubjective level, a similar fantasy is perpetuated whereby one seeks in
the other what the other does not possess. In shifting the burden of
fulfilment, knowledge, redress, or whatever it is which is sought, onto
another, the subject reinforces the ideological fantasy of the other/the
master/the saviour, and experiences an illusory sense of liberation and
immunity from responsibility and action.

Only by traversing the fantasy, by acknowledging the basic gap or lack
in both subject and object, is the possibility of love opened; when "all the
burden falls back upon the subject since he renounces any support in the
Other" (Žižek, 2001:59). The imperfection and incompleteness of the
subject, the impossibility of fully penetrating the kernel of one's being,
and the simultaneous acknowledgement of a similar lack in the other,
would appear to attest to an utter incommensurability between subject and
object, between self and other; but it is in the celebration of this very
impossibility and inaccessibility that Žižek locates "love's most sublime
moment" (Žižek, 2001: 58):

> What defines love is this basic discord or gap...the lover seeks in the
> beloved what he lacks, but as Lacan puts it, 'what the one lacks is not what
> is hidden within the other'...the only thing left to the beloved is thus to
> proceed to a kind of exchange of places, to change from the object into the
> subject of love, in short: to return love...by reaching his hand back to the
> lover and thus answering the lover's lack/desire with his own lack (Žižek,
> 2001: 58).

While Žižek is often critical of deconstruction, and of Derrida in particular,
the above statement resounds strongly with Derrida's reflections on love
and friendship. Derrida explores the concept of love/friendship through a
reading of Plato and Aristotle, but especially through a reading of
Nietzsche, and his conclusion of love as an act echoes the image of the

hand being reached back to the lover: "life, breath, the soul, are always and necessarily found on the side of the lover or of loving…one can love being loved – or to be lovable – but loving will always be more, better and something other than being loved" (Derrida, 2005: 10).[11] The focus on loving over the desire to be loved resounds with Nietzsche's statement that "the demand to be loved is the greatest kind of arrogance" (Nietzsche, 1984: 239), and it is also for Žižek the gesture wherein genuine love emerges, and which reverses the status of the loved one from object to subject:

> I am truly in love not when I am simply fascinated by the agalma of the other, but when I experience the other, the object of my love, as frail and lost, as lacking 'it', and my love none the less survives this loss…we now have two loving subjects instead of the initial duality of the loving one and the loved one the object of love…[the object of love] thus acquires the status of another subject (Žižek, 1999: 164).

Lacan maintains the distinction between the self and the other within the experience of love, but he also stresses the transference of attention to the being of the other as central to this experience: "Love, now no longer conceived of as a passion, but as an active gift, is always directed, beyond imaginary captivation, towards the being of the loved subject" (Lacan, 1991: 276), and he reiterates the focus of this direction: "Love aspires to the unfolding of the being of the other" (Lacan, 1991: 277). The transformation of the object into a subject described above echoes Buber's differentiation between the "I-It" relationship which objectifies the other, and the "I-Thou" experience wherein the other is embraced as a self. Žižek may be considered cynical about human relationships, communication, and the possibility of love; Kearney refers to his "uncompromising scepticism" and "nihilistic cynicism", and he quotes the criticism of M. Brockelman for "his insistence upon the total 'unrepresentability' of the…subject" (Kearney, 2003: 257). However, in highlighting the difficulties, ambiguities, and failures inherent in the reality of human experience, Žižek simultaneously attests to the intrinsic urgency of love for human living, and to his persistent conviction in the possibility of love.

---

[11] A statement by Kearney suggests the link between the thoughts of Derrida and Žižek here: "Desire of the other as separate and transcendent is desire as gift rather than appropriation" (Kearney, 2001: 69).

SECTION III:

POETRY

CHAPTER SEVEN

WILLIAM WORDSWORTH

The centrality of language to human experience, its expression, its communication, and its analysis, and the limitations of this phenomenon in fully realising the symbolization of being in the world, provides a link between the disciplines of philosophy, psychoanalysis, and poetry. While all three attempt to express, question, and reflect upon the human condition, the distinction of the poetic word as a medium with a unique potential to disclose and articulate the truth of being human, is asserted by many philosophers and psychoanalysts, including the writers explored in previous chapters. Nussbaum, asking "if it is love one is trying to understand, that strange unmanageable phenomenon or form of life", states that while "literary form is not separable from philosophical content", the language of literature may enable a greater understanding:

> there may be some views of the world and how one should live in it – views, especially, that emphasize the world's surprising variety, its complexity and mysteriousness, its flawed and imperfect beauty – that cannot be fully and adequately stated in the language of conventional philosophical prose...but only in a language and in forms themselves more complex, more allusive, more attentive to particulars (Nussbaum, 1992: 3).

Nietzsche, although somewhat critical of poets in some ways, himself adopted a poetic form in his use of aphorisms, his *Zarathustra* reads like a confessional lyric poem, and he admits that "there are so many things between heaven and earth which only the poets have let themselves dream!" (Nietzsche, 2003a: 150). Freud speaks enviously of the relative ease with which poets discovered and expressed truths of the human condition: "Everywhere I go I find that a poet has been there before me",[1] and goes on to explain: "We laymen have always been intensely curious to know...from what sources that strange creature, the creative writer, draws his material, and how he manages to make such an impression on us with

---

[1] This is a caption on a wall of the Freud Museum in Vienna.

it and to arouse in us emotions of which, perhaps, we had not even thought
ourselves capable" (Freud, 1995: 436). In his study of love "as an
experience common to all human beings", the contemporary psychoanalyst,
Andre Green, echoes the sentiments of Freud as he humbly asserts that
"the creation of poets goes far beyond the psychoanalytic interpretation of
love":

> I think that art, mainly literature, and especially poetry, undoubtedly gives
> a better introduction to the knowledge of love, which we grasp by
> intuition...the detour through imaginative and poetic language of a very
> general human experience has proved to be more efficient than the ideas
> born from an experiment which has undeniably committed itself to the
> most constant and careful investigation of love relationships (Green and
> Kohun, 2005: 5).

Buber sees in lyric poetry "the tremendous refusal of the soul to be
satisfied with self-commerce", and a manifestation of relation as essential
to human being: "Poetry is the soul's announcement that even when it is
alone with itself on the narrowest ridge it is thinking not of itself but of the
Being which is not itself" (Buber, 2004: 213). In an interview with
Richard Kearney, Ricoeur offers his reflections on the "prejudice and
bias" of ordinary language, and concludes that:

> we need a third dimension of language which is directed...towards the
> disclosure of possible worlds...this third dimension of language I call the
> mytho-poetic. The adequate self-understanding of man is dependent on this
> third dimension of language as a disclosure of possibility (Ricoeur, 1991:
> 490).

Ricoeur states that "the philosopher relies on this capacity of poetry to
enlarge, to increase, to augment the capacity of meaning of our language"
(Ricoeur, 1991: 450). Both Lacan and Žižek turn to poetic devices to
explore the unconscious process at work.[2] The power of poetry to disclose
truth, to lift the veil of accustomed modes of seeing, and to express new
visions of possibility and reality, is aptly described by Guillaume
Apollinaire as he gives his definition of the poet:

---

[2] Lacan refers to "metaphor" and "metonymy" as modes of language which may
aid understanding, and makes direct use of poetic references to elucidate his
thought; Žižek turns to Wordsworth's lines, "On Boating", to discuss the co-
existence of the sublime and the monstrous in human experience.

Poets are not simply men devoted to the beautiful. They are also and especially devoted to truth, insofar as the unknown can be penetrated, so much that the unexpected, the surprising, is one of the principal sources of poetry...since men must live in the end by truths in spite of the falsehoods with which they pad them, the poet alone sustains the life whereby humanity finds these truths.[3]

The quest for understanding, of the subject and the world, which is explored through philosophy and psychoanalysis, is also central to the poetic act, its creation and its reception. Adrienne Rich, in a reflection on her developing attraction to poetry, points to its potential revelation and interpretation of human understanding:

Poetry soon became more than music and images; it was also revelation, information, a kind of teaching...I thought it could offer clues, intimations, keys to questions...*What is possible in this life? What does "love" mean, this thing that is so important? What is this other thing called "freedom" or "liberty" – is it like love, a feeling? What have human beings lived and suffered in the past? How am I going to live my life?* (Rich, 2004: 505).

Thus poetry is another mode whereby the human being seeks understanding, of the self, the other, and the world, and it addresses and explores the questions which inspire philosophy and psychoanalysis in all aspects of inquiry, albeit in its own unique way.

Wordsworth is a poet who radicalized the poetic experience in its content, method and purpose, and who, anticipating the philosophers and theorists of the previous sections, posited truth as the ultimate *raison d'être* of thought and of the poetic act: "poetry is the most philosophical of all writing...its object is truth...not standing upon external testimony, but carried alive into the heart by passion; truth which is its own testimony" (Wordsworth, 1984: 605). The world of the late eighteenth century which formed the background of Wordsworth's poetic work was the scene of turbulent change, violence and upheaval. It saw the questioning of European thought in philosophy, politics, and literature, as revolutionary ideals of individual freedom and social change propelled revolt against established orders. Revolutions in America and France hinted at a possible new and bright socio-political future. A revolutionary spirit permeated the political and social realm, with a commitment to replace long-accepted traditions of government, society and individuality with the radical embrace of the ideals of freedom, equality and fraternity. Enthusiasm for

---

[3] This quotation is taken from an excerpt from "The New Spirit and the Poets", chapter 9, in *Poetry in Theory: An Anthology 1900-2000*, ed. Jon Cook.

change expressed itself in revolutionary action which was often ambiguous in its methods, and the ensuing devastation and brutality of the reign of terror across Europe led to disillusionment among many who had supported the revolutionary dream. For those, the idealistic dreams of this period were followed by uncertainty and incomprehension in the face of the violence and bloodshed which seemed to mock the very concepts which inspired them; words like liberty, equality, and fraternity sounded hollow in the aftermath of war and terror.

The life of Wordsworth spans this period of transition from unfettered hope and determined optimism to acknowledgement of the human cost of revolt and industrialisation, and many Wordsworthian commentators situate their analysis of his work within this framework. Thus, explorations and interpretations have dealt with his poetry as a portrayal of his shifting political views, his embrace of solitude as a gradual detachment from the complexities of a changing civilized world, and the personal conflicts and failures which are variously attributed to the writer of the poems.[4] The reading of Wordsworth's poetry for the purposes of this study does not pursue this analysis except as it impinges on the thesis question, and concurs with the poet's claim that "All men ought to be judged with charity and forbearance after death has put it out of their power to explain the motives of their actions" (Wordsworth, 2002: 126). Suffice to suggest that the poet, faced with concrete examples of the failure of theoretical ideals of equality and fraternity, sublimated these values into a love of the world and its inhabitants which confronted him in reality. In the words of David Bromwich, "he began as a moral thinker about society, and ended as a moral thinker about personal experience" (Bromwich, 2000: 74). Like Freud later, he rejected the doctrine of "universal love" while concentrating on his personal reaction to the flesh and blood characters of his actual experience. This resounds with Buber's positing of genuine relationship and experience of love in the practical, concrete situations of lived experience. While Wordsworth's poetry is radically personal, exploring questions of humanity through a persistent examination of his own psychological and emotional development, the emphasis here is on the poetic word rather than the character of the writer.

The political and social upheaval that characterized the end of the eighteenth century was paralleled by major changes in European thought, particularly articulated in philosophy and literature, and combining to

---

[4] The concentration on the personality of the poet is evident in the following works: Paul Hamilton's *Wordsworth, 1986*; David Bromwich's *Disowned by Memory: Wordsworth's Poetry of the 1790s, 2000*. Such psychobiographical readings are contested by critics as diverse as Eliot and Roland Barthes.

epitomize the period defined as romanticism. Stuart Curran, in the preface to *The Cambridge Companion to British Romanticism,* describes this period as "a crucial transition between an Enlightenment world view and the values of modern, industrial society" (Curran, 2005: xiii). The disillusionment which followed the revolutionary attempts at political democracy and individual freedom did not diminish the impact of the new vision of the subject, and the subject's place in the world. The concept of subjectivity took on new meanings which suggested an inter-weaving of freedom and responsibility, the acknowledgement of the powers of the imagination, and the prominence of feeling and passion as primary factors in the acquisition of knowledge about the human being in the world, over the one-sided adherence to reason as the repository of truth and knowledge. Irving Singer considers the new importance given to the emotions to be central to the romantic vision: "What distinguished Romanticism from earlier forms of idealism...[was] the extraordinary importance that was given to feeling rather than reason", and he continues to explain that this did not translate into a negation of reason altogether: "It is not the case that the Romantics believed that 'feeling is all', as some commentators have suggested, but only that feeling is primary, both in morals and in the acquisition of knowledge about the world" (Singer, 1984: 285-6). The elevation of the imagination is seen by P.M.S. Dawson as also crucial to the romantic achievement: "The Romantics' faith in the power of imaginative vision to transform the world is the source of some of their greatest achievements", and he suggests that this was a political as well as a poetic ideal of romanticism: "In a society whose practices and beliefs constituted a denial of the human imagination and creativity it was the poet's role to keep open a sense of alternative possibility" (Dawson, 2005: 71,73). An attempt to reunite what had previously been dissected, heart and mind, body and soul, passion and reason, human being and nature, inspired the philosophy and literature of this period, and Wordsworth, as the "historian of the heart", sought, through autobiographical narration, self-analysis, and the development of a personal poetic and linguistic vision, to give expression to the tenets of the romantic period. Focusing upon personal experience and an increase in self-consciousness, Wordsworth's poetry embodies an analysis of the past by the present, "emotion recollected in tranquillity" (Wordsworth, 1984: 611); an accommodation of unconscious influences and motivations on mood and behaviour, and a narration of dreams and memories as a route towards self-discovery. The deepening insights into the psychological development of the human being which are enabled by this poetic endeavour are paralleled by a similarly increasing uncertainty of self-definition which foreshadows Nietzsche's introspective analysis and rejection of traditional understanding of selfhood and subjectivity. Harold Bloom comments on "a very complex nineteenth century questioning of the notion of a single, separate self, a questioning that culminated in the analytics of Nietzsche, Marx and Freud, but which may be stronger in the poets even than it was in the great speculators" (Bloom, 1976: 135).

Anticipating Freud and the psychoanalytic techniques of free-association and interpretation, Wordsworth's poetry is a searching and a poised act of self-examination. The similarities between Wordsworth, and Freud and Nietzsche, are highlighted by Bloom when he seeks to define his understanding of "strong poets"; he states that "strong poets present themselves as looking for truth 'in the world'… two of the strongest poets in the European Romantic tradition [were] Nietzsche and Freud" (Bloom, 1976: 2). The urgency of the search for truth is proclaimed by Wordsworth: "Intelligent lovers of freedom are from necessity bold and hardy lovers of truth" (Wordsworth, 1984: 668). The commitment to self-analysis and introspection evident in Nietzsche and Freud is foreshadowed by Wordsworth's intense preoccupation with personal reflection and autobiographical reference as a source of his poetic truth. He asserts the value of humility and honesty in a questioning of the inner self as prerequisite to truth and love:

> …true knowledge leads to love,
> True dignity abides with him alone
> Who, in the silent hour of inward thought,
> Can still suspect, and still revere himself,
> In lowliness of heart (Wordsworth, 1984: 31).

The inner quest which the poet undertakes involves both mind and heart, as Wordsworth professes his conviction that the soul arrives at truth through both emotion and reason, and that knowing accompanied by feeling enables the experience of empathy that underlies caring and love.

Neglect of the Heart

> The differences, the outside marks by
> which,
> Society has parted man from man,
> Neglectful of the universal heart
> (Wordsworth, 1984: 574).

Reacting against classicism and the Enlightenment, with its emphasis on rationality, order, and inevitable social progress, romanticism promoted the primacy of subjectivity, unfettered imagination, and emotional spontaneity. As the acknowledged standard-bearer of romanticism in English literature, Wordsworth seeks a new definition of the poet, his/her work, and his/her method. In The Preface to the "Lyrical Ballads" (1802), co-authored with Samuel Coleridge, Wordsworth provides a manifesto in defence of his art which differs radically from the measured ornamentation and rigid conventions implicitly accepted by the prevailing literary canon. He champions a more realistic and naturalistic type of writing and argues that the exposition of the heart of man is central to the poetic process: "my theme / No other than the very heart of man" (Wordsworth, 1984: 575). The acknowledgement of feeling and passion as integral to human experience leads Wordsworth to examine the hitherto neglected possibilities implicit in a recognition of the heart as the seat of a different level of knowledge, and he defines his vision of poetry accordingly: "Poetry is passion: it is the history or science of feelings" (Wordsworth, 1984: 594). He proposes an expansion of philosophy to integrate this hitherto neglected source of truth: "philosophy enlightened by the affections" (Wordsworth, 1984: 668). In his role as a teacher and trainer of psychoanalysts, Lacan makes a similar plea: "I urge you...at the heart of your own search for the truth, to renounce quite radically...the use of an opposition like that of the affective and the intellectual...by using it one gets into a series of blind alleys" (Lacan, 1991: 274). The enlightenment and understanding ensuing from "the affections" is shown by Wordsworth to be primarily sourced in the capacity to love; his poetry centres on the essential necessity of a willingness and a commitment to feel a sense of love of life in all its manifestations, resounding with Nietzsche's *amor fati*, and it therefore examines the phenomena, personal and cultural, which hinder this possibility. In an implicit critique of "what is now called science", Wordsworth argues that it needs "to put on...a form of flesh and blood" in order to address the complexities and diversities of its subject (Wordsworth, 1984: 607). In contrasting "the knowledge both of the Poet and the Man of Science", Wordsworth puts forward his conception of the poet and his work:

> The Man of Science seeks truth as a remote and unknown benefactor; he cherishes and loves it in his solitude: the Poet, singing a song in which all human beings join with him, rejoices in the presence of truth as our visible friend and hourly companion. Poetry is the breath and finer spirit of all knowledge; it is the impassioned expression which is in the countenance of all Science...the Poet binds together by passion and knowledge the vast

empire of human society...Poetry is first and last of all Knowledge – it is
as immortal as the heart of man (Wordsworth, 1984: 606).

Wordsworth's insistence on the heart as the essence of the poetic act is
later echoed by Derrida in his response to the question "What is poetry?"
in 1998; he questions the possibility of an answer, but insists that any
attempt involves knowing "how to renounce knowledge"; thenceforth he
offers his response: "I call a poem that very thing that teaches the heart,
invents the heart, that which, finally, the word heart seems to mean and
which, in my language, I cannot easily discern from the word itself"
(Derrida, 2004: 536). Wordsworth's admonishment against the one-sided
emphasis of science is based on its neglect of the heart, and he sees this
bias as detrimental to human knowledge and truth:

> Our meddling intellect
> Mis-shapes the beauteous forms of things;
> We murder to dissect.
> Enough of science and of art;
> Close up these barren leaves;
> Come forth, and bring with you a heart
> That watches and receives (Wordsworth, 1984: 131).

His plea for recognition of the heart's knowledge resounds with the ideas
of the seventeenth century philosopher, Blaise Pascal, whose writings
exerted a significant influence on romanticism, and particularly on the
work of Rousseau. Pascal asserted the dominating faculty of the
imagination in the complex quest for truth, and he posited the intuitive
mind as a necessary correlation to rational thought: "the heart has its
reasons which reason itself does not know" (Pascal, 1999: 150-158); the
paradoxical inter-twining of passion and reason is echoed later by
Nietzsche in his attack upon the degradation of passion and the
misunderstanding of reason: "As if every passion did not have its quantum
of reason" (Nietzsche, 1968: 208). Wordsworth elevates the imagination to
a position of power and revelation which enhances awareness, of self, of
others, and of the natural world: "the power of the human imagination is
sufficient to produce such changes even in our physical nature as might
almost appear miraculous" (Wordsworth, 1984: 611).

Wordsworth's embrace of the truth of emotional experience is a
consistent commitment throughout his work: In his essay, "Wordsworth's
Poetry to 1798", Duncan Wu refers to this pervasive concern: "From his
earliest writings to his last...he was endowed with an intuitive
understanding of the human mind, and from the first attempted to describe

the inner truth of the emotions" (Wu, 2003: 26). In embracing the world of emotion and imagination, the poet inevitably focuses on internal experience, resulting in a self-examination that necessitates an exploration of his personal past through the power of memory and interpretation. Through memory the adult mind contends with its childhood origins. In this way, an integration of the self is attempted, where earlier experiences, events and encounters are revisited with the objectivity which distance, temporal and spatial, facilitates. Simultaneously, the present circumstances of the poet are opened to inquiry and understanding when viewed against the background of the past. The resulting narrative of the self, which is expanded to accommodate on-going interpretation and understanding, resounds with Ricoeur's thesis on narrative identity and the importance of memory in formulating that identity.

Inevitably, in the light of new thinking characteristic of this period, the concept of childhood and the significance of early experience took on a different meaning and importance than had hitherto been contemplated, and the psychological and emotional significance of this period of life became a subject of study across diverse disciplines. This later became a cornerstone of Freud's psychoanalysis with its emphasis on explaining mental and emotional distress through a re-narration of past experiences in a therapeutic setting, its insights into the phenomena of memory, forgetting, and repetition, and its recognition of the unconscious as a powerful factor in human experience. For Wordsworth, the child embodies all the possibilities for freedom, creativity and enthusiastic curiosity, which are later diminished to varying degrees by the gradual immersion in civilization; the child is an earlier self unburdened by the consciousness of adult cares. Buber sees the development of the child as being impacted by both nature and society: "He is educated by the elements, by air and light and the life of plants and animals, and he is educated by relationships" (Buber, 2004: 107). Arguing for the intelligence of the body as a source wisdom, Nietzsche looks to the truth of the child: "I am body and soul' – so speaks the child. And why should one not speak like children?" (Nietzsche, 2003a: 61). While Freud did not idealize childhood in this way, his analysis of the influence of earlier life-events and trauma, and the conflict between the individual and civilization, resounds with Wordsworth's thesis. For Freud, the process of socialization involves the internalization of injunctions and expectations which restrict the unbounded freedom and curiosity of the child's initial experience of the world; there is a gradual awareness that certain experiences, feelings, and desires are at variance with social mores, and hence the repression of certain aspects of the self. Wordsworth's glorification of childhood appears to refer to the innocence and creativity which precedes the demands of socialization, a phase which might be seen to be lost as the child enters the Lacanian realms of the imaginary and the symbolic. Both Wordsworth and Freud discern a loss of self, to varying degrees, in the social adaptation of the human being, and a diminished self lacks the integration which enables the experience of love, of oneself and of others. Both writers point to this consequence; Wordsworth confronts it in his analysis of his own development, while Freud encounters it in the distress of his patients as they attempt to express their concerns through the transference of love onto the analyst. Echoing the thought of both writers, Nietzsche offers his reflections on childhood: "The child is innocence and forgetfulness, a new beginning, a sport, a self-propelling wheel, a first motion, a sacred Yes" (Nietzsche, 2003a: 55).

According to Wordsworth, the new orientation of poetic expression which he advocates, necessitates the cultivation of a different poetic language, an articulation of human experiences grounded in the actual lives of ordinary people; he wants "a selection of the language really spoken by men" (Wordsworth, 1984: 602). The necessary relationship between understanding and language, later developed in the thought of the philosophers and theorists of the previous sections, is explored by Wordsworth as he examines "in what manner language and the human mind re-act on each other" (Wordsworth, 1984: 596), and he seeks a language which reflects and resounds with the lived activity which he observes around him. This leads him to concentrate his attention on the individuals who inhabit the landscape of hills and valleys to which he is consistently drawn. His sources of inspiration therefore differ radically from that of his predecessors, but Wordsworth argues against any exclusion from his poetic explorations: "It is the honourable characteristic of Poetry that its materials are to be found in every subject which can interest the human mind" (Wordsworth, 1984: 591). The inclusive nature of poetry is also attested by the Irish poet, Seamus Heaney, when he says: "Poetry, let us say, whether it belongs to an old political dispensation or aspires to express a new one, has to be a working model of inclusive consciousness" (Heaney, 2000: 572).

Creating a new poetic vision, in content and form, Wordsworth combines the narrative style of the ballad with the lyric's emotional content; both forms had been considered inferior to the strict demands of serious poetry, but Wordsworth defends his position while acknowledging the impact of rigid prejudice in depreciating something new and unfamiliar: "that most dreadful enemy to our pleasures, our own pre-established codes of decision" (Wordsworth, 1984: 591). The difficulty inherent in a renunciation of the familiar is also noted by Freud: "Hardly anything is harder for a man than to give up a pleasure which he has once experienced. Actually, we can never give anything up; we only exchange one thing for another" (Freud, 1995: 438). Consequently, what is radically new is often dismissed as untenable; as Nietzsche says, "to hear something new is hard and painful for the ear; we hear the music of foreigners badly" (Nietzsche, 2003: 115). Wordsworth is committed to the embrace of a new poetic vision which involves "breaking the bonds of custom" whereby one tends "to dwell upon those points wherein Men differ from each other, to the exclusion of those in which all Men are alike" (Wordsworth, 1984: 658). The acknowledgement of universal experiences of thought and feeling, regardless of social role or status, enables a recognition of one's own needs, desires, fears, strengths and weaknesses reflected in the other, and according to Wordsworth, results in understanding, empathy, compassion, and ultimately love of the other and the self. This resounds with Žižek's argument that love is only possible in an acceptance that the other/beloved does not possess the attributes and solutions which are felt lacking in the self. The willingness to recognize the frailty, fallibility, confusion and conflict which may appear in the other, as also definitive of the self, enables the possibility of approaching the other, not as a receptacle of disowned projections, but in an openness and vulnerability to alterity and difference in oneself and others; in the words of Ricoeur, it is the attempted acknowledgement of "oneself as another". The revolutionary nature of this poetic vision, its rejection of established criteria and restrictions, inevitably provoked disdain and ridicule. Wordsworth retorts with a psychoanalytic interpretation of projection which often underlies the critic's scorn: "The lash, which they are aiming at my productions, does, in fact, only fall on phantoms of their own brain" (Wordsworth, 1984: 640). His near-contemporary, William Blake, puts it thus: "O'er my sins thou sit and moan: / Hast thou no sins of thy own? / O'er my sins thou sit and weep, / And lull thy own sins fast asleep" (Blake, 2004: 90). Acknowledging the attraction of familiarity and repetition, later explored by Freud as the compulsion to repeat, Wordsworth accepts the difficulties inherent in moving beyond habitual pleasure and security: "we not only wish to be pleased, but to be pleased in that particular way in which we have been accustomed to be pleased" (Wordsworth, 1984: 614). Thereby, he acknowledges the obstacles which hinder the growth of understanding, openness, and vulnerability, and which diminish the capacity to love.

The world of nature, its magnificence and power, its turbulence and gentleness, and its particularity and universality, provides the canvas upon which Wordsworth paints the human experience: "Poetry is the image of man and nature" (Wordsworth, 1884: 605). Through his own love of nature and through an exploration of his own psyche, Wordsworth expresses through his poetry a conviction that love is a powerful, if sometimes elusive, instrument of mediation between self and the universe, between self and others, and between the disparate complexities of the individual psyche. The celebration of love which underlines Wordsworth's poetry is characteristic of romanticism in general, according to John Jones, in his analysis of the period: "The work of the Romantics, poets and novelists, celebrates the fact of love, as once marvellously evident and difficult beyond despair, and about which the age immediately preceding them had been less than honest" (Jones, 1970: vii). In an attempt to approach a more honest analysis of love Wordsworth sources his investigations in an encounter with his own inner realities, and his poetry moves across the inner and outer landscapes combining an observation and a translation of the relations between the private individual and the characters which inhabit his/her world, and the interactions between the human being and the natural world. The connection between love of nature and love of man is a persistent theme in his poetry, as stated by John Beer when discussing Wordsworth's faith in the lessons of the heart:

> Wordsworth believed that in attending to the motions of his own heart he was making a study that could be of value to all his fellow human beings. He hoped, among other things, to show by this study how the love of nature…must inevitably lead to the love of man (Beer, 1978: 13).

The concept of love is therefore central to Wordsworth's work, and in his poetic study of human nature and his exploration of the mind and heart, he portrays both the possibilities of its experience and the obstacles which sometimes prevent its realization.

Loss

> Whither is fled the visionary gleam?
> Where is it now, the glory and the
> dream? (Wordsworth, 1984: 298).

Impermanence and transience, as inescapable realities of the human condition, propel an equally real desire to transcend the sorrow and limitation which often accompanies a realization of finitude and unpredictability; literature abounds with diverse approaches to this perennial conflict: "The immortal Mind craves objects that endure"

(Wordsworth, 1984: 287). Wordsworth's encounter with the vicissitudes characteristic of life in all its forms is explored on one level through his favourite image of the daffodil; contemplation of the beauty and splendour of a daffodil-filled meadow instills a momentary joy: "A poet could not but be gay / In such a laughing company" (Wordsworth, 1984: 303), and the memory of this joy retains the power to soothe in times of solitude and reflection. However, the imagery of the daffodil evokes the sentiments of an earlier poet, Robert Herrick, when he immortalizes the flower as a symbol of the brevity of life:

> We have short time to stay, as you,
> We have as short a spring;
> As quick a growth to meet decay,
> As you, or anything (Herrick, 1919: 252).

The sorrow pertaining to a confrontation with change and death is intensified to unbearable proportions when it involves loss of the beloved. In the sonnet "Surprised by Joy" (Wordsworth, 1984: 334), Wordsworth expresses his personal anguish and inconsolable grief in the face of such loss. The death of his beloved daughter, "my most grievous loss", is "the worst pang that sorrow ever bore", and there is no compensation to be found in memory or forgetfulness. The poet realizes that this loss is final, and its pain a constant companion: "neither present time, nor years unborn / Could to my sight that heavenly face restore". A momentary relief from this grief, a fleeting encounter with joy, results from an involuntary forgetting of his loss, but only serves to reprimand the poet for his perceived disloyalty, as he admonishes himself for being "beguiled" and "blind". In the wake of such irreparable loss, described in a letter as "oppressed with sorrow and distracted with anxiety" (Wordsworth, 2002: 110), and in the alternating responses of denial, anger and incomprehension, the experience of love is revealed as potentially fraught with risk, pain, and personal fragmentation.

Freud describes the human response to loss, whether real or perceived, as having two possibilities; when the loss is experienced as unbearable, the subject/patient refuses to accept its reality, an experience described by Wordsworth as "unwilling to forego, confess, submit" (Wordsworth, 1984: 448), and adopts as a coping mechanism the introjection of the lost object into the self; the subject subsequently directs the anger, depreciation and loathing evoked by the loss onto this introjected aspect of the self. The possibility of love, of self and others, is sabotaged as the self becomes the target of attack and condemnation. Wordsworth sees this reaction as understandable and universal; "Man / As long as he shall be the Child of

Earth, / Might almost 'weep to have' what he may lose" (Wordsworth, 1984: 435). According to Freud's analysis, the resulting *melancholia* can only be alleviated by a conscious acceptance of the loss, a working through the grief, and a letting go of the loved object: in the words of the poet, "grief will have its course" (Wordsworth, 2002: 83). Herein lies the work of mourning which is essential to psychological recovery. For Freud, the psychoanalytic encounter provides a potential space for such healing, as it offers an exploratory relationship based on acceptance, openness and understanding; similarly, Wordsworth addresses his recollections, confusions and reflections to a beloved friend, usually Coleridge or his sister Dorothy, confident in the power of their love to support his often painful and uncertain explorations.

Through the poems collected in the "Lyrical Ballads", Wordsworth is committed to acknowledging the lives of those who exist beyond the social order of identity and recognition, and through an imaginative sensitivity to human suffering, he attains an emphatic understanding of the experience of loss and the possibility of mourning. Particularly in the narrative poems, we are presented with characters who have experienced separation and loss to varying degrees: like "Michael", who grieves for his lost son, and who endures the heart-breaking sorrow only through the power of love: "There is a comfort in the strength of love; / 'Twill make a thing endurable, which else / Would break the heart" (Wordsworth, 1984: 236), Margaret, of "The Ruined Cottage", frozen in time and space as she dementedly awaits the return of her long-departed husband, and whose psychological fragmentation and despair is mirrored in the signs of ruin and decay imprinted on her cottage: "About the fields I wander, knowing this / Only, that what I seek I cannot find" (Wordsworth, 1984: 40), and "The Old Cumberland Beggar", bereft of name and home, who unknowingly elicits the poet's emphatic feeling and reflection on the universality of human needs and desires:

> ...the poorest poor
> Long for some moments in a weary life
> When they can know and feel that they have been
> Themselves the fathers and the dealers out
> Of some small blessings, have been kind to such
> As needed kindness, for this single cause,
> That we have all of us one human heart (Wordsworth, 1984: 53).

These characters portray varying levels of alienation and dislocation, from community, purpose, or self, which accompanies the "progress" and materialism of industrialization, and the estrangement between the subject and the environment is depicted by the poet as an emotional and personal loss.[5] According to David Bromwich, these characters, particularly the Cumberland beggar, portray an image of humanity which exists outside of conventionally assumed categories: "what is suspended is the rational conception of a person, a plan of life, a social context with intelligible meanings and obligations", (Bromwich, 2000: 5), and yet these poems "make us know more deeply certain feelings that belong to humankind" (Bromwich, 2000: 97) The narrative element of these poems gives voice to these otherwise silent and ignored experiences of human sorrow, and manifests the connection between mourning and language which became central to psychoanalytic practice. In "The Idiot Boy" Wordsworth presents the inner world of a boy whose linguistic limitations prevent expression and communication; Johnny's speech is beyond the reach of the untrained ear. However, the mother's love for her son gives her access to his thoughts and feelings, and his humanity is dignified by the language through which this understanding is described. The language and subject-matter of these poems resulted in rejection and criticism which Wordsworth answers with his radical philosophy of poetry as "a natural delineation of human passions, human characters, and human incidents" (Wordsworth, 2002: 50). This is the claim asserted in the preface to the collection, and through the poems this claim is reiterated and justified as the poet argues for the dignity of all human beings regardless of social definition:

> ...'Tis Nature's law
> That none, the meanest of created things,
> Of forms created the most vile and brute,
> The dullest or most noxious, should exist
> Divorced from good, a spirit and a pulse of good,
> A life and soul to every mode of being
> Inseparably linked (Wordsworth, 1984: 51).[6]

Wordsworth's aim is to highlight the universality of human experience, and "to shew that men who do not wear fine cloaths can feel deeply"

---

[5] The alienation of the individual in modern times is a theme explored in many literary and philosophical works, and is a basis of Eliot's poem, "The Wasteland", which will be examined in the next chapter.

[6] These lines address the ambiguities of the human condition explored by the writers of previous sections; the proximity of good and evil as outlined by Nietzsche and Ricoeur, the co-existence of the sublime and the monstrous as discussed by Žižek, and the call for a realistic appraisal of human nature by Freud.

(Wordsworth, 2002: 65). These thoughts provide a visionary contrast to the technological and utilitarian attitude which became popular in the service of the industrial revolution and its aftermath, and the poet's opposition to prevalent thinking is a significant characteristic of romantic poetry. This is the argument proffered by Dawson, in his essay "Poetry in an Age of Revolution":

> The real focus of the Romantics' critique of their age is on the moral and social values in whose name both the increase of industry and the rationalization of agriculture took place. These social tendencies implied a redefinition and a revaluation of human nature and of the human person to which the poets were all finally opposed (Dawson, 2005: 67).

The interdependence of human subjects, the mediation necessary for identity and recognition,[7] and the universal dignity of each human being, underlie Wordsworth's sense of love which opens an alternative path to understanding: "we have all of us one human heart" (Wordsworth, 1984: 53), and which recalls Buber's vision of the I-Thou relationship as prerequisite to genuine encounter, and other philosophical reflections on love and friendship.[8] He hopes, through his poetry, to enhance the recognition of this intersubjectivity:

> I hope…they may…in some small degree enlarge our feelings of reverence for our species, and our knowledge of human nature, by shewing that our best qualities are possessed by men whom we are too apt to consider, not with reference to the points in which they resemble us, but to those in which they manifestly differ from us (Wordsworth, 2002: 66).

The understandable reluctance to expose the self to the vulnerability inherent in love, its potential transience and infirmity, and "the impotence of grief" (Wordsworth, 1984: 43) in the experience of loss, are obstacles to the repeated embrace of love in its totality. Wordsworth's commitment to the significance of love does not negate the difficulties which this implies, and some of his greatest poems, such as "The Prelude" and the "Immortality

---

[7] The interdependence of identity and recognition is a theme explored by Ricoeur throughout his philosophical writings, for example *Oneself as Another* and *The Course of Recognition*. It is also relevant to Lacan's exposition of the mirror stage wherein the child/adult increasingly seeks recognition of identity and worth in the reflection of others.

[8] For example, Heidegger's concept of "care", Derrida's reflections on "the gift" and "forgiveness", and Foucault's critique of institutional violence directed against the unacceptable 'other', whether criminal, madman, or political rebel.

Ode", can be seen as an attempt to work through the process of grief pertaining to loss and change, and ultimately to enhance self-understanding.

The autobiographical and confessional nature of Wordsworth's poetic inspiration portrays a commitment to introspective analysis and questioning, and a persistent revisiting of past experiences in order to map the poet's development and elicit greater understanding of his emotional and mental constitution. An examination of the different developmental phases of a life inevitably confronts the poet with the reality of loss; every life is marked with little deaths as growth and change imply the necessity to relinquish the familiar in an embrace of the new. When loss is experienced as an involuntary removal of that which is held dear, the human response is to resist the perceived stealth of what is considered essential to the self through whatever means present themselves: flight from reality takes many forms, and Wordsworth acknowledges this human trait:

> And is there one, the wisest and the best
> Of all mankind, who does not sometimes wish
> For things which cannot be, who would not give,
> If so he might, to duty and to truth
> The eagerness of infantile desire?
> (Wordsworth, 1984: 392).

The joys and sufferings which compose the lived experience of the human being are seen by Wordsworth as being vulnerable to loss and change:

> Unhappy man! Thy sole delightful hour
> Flies first; it is thy miserable dower
> Only to taste of joy that thou may'st pine
> A loss, which rolling suns shall ne'er restore
> (Wordsworth, 1984: 20).

The process of growth in the human being as well as in the world of nature, involves a simultaneous shedding of the old in an accommodation of the new, and the ebb and flow which permeates all of life is sometimes reflected in emotional reactions: "As high as we have mounted in delight / In our dejection do we sink as low" (Wordsworth, 1984: 261). Maturation implies a subtle distancing from infancy, childhood and youth, but the changes and losses which are wrought in the human experience do not have the consolation of retrieval or renewal that nature enjoys.[9] As

---

[9] Adam Phillips suggests an interesting analysis of the losses implicit in the inevitable transition from childhood passion and intensity to adult compromise and

Thomas Kinsella reflects in his poem "Mirror in February", facing his middle-aged face in the mirror, "I read that I have looked my last on youth / And little more; for they are not made whole / That reach the age of Christ", and in contrast to the rejuvenation of the trees outside his window, he resigns himself to the reality that he is "not young, and not renewable, but man" (Kinsella, 1996: 54). The inevitability of loss, and in particular the loss of unconscious and unquestioned union and integration with the natural universe which characterizes the child's experience, "the radiance which was once so bright", is a central theme explored in the "Immortality Ode" (Wordsworth, 1984: 297): "But yet I know, where'er I go, / That there hath passed a glory from the earth". As an adult poet eliciting the power of memory to enhance self-understanding, Wordsworth evokes images, of people, places and events from his earlier self, and from contemplation on this period of life, he develops a conviction that it is a stage of unrepeatable innocence, creativity and freedom. Freud questions this evocation of childhood and refers to the impact of retrospection in the formation of adult memories of earlier experiences: "This age of childhood, in which the sense of shame is unknown, seems a paradise when we look back upon it later, and paradise itself is nothing but the mass-fantasy of the childhood of the individual" (Freud, 1997: 139, 140). Yet, echoing Wordsworth's reference to "the radiance" of the child, Freud also laments the "influence" of forces such as "religious education" which results in "relative atrophy" in the adult subject: "Think of the depressing contrast between the radiant intelligence of a healthy child and the feeble intellectual powers of the average adult" (Freud, 1995: 715). The attributes of childhood which Wordsworth laments, "The things which I have seen I now can see no more", precede the development of "the sense of shame" resulting from the constraining and limiting influences of a gradual adaptation to social life, with its demands for conformity and acquiescence,[10] and convince the poet that the child is the "best philosopher", (Wordsworth, 1984: 299), having a wisdom which is not distorted by external and conflicting expectations. Buber echoes this sentiment, stating that in attempting an understanding of the human subject, and especially the development of the human relationship to

---

disillusionment; he suggests that writers such as "Rousseau...Blake... Wordsworth...and Freud...seemed to retell the biblical story of the Fall...in this tradition...there is a new fall, the fall into adulthood...the fall out of childhood" (Phillips, 2005: 71).

[10] One is reminded here of Lacan's mirror stage when the child loses contact with the real self and enters the imaginary and symbolic realms wherein one's identity is increasingly mirrored through the recognition of others.

others and to the world, "We receive fuller knowledge from the child" (Buber, 2004a: 26). Using his personal memories, Wordsworth associates childhood with unfettered imagination, primary feeling, and the possibility of union with the expansive world of nature: "A child, I held unconscious intercourse / With the eternal Beauty, drinking in / A pure organic pleasure" (Wordsworth, 1984: 390). With the loss of the intensity of instinctual drives and the oceanic feeling of being at one with the universe,[11] Wordsworth discerns in the transition to adulthood a substitution of learned behaviours, adherence to social norms, and preoccupation with material affairs: "Shades of the prison-house begin to close / Upon the growing boy". Meanwhile, the urgency of loss is temporarily repressed and denied, "doomed to sleep" (Wordsworth: 1984: 390), only to surface in dreams and memory, and in a yearning to re-capture some of the magic of this lost time when "I conversed with things that really are" (Wordsworth, 1984: 402). The reference to "things that really are" suggests a parallel to Lacan's differentiation of the real from the imaginary and the symbolic, and his exposition of the mirror stage as the developmental moment when the real is distorted and overshadowed by the attraction of the image. Lacan links this development with the growing awareness of loss, a sense of lack, and the birth of desire which is often misinterpreted and directed away from its real target and onto an illusory other who will fulfill this lack. The repression of these early memories, these "days / Disowned by memory" (Wordsworth, 1984: 391), through being split off from awareness, constitutes a fragmentation of identity and personality, a "wavering of my mind" (Wordsworth, 1984: 391), and an alienating dejection which thwarts love of self and one's surroundings. A sense of estrangement from parts of the self, from objects of love, and from the harmony of nature, combines with a nostalgia for what is lost, and in Wordsworth this nostalgia is strengthened to become a determined commitment to employ the power of memory as a method of restoring that which is gone. In his analysis of the poet's work, and in particular "Tintern Abbey" as a poem deemed to be unsurpassable as a poem of memory, Harold Bloom credits Wordsworth, along with Nietzsche and Freud, with radically expanding the concept of memory through addressing the complexities, defenses and repressions which impact on this phenomenon (Bloom, 1976: 52).

The attempted recovery of these early years, through reflection, revisiting, and memory, while never fully achievable, "We see but darkly /

---

[11] Freud referred to the narcissism which can be traced to the feeling of omnipotence and self-centeredness which characterizes early childhood.

Even when we look behind us" (Wordsworth, 1984: 417), is deemed by Wordsworth to be essential to self-knowledge and integration: "to understand myself" and "to know / with better knowledge how the heart was framed" (Wordsworth, 1984: 391). This is the work which he undertakes in his autobiographical poem "The Prelude". He is aware of the difficulty of this project, "hard task to analyze a soul" (Wordsworth, 1984: 398), and anticipating the environment of a psychoanalytic encounter, he adopts a confessional tone in addressing an emphatic listener whose presence, real or imagined, enables understanding and interpretation. As a reading of his own psychic processes, the self-initiated self-exploration undertaken by the poet is a paradigm of the psychoanalytic rule of free-association on which Freud bases the success of the analytic encounter. It is an example of an important shift of focus in romantic poetry, as the emphasis is changed from its mimetic qualities, its mirroring of the external world, to an illumination of the inner experience, the growth of the poet's mind and the development of the self. A recollection and appreciation of one's past enables an understanding of one's present situation – a central tenet of Freudian psychoanalysis – and the poet "endeavoured to retrace / My life through its first years" (Wordsworth, 1984: 392) in order to discover "the individual hour in which / His habits were first sown" (Wordsworth, 1984: 397). "The Prelude", therefore, anticipates the general Freudian acceptance of the importance of childhood in the adult psyche, but it also adheres to Nietzsche's doctrine of the eternal recurrence, the acceptance and integration of all aspects of one's fate, one's life.

This attempted integration involves a recognition and a re-evaluation of ideals and dreams which are sometimes betrayed or lost through the contingencies of reality, inner and outer experiences. The courage to accept the possibility that one's convictions and hopes are susceptible to correction and revision requires an honest appraisal of one's past and present, in the emotional, spiritual, and physical realms, and in the case of Wordsworth, a determination to transcend and transform loss, failure, and betrayal into a reconciling triumph. In Books IX and X of "The Prelude", the poet describes the youthful search for meaning and purpose within the given circumstances of life, in his case, amid the contradictory ideals and methods of the French Revolution: "I looked for something that I could not find' (Wordsworth, 1984: 510), and the difficulty in matching one's inmost thought and feelings with those of popular opinion: "impotent to make my hopes put on / The shape of theirs, my understanding bend / In honour to their honour" (Wordsworth, 1984: 515). The temptation to escape the pain of solitude through immersion in the "crowd" is explored by Buber as an obstacle to genuine relationship, and results in Nietzsche's "herd-mentality". By contrast, the experience of emotional and intellectual intimacy which accompanies transitory periods of shared commitment and hope has the power to transcend human isolation and mistrust: "Bliss was it in that dawn to be alive, / But to be young was very heaven" (Wordsworth, 1984: 550). The alternation of certainty and doubt, of hope and despair, suggests to the poet that his mind is divided and conflicted: "Having two natures in me, joy the one, / The other melancholy", and he struggles with "false imagination" and "the errors into which I was betrayed / By present objects, and by reasonings false" (Wordsworth, 1984: 554). The reality of psychic conflict and the fragmented multiplicity of the self are key themes in the work of Freud and Ricoeur, and Wordsworth attempts to transcend the potential distortions and limitations which may be unconsciously assumed in the absence of awareness and understanding.

The poetry of Wordsworth confronts the reality of loss and separation in human life, in relationship, in ideals, and in a persistently changing sense of self which is sometimes susceptible to betrayal when "the pledges interchanged / With our inner being are forgot" (Wordsworth, 1984: 417). Using his personal development and memory as a paradigm, he gives an honest exposition of the anger, confusion and despair which ensue from these experiences: "Thus strangely did I war against myself" (Wordsworth, 1984: 560), but he searches for a power which can transform such loss into a triumph of restoration. This power he identifies as love, love of nature and love of human beings. His love of nature, as a power and harmony pervading all of life, is a commitment to Nietzsche's *amor fati*, as he acknowledges that this life, this world, is the ground of human experience: "in the very world which is the world / Of all of us, the place in which, in the end, / We find our happiness, or not at all" (Wordsworth, 1984: 550). Buber agrees with this assertion: "human life exists, though brokenly, in the world" (Buber, 2004: 109), while Nietzsche echoes this sentiment stating that human "happiness should smell of the earth and not of contempt for the earth" (Nietzsche, 2003a: 140), and he claims that "a good, human thing was the world to me today, this world of which so many evil things are said' (Nietzsche, 2003a: 206). For Wordsworth, it is only in the "familiar face of life", the ordinary and commonplace, that love can be discovered and experienced, and despite the vulnerability which characterizes human existence, he insists on the power of love to maintain hope and resilience: "To fear and love / To love as first and chief, for there fear ends" (Wordsworth, 1984: 582).

Solitude and Attachment

> Points have we all of us within our
> souls
> Where all stand single (Wordsworth,
> 1984: 409).

The gradual repression of instinctual "appetites", "glad animal movements", and "the coarser pleasures2 through which the young child apprehends the environment (Wordsworth, 1984: 133), results from internal and external pressures to adjust to the social world; it is "the inevitable yoke" (Wordsworth, 1984: 300). The above quoted words bring to mind Nietzsche's analysis that man has raised himself too much above the animal, and that this distorted view of human nature which denies the often unconscious impact of natural instincts and drives, has diminished the capacity of fully loving and embracing life in its complexity. The artifice of social life, with its attending values and expectations, becomes an unconscious burden which restricts individuality and creativity:

> Full soon thy soul shall have her earthly freight,
> And custom lie upon thee with a weight,
> Heavy as frost, and deep almost as life
> (Wordsworth, 1984: 300).

The negation of certain aspects of humanity, where "the true and the false [become] so inseparably interwoven" results in a "thrusting out of sight the plain humanities of nature by a motley masquerade of tricks" (Wordsworth, 1984: 617). The repression of "the plain humanities of nature" is the demanded price of socialization and civilization, as Freud convincingly argues in *Civilization and its Discontents.* At each developmental stage, the child surrenders something of the "bliss" and "glory" of "a time when meadow, grove, and stream, / The earth, and every common sight, / To me did seem / Apparelled in celestial light" (Wordsworth, 1984: 297), until eventually this vision of life fades from awareness: "At length the Man perceives it die away, / And fade into the light of common day". In Freudian terms, the superego exerts an increasing influence as the child/adult accommodates itself to the demands of civilization, and authenticity is replaced by imitation and performance: "As if his whole vocation / Were endless imitation" (Wordsworth, 1984: 300).

The confining boundaries of socialization, experienced in education, employment and family life, diminish the subject's freedom to express and to act on individual feeling and desire, as conformity and popularity take precedence over personal values and original thought. This jeopardizes the possibility of love between unique subjects, as "the dreary intercourse of daily life" (Wordsworth, 1984: 135) overshadows "the primal sympathy" (Wordsworth, 1984: 302) which discerns in nature and humanity a force of beauty and of love:

> The insinuated scoff of coward tongues,
> And all that silent language which so oft
> In conversation betwixt man and man
> Blows from the human countenance all trace
> Of beauty and of love (Wordsworth, 1984: 404).

These lines resound with Buber's contention that much of human conversation is motivated by utility, promotion of self image, and fear of disclosure of vulnerability and imperfection; it is a pseudo-dialogue which precludes genuine communication between self and other, and it is, in Lacanian terms, "empty speech" which seeks to hide or disguise personal truth. Thus, life can be diminished to a futile struggle to gain acceptance, security, and admiration, through an endless series of performances and projects:

> Then will he fit his tongue
> To dialogues of business, love, or strife;
> But it will not be long
> Ere this be thrown aside,
> And with new joy and pride
> The little Actor cons another part,
> Filling from time to time his 'humorous stage'
> With all the Persons, down to palsied Age,
> That Life brings with her in her Equipage
> (Wordsworth, 1984: 300).

The preoccupations and demands of social life, "Empty noise / And superficial pastimes" (Wordsworth, 1984: 410), are also sought as a protection against the pain of solitude wherein one may be faced with a frightening realization of vulnerability and need, and an awareness that "every soul is a world of its own" (Nietzsche, 2003a: 234). The subject, while inherently alone and separate, physically and psychologically, nevertheless is imbued with the drive to connect with what is exterior to itself. Wordsworth echoes Nietzsche's doctrine of the will to power when he states that "there is an active principle alive in all things" which seeks to move beyond itself:

> All beings have their properties which spread
> Beyond themselves, a power by which they make
> Some other being conscious of their life
> (Wordsworth, 1984: 676).

This urge to connect, to make an impact on the other, as it is perceived in the natural and the human domain, is intrinsic to human existence: "for we live by hope / And by desire; they are the very blood / By which we move" (Wordsworth, 1984: 677), and thus the reality of human solitude is constantly resisted and denied. This is the paradoxical nature of the human being, and in acknowledging the apparent contradiction Wordsworth does not negate the validity of either solitude or connection. The conflicting desires for solitude and community, and the simultaneous fears of isolation and engulfment, are explored by the poet in his quest for self-knowledge. According to Jones, this dilemma is central to Wordsworth's self-analysis: "Solitude and attachment, the huge abstractions moving through Wordsworth's life and poetry" (Jones, 1970: 48). The poet confronts the repercussions of this conflict through a persistent attempt at deciphering, through reflection, memory and analysis, his own psychic interiority as it reveals itself in honest contemplation: "What distinguishes Wordsworth is the enormous importance which he attaches to introspection, or the inward eye" (Jones, 1970: 92). The poet concludes that the real difficulties and conflicts exist within:

> When men in various vessels roam the deep
> Of social life, and turns of chance prevail
> Various and sad, how many thousands weep
> Beset with foes more fierce than e'er assail
> The savage without home in winter's keenest gale
> (Wordsworth, 1984: 14)

According to the poet, the only possibility of approaching an understanding of human nature is through self-exploration, "by stripping our own hearts naked" (Wordsworth, 1984: 622), and succumbing to the perils and insights which solitude can provide: "Nor star nor needle know the tempests of the soul" (Wordsworth, 1984: 27).

The introspection pursued by Wordsworth in a search for self-understanding, where "we have traced the stream / From darkness, and the very place of birth / In its blind cavern" (Wordsworth, 1984: 583), resounds with the psychoanalytic process of remembering and interpreting, as illusions and repressions give way to expression and integration. Thus Wordsworth addresses his doubts and confusions to an understanding and attentive observer and listener, he freely explores the multi-faceted nature of his emotional and mental development, and he is rewarded with insights which are difficult to accept but which contain the source of true liberation. In Book XIII of "The Prelude", he reflects on one such discovery, the realization of personal freedom and responsibility, and anticipating Lacan's assertion that the patient must eventually relinquish the illusion of "the one supposed to know", and look to his/her own heart and desire, Wordsworth argues that imagination and love are "each in each", and can only be developed in a spirit of individual and personal truth:

> Here must thou be, O Man!
> Strength to thyself; no Helper hast thou here;
> Here keepest thou thy individual state:
> No other can divide with thee this work,
> No secondary hand can intervene
> To fashion this ability. 'Tis thine
> In the recesses of thy nature, far
> From reach of outward fellowship,
> Else 'tis not thine at all (Wordsworth, 1984: 583).

However, having gained this sense of self-responsibility and self-ownership, the subject is enabled to experience the joy and transformation of love in honest relationship, (honest because it is not masking need or fear). The connection between self-awareness and the embrace of the other underlies the explorations of Wordsworth's poetry, and is particularly portrayed in "The Prelude"; as Gill explains, "Tracing the development of his poetic imagination Wordsworth needs to demonstrate that its growth involved the embrace of other human beings, that its power stemmed not from solipsistic self-communing but from its human centredness" (Gill, 1991: 74). An acceptance and an understanding of the self enable an acceptance and a love of others in their 'human, all too human' realities.

Through an imaginative encounter with the inner self and a corresponding openness to the power of the natural world, Wordsworth establishes the possibility of synthesis and reconciliation of apparent opposites; his poetry is essentially a poetry of mediation. The psychoanalyst, Anthony Storr, in his exploration of the joy and pain of solitude, refers to the human desire for "wholeness or integration; a condition in which the different elements of the psyche, both conscious and unconscious, become welded together in a new unity", and he points to Wordsworth's "Prelude" as an example of this process (Storr, 1997: 193). In this quest for unity and integration, Wordsworth questions the reality of intransigent binaries, and destabilizes the perceived boundaries between human and non-human, small and great, outer and inner, and especially solitude and connection. Echoing the poet's attempt at synthesis and wholeness, Storr explains the elusiveness of this goal while emphasizing its significance:

> Man's adaptation to the world is largely governed by the development of the imagination and hence of an inner world of the psyche which is necessarily at variance with the external world. Perfect happiness, the oceanic feeling of complete harmony between inner and outer worlds, is only transiently possible. Man is constantly in search of happiness but, by his very nature, is precluded from finally or permanently achieving it in either interpersonal relations or in creative endeavour…The happiest lives are probably those in which neither interpersonal relationships nor impersonal interests are idealized as the only way to salvation. The desire and pursuit of the whole must comprehend both aspects of human nature (Storr, 1997: 202).

To strengthen his argument, Storr closes his reflection with the following lines from the "Prelude":

> When from our better selves we have too long
> Been parted by the hurrying world, and droop,
> Sick of its business, of the pleasures tired,
> How Gracious, how benign, is Solitude
> (Wordsworth, 1888: 587).

In his extensive commentary on *The Nature of Love,* Irving Singer points to the "Romantic preoccupation with oneness [as] a reaction against the dualism of the seventeenth and early eighteenth centuries", and sees the role of the imagination as that of enabling harmony and unity of phenomena which previous philosophies had dissected: "Imagination assumed its central importance because it seemed, by its very nature, to unify the categories of sense and intellect, passion and rationality, matter and mind2 (Singer, 1984: 288). For Wordsworth, his abiding love of nature encompasses a love of all of life, and thus obliterates the separation of the human and the material world. His love of nature leads him inevitably "to the love of human Kind2 (Wordsworth, 1984: 501), and to an appreciation of love expressed in simplicity and humility, in the "little, nameless, unremembered acts / Of kindness and of love" (Wordsworth, 1984: 132). An appreciation of the ordinary, the simple, and the often unnoted expressions of kindness and love, is also seen by Nietzsche as crucial to our humanity: "Goodwill…I mean those expressions of a friendly disposition in interactions, that smile of the eye, those handclasps, that ease which usually envelops nearly all human actions…it is the continual manifestation of our humanity" (Nietzsche, 1984: 48). The belief in the innate goodness of the human being and the capacity for benevolence and love amidst the inevitable frustrations and failures characteristic of human life, is seen by Stephen Gill as a prevailing conviction throughout the poet's work: "Across his creative lifetime Wordsworth returned repeatedly to meditations on such topics as the relation of human beings to their world, the function of moral development, and the core values which give life its worth" (Gill, 2003: 157). Love of life, in its natural and human manifestations, is one such core value: "We live by admiration, hope, and love" (Wordsworth, 1858: 345). The reality of pain and suffering, of doubt and uncertainty, "The still, sad music of humanity" (Wordsworth, 1984: 134), does not preclude the possibility of a "cheerful faith that all which we behold / Is full of blessings" (Wordsworth, 1984: 135), and this faith is enhanced by momentary feelings of harmony wherein "We see into the life of things" (Wordsworth, 1984: 133). What is then seen, realized, and embraced as a vision of life is the centrality and significance of love as the often difficult, elusive, and thwarted experience of human being:

> From love, for here
> Do we begin and end, all grandeur comes,
> All truth and beauty, from pervading love,
> That gone, we are as dust (Wordsworth, 1984: 582).

CHAPTER EIGHT

T.S. ELIOT

The world of Western Europe which encapsulated the romantic era gradually settled into a period of relative stability and confidence as nation states solidified their positions and began to enjoy a sense of security in the aftermath of revolutionary wars.[1] An optimistic and self-congratulatory attitude, suggesting lasting achievement and on-going progress issuing from a rationalized world, began to express itself in the political, economic and scientific realms, and this was reflected in literature as in other art forms. This attitude of optimism and certitude boasted unprecedented advancement in all areas of human endeavour, and this uncritical idealism and metaphysical transcendence characterized intellectual activity in the literature and philosophy of Western Europe throughout the second half of the nineteenth century.

However, rumblings of discontent and doubt tentatively questioned the validity of this definitive vision of reality, and Nietzsche's onslaught on the metaphysical tradition came before the turn of the century. Gadamer refers to the impact of Nietzsche's "radical questioning": "Nietzsche was less the inventor of some other particular philosophical doctrine than the symbolic expression of the crisis of modern life" (Gadamer, 1991: 218). James McFarlane, co-editor of *Modernism: A Guide to European Literary 1890-1930*, credits Nietzsche with "a uniquely influential role in the Modernist period [due to] his ruthless questioning of the nineteenth century's *idées recus*, [and] his total repudiation of traditional morality" (McFarlane, 1991: 79). Another contributor to this volume, Alan Bullock, asserts that Freud exerted a uniquely significant influence on this period: "No single man, probably, has exercised a greater influence on the ideas, literature and art of the twentieth century than Freud" (Bullock, 1991: 67).

---

[1] The solidification of nation states in this period was considered by Nietzsche to foster estrangement and disintegration; he refers to "the morbid estrangement which the lunacy of nationality has produced and continues to produce between the peoples of Europe", and he claims that this is "only an interlude" preceding an acknowledgement that *"Europe wants to become one"* (Nietzsche, 2003: 189).

A combination of social developments and individual discoveries heralded a gradual unmasking of the illusions supporting traditional values and doctrines; the growing social fragmentation, which paralleled the increasing industrialization and mechanization of work and labour, suggested that progress might be ambiguous and double-edged, while the writings of Marx, Freud and Nietzsche forced a revolutionary challenge to human mastery and knowledge, as Darwin and Einstein offered scientific evidence of misunderstanding and misinterpretation. According to Peter Child's analysis, in his delineation of this period, certain writers effected radical change:

> Certain writers in different fields did change the world in the sense at least of massively altering people's most fundamental interpretations of 'reality'. Not least in any such list would be the six figures...Freud, Darwin, Saussure, Nietzsche, Einstein and Marx...in terms of politics and history, psychology, philosophy, language and science (Childs, 2000: 26).

The role of writers in foreseeing, reflecting and effecting change, particularly in this period of increasing questioning and revaluation is also highlighted by Bullock, in his analysis of modernity:

> It is more likely that the artists, the writers and the thinkers of the 1900s with their more highly developed sensitivity were responsive to trends and conflicts – social, moral, intellectual, spiritual – already beginning to appear over the horizon, and sought for new forms, new languages, in which to project these in advance of their time (Bullock, 1991: 69).

The failure of secularization and technological progress to provide coherent and consistent meaning relating to questions of truth, subjectivity, and tradition, culminated in the incomprehensible horror of World War 1. Conventional norms of individual responsibility and social control buckled under the shocking realization of their failure, and disenchantment with traditional versions of progress and achievement fostered a rejection of established modes of thought and a determination to explore new, "modern", perspectives in viewing and interpreting the new reality which presented itself.

Experimentation, in thought, language, and activity, became characteristic of the "new" era, and this was central to radical developments in all areas of the arts; as such, modernist literature sought to break away from the restricting adherence to preceding traditions, and to creatively respond to the realities of fragmentation and ephemerality which threatened personal and social stability. In the realm of poetry, the search for a revolutionary artistic expression was initiated especially by the American poet, Ezra Pound, as he and his followers repudiated what they saw as the dishonest sentimentality and subjective emotionalism of Wordsworth's romanticism. While Wordsworth saw his poetic vision as a break from his immediately preceding tradition, and although his poetic project involved a revolutionary creation in form and content, the romantic tradition which he had initiated was now deemed to have lost its energy and relevance. The autobiographical nature of romantic poetry, with its narrative and lyrical emphasis, and its pastoral conventions and traditional regularity of rhythm and rhyme, were now considered inadequate to address the modern experience, and a new poetic discipline was inaugurated wherein language and voice were subjected to experimentation and renewal.

As with any historical or literary period, the modernist label is suffused with complexity and contradiction, and its use is inevitably limited to retrospective analysis and interpretation. Most commentators on the period acknowledge the difficulties involved in any attempt to categorize an interpretation of modernism into neat precisions of either time or definition; the seeds of modernism lie beyond the obvious rejection of romanticism and classicism; the concerns and methods of its now-identified intellectual and literary exponents defy any uniform classification; and the reverberations of its radical experimentation and exploration continue to exert an impact in "postmodern" experience. The paradoxical nature of the modern tradition is central to the study of the period by Malcolm Bradbury and James McFarlane:

> The period we are calling the Modern shows us not the mere rehabilitation of the irrational after a period of ordered Realism, or for that matter the reverse, a period of Classicism after a phase of Romanticism, but rather a compounding of all these potentials: the interpenetration, the reconciliation, the coalescence, the fusion – perhaps an appallingly explosive fusion – of reason and unreason, intellect and emotion, subjective and objective (Bradbury and McFarlane, 1991: 48).

The "explosive fusion" was particularly evident in the growing search for new linguistic possibilities deemed necessary to symbolize the experience of thought and feeling which was inaccessible to traditional language usage, and the poetic genre was one significant vehicle of this exploration.

The publication of T.S. Eliot's "The Waste Land" in 1922 is often cited as the inaugural moment in the development of modernist poetry, and in its form and structure, its imagery and references, it epitomizes the successful expression of Pound's stated poetic requirements. Lyndall

Gordon, in her account of the poet's life, describes it as "the poem that fired the imagination of the 'lost' generation" (Gordon, 2000: 146). The poetry of Eliot grapples with the apparent absence of meaning in modern life; it exposes the personal and social fragmentation and disenchantment often masked by assumed conventions in behaviour, communication, and relationships; and it explores the diverse impediments to authenticity and integrity in the private and public expression of experience. J.C.C. Mays sees this as the achievement of Eliot's poetry: "He is a great modern poet for the reason that he translated the sad accidents of his own life into poetry in a way that miraculously contained the exultation and despair of a generation" (Mays, 2006: 110-111). In form and content, Eliot's poetry launched a uniquely original and unfamiliar interpretation and portrayal of modern reality. The personal voice, the Wordsworthian "I", was replaced by a diversity of voices and personas, reflecting the absence of a unified, harmonious self; the beauty of the pastoral landscape was foreshadowed by the drab, disparate, sprawling sterility of urban development, and the pleasurable sound effects of familiar rhythm and structural constancy gave way to an unpredictable multiplicity of contrasting styles and a reversal of traditional associations of sequence and destination.[2]

The urgent necessity of initiating a new poetic tradition is the logical supplement to the realization that the old conventions and assumptions no longer served to express and embrace a new world devoid of prescriptive rules and values: "We cannot revive old factions / We cannot restore old policies / Or follow an antique drum" (Eliot, 2004: 196). Eliot's use of language to accommodate the new realities in poetic form results in a radically different achievement, an achievement that reverberates through linguistic explorations, in philosophy and in literature, to the present day. Eliot espoused an "Impersonal theory of poetry" which questioned the relation of the poem to its author, stating that "Honest criticism and sensitive appreciation is directed not upon the poet but upon the poetry" (Eliot, 1975: 40), and he disputed Wordsworth's poetic formula of "emotion recollected in tranquility": "For although every poet starts from his own emotions, his struggle must be to transmute his personal and private agonies into something rich and strange, something universal and impersonal" (Eliot, 1975: 17).[3] However, Eliot acknowledged the revolutionary poetic vision of the romantic poet, and he concurred with

---

[2] This is not to deny that modern poetry also built upon the Romantic tradition. The influence of the Romantic inheritance on modern poetry is explored by Cleanth Brooks in *Modern Poetry & the Tradition*.

[3] This is a quotation from Frank Kermode's introduction to the *Selected Prose of T.S. Eliot*.

Wordsworth's insistence on the use of language reflecting common speech:

> While poetry attempts to convey something beyond what can be conveyed in prose rhythms, it remains, all the same, one person talking to another...the immediacy of poetry to conversation is not a matter on which we can lay down exact laws. Every revolution in poetry is apt to be, and sometimes to announce itself to be a return to common speech. That is the revolution which Wordsworth announced in his prefaces, and he was right (Eliot, 1975: 111).

However, as Eliot points out, "meanwhile the spoken language goes on changing" (Eliot, 1975: 112), and this change is often a reflection of alterations in every sphere of human living. In his essay "Eliot as Philosopher", Richard Shusterman points to Eliot's attempted fusion of tradition and interpretation, comparing it with the hermeneutical philosophy of Gadamer, and states that "as Eliot recognized with Wittgenstein, since language depends on social use, its meaning changes over history through the changing situations and applications which it must address" (Shusterman, 2006: 41). Thus, in the perceived unfamiliarity of a new age, a new poetic form is deemed essential. According to Helen Gardner, one of the earliest commentators on Eliot's work, the poet has "effected a modification and an enrichment of the whole English poetic tradition" (Gardner, 1972: 2). Poems such as "The Waste Land", "The Love Song of J. Alfred Prufrock", "Four Quarters", and "The Hollow Men", wrestle with the uncharted territory of social and individual disenchantment and dissolution, the eclipse of personal and collective meaning and purpose, and the alienation of the subject from previously assumed sources of direction and support.

Sterility, meaninglessness, bleakness and brokenness, are the recurring images pervading Eliot's modernist vision.[4] Unity and coherence are confined to the poetic structure, while disintegration and dissonance ground the thematic backdrop. Whence the possibility of love in this portrayal of reality? The vision of life, in the physical, psychological, and spiritual spheres that are explored and interpreted in Eliot's work, may be

---

[4] The sense of meaningless, despair and bleakness which is characteristic of much modernist literature is reflective of "a world threatened by disintegration": this is the description of Albert Camus in his Nobel speech, and as a representative of a later generation of modernists, he offers the following understanding of the disillusionment of the age: "I think that we should understand – without ceasing to fight it – the error of those who in an excess of despair have asserted their right to dishonour and have rushed into the nihilism of the era" (Camus, 1957: etext).

described as a world reflecting the absence of love; this absence is palpable in the feigned attempts at communication between human beings, in the ceaseless longing for security and permanence, and particularly in the self-disgust which is only fleetingly averted through momentary immersion in social niceties and pseudo-communication: "We grope together / And avoid speech" (Eliot, 2004: 85). Gardner argues that "love, including in itself all other virtues", is a central theme of Eliot's poetry, from its absence in the earlier poems, "where faith and hope and love are known in terms of their opposites", and which "compelled him to contemplate another vision", to the conclusion of the "Four Quartets", that "All shall be well, when all is gathered in love, and the rose, the symbol of natural beauty and natural love, is one with the fire, the love by which all things are made" (Gardner, 1972: 185). A reading of Eliot's poetry therefore enables an investigation of the obstacles to love, the resulting personal and collective malaise, and thus indirectly highlights the urgency and persistence pertaining to an inescapable search for love's possibility.

Fragmentation

> These fragments I have shored against
> my ruins (Eliot, 2004: 75).

The sense of fragmentation reflected in the social and personal reality of the early twentieth century is captured in its essence in the words of a near contemporary of Eliot, W.B. Yeats: "Things fall apart; the centre cannot hold" (Yeats, 1967: 99). The collapse of the "centre", the systems and structures hitherto credited with authority and management in the political, social, economic and personal realms of human existence, expressed itself in undeniable terms of material destruction and financial ruin which characterized the early twentieth century: "an age which advances progressively backwards" (Eliot, 2004: 161). The urban hell of London city epitomized for Eliot the post-war reality of devastation and failure, and the city is the canvas upon which he portrays the human face of this alienating environment. It is representative of the "Unreal City" and the corresponding unreality of the human experience within its confines: "I was neither living nor dead" (Eliot, 2004: 62). In an essay titled "The Poetry of the City", G.M. Hyde argues that "the Modernist literature was born in the city and with Baudelaire – especially with his discovery that crowds mean loneliness and that the terms 'multitude' and 'solitude' are inter-changeable for a poet with an active and fertile imagination" (Hyde, 1991: 337). The words of Nietzsche point to the experience of loneliness amid the pseudo-camaraderie to which one does not really belong: "to be thus in company is truly more lonely than to be alone" (Nietzsche, 2003a: 177). Loneliness, anonymity, and isolation characterize the modernist world, and suggest what Buber refers to as one of the "epochs of homelessness" in "the history of the human spirit" (Buber, 2004: 150). Eliot paints the death-in-life landscape of "half-deserted streets" and "sawdust restaurants with oyster-shells" (Eliot, 2004: 13), and discerns behind the stagnating concealment of "fog" and "smoke" another landscape of disunity, conflict and confusion. This is the subject of R.D. Laing's aptly titled book *The Divided Self.* It is the intensely self-conscious alienation of personal psychic fragmentation, the split self of public compliance and civility and private turmoil and rebellion. Peter Childs links this modernist depiction of the fragmented self to the unavoidable influence of Freud's insights: "With the publication of Freud's work, *The Interpretation of Dreams*, 1899, it became clear to many writers that there wasn't a unitary narrative self to which each of us might conform...the self was not fixed and stable, but evolving, fluid, discontinuous and fragmented" (Childs, 2000: 51). It is in this psychological, emotional and mental breakdown of purpose and direction that Eliot situates the collapse of the centre, and his poetry explores the alternating efforts and impasses which characterize the hidden experience of that inner desolation.

In a poem which encapsulates the inner torment of the modern subject, "The Love Song of J. Alfred Prufrock", Eliot posits in the title the dilemma of human desire and social demand. The poem is titled "love son", suggestive of the significance of love in the maintenance of life, but the emotions and thoughts expressed through the poem's persona highlight the obstacles and rationalizations which silence the henceforth repressed desire and fundamental need to love and to be loved underlying the psychic conflict of the split self, the "you and I" of Prufrock's monologic ruminations. The poem therefore undertakes to articulate the unsayable, to symbolize the unconscious flow of conflicting thoughts and emotions, "to make audible or perceptible the mind's inaudible conversations" (Bradbury and McFarlane, 1991: 49). The impossibility of comprehensive articulation, the ceaseless conflict between desire and fear, and the apparently futile attempts to reconcile personal integrity with public image, are explored by Eliot in this early poem, and these themes are consistently developed throughout his poetic career: "Themes and approaches which preoccupied him to the end of his career already emerge in "Prufrock", the opening poem of the first book...it strikes the tone of effort and the futility of effort which is central to Eliot's writing" (Mays,

2006: 110-111). The resulting malaise pervading the individual and his environment is symptomatic of un-lived life, and this is "a central, recurring theme of Eliot's poetry" according to Raine: "Prufrock's failure to seize the day, his resolve to remain repressed, avoiding the element of risk that is part of truly living, is something Eliot was to return to" (Raine, 2006: 2).

The persona of the poem exudes a fearful timidity portrayed in a repressed yearning to connect and to communicate, to speak and to be heard, to reveal and to be affirmed. These desires, suggestive of innate human needs, (as explored by all the writers outlined in this study), are couched in persistent self-questioning and procrastination: " 'Do I dare? and 'Do I dare?'"(Eliot, 2004: 14). The risk being questioned is that of vulnerability in the awareness that one cannot predict or control the reaction of another; but Prufrock projects his own self-depreciation and self-loathing onto any encountered other and imagines the expected rejection by the other as a repetition of his own self-criticism: "I should have been a pair of ragged claws / Scuttling across the floors of silent seas" (Eliot, 2004: 15). Here the voice of the internal superego is berating and dismissive, resulting in a paralysis which makes action impossible. Freud's description of the "ego ideal"[5] as an agency corresponding to "what we call our 'conscience'", suggests a self-consciousness which is sometimes experienced in "delusions of being …watched", judged, and evaluated: "A power of this kind, watching, discovering and criticizing all our intentions, does really exist. Indeed, it exists in every one of us in normal life" (Freud, 1995: 559). This perceived awareness of a watchful gaze, judging our actions, is also suggested by Lacan's big Other. Eliot's portrayal of the self is that of a battleground between desire and social constraint, or as Freud described it, between the id and the superego. Prufrock's self-image, which he attempts to conceal even from himself, is

---

[5] Ambiguity pertains to the notion of the "ego-ideal", as Freud's reference here suggests strong links with a berating super-ego. However, Lacan sees the development of the "ego-ideal" as contingent on maturation and self-striving, and he links its acknowledgement with the desire and the possibility of love. On one level, the "ego ideal" is at a distance from the reality of the self, and therefore may be suggestive of a false or a public image which disguises the perceived fallibility and flawed nature of the self; there is thus a gap between the desired presentation of the subject and the privately-held images of the self. On another level, the "ego-ideal" is a goal that is striven towards, a goal that is never permanently reached, as the nature of the organism insists that it continually seeks to expand and to grow. Nietzsche's doctrine of the will to power and Lacan's reflections on "desire" are evoked here.

that of a worthless coward living his life in carefully rehearsed performances, patterned responses, and adherence to empty rituals of trivial routines: "I have measured out my life with coffee spoons" (Eliot, 2004: 14). The image of the "coffee spoons" is an example of Eliot's formulation of the "objective correlative" whereby emotion is expressed through "a set of objects, a situation, a chain of events which shall be the formula of that particular emotion; such that when the external facts, which must end in sensory experience, are given, the emotion is immediately evoked" (Eliot, 1975: 48). Murdoch explains it thus: "[With] T.S. Eliot's 'objective correlative' we see through, pass through, the busy multiplicity of particulars and contemplate, touch, become one with, 'the thing itself'" (Murdoch, 1993: 59). The ironic juxtaposition of the trivial action and the measurement of a life evokes the regret and despair of a humdrum existence and a wasted lifetime. The rigorous shielding of the self in habitualisation, of behaviour, speech, appearance and image, defensively blocks an opening of the self to the other, and therefore poses an obstacle to the experience of love.

Prufrock's fear of vulnerability and failure to embrace risk is coupled with an obsessive concern with outward appearance, public image, and the conformity to expected behaviours: "Shall I wear my hair behind? Do I dare to eat a peach?" (Eliot, 2004: 16). The repression of his innate needs is reflected in the prudery suggested by the symbolization of his name, and Prufrock baulks at the exposure of his "all too human" reality. Freud's concept of repression and its resultant neuroses is here manifested in poetic form; the conflict between the desire to connect and the fear of ridicule and rejection confines Prufrock to an endless internal monologue which defies decision and resolution, "a hundred visions and revisions" (Eliot, 2004: 14), and which subtly erodes any hope of reconciliation between these warring psychic forces. Exposure of his real self is perceived as a potential assault on his conventional image; he does not dare "disturb the universe" (Eliot, 2004: 14), because he is aware of the fixed identity which has been imposed on him through habit and routine:

> And I have known the eyes already, known them all –
> The eyes that fix you in a formulated phrase,
> And when I am formulated, sprawling on a pin,
> When I am pinned and wriggling on the wall,
> Then how should I begin
> To spit out all the butt-ends of my days and ways?
> And how should I presume? (Eliot, 2004: 15).

The inner torment of his self-conscious sense of inadequacy and his conviction that he is trapped in the critical and disapproving gaze of others is poignantly captured in the imagery of the above lines: the alliteration, assonance and cacophony in words such as "fix", "formulated", "pinned", "sprawling", and "wriggling" convey the tortured psychic incarceration which defines Prufrock's fragmented existence. The maintenance of this identity, although restrictive, painful, and unflattering, appears preferable to the risk of annihilation which its withdrawal would entail. Prufrock's fixed identity is impervious to the change, growth and transformation involved in an openness to loving others and accepting love. It negates and suppresses the desire for the experience of love. Moody suggests that this is the key to Prufrock's fear: "Prufrock's fear is a fear of the human city and of human relations. More particularly, it is a fear of being not understood, not recognized; and so of losing identity, of becoming a non-person", and he goes on to equate this with the desire to be accepted and loved: "It is apparent that the root of his fear is in the primary human need to be loved" (Moody, 1996: 184,185). This resounds with Ricoeur's exploration of the concept of identity, and his understanding that one's identity is often precariously dependent on the "fragile opinion" of the other (Ricoeur, 2002: 121). Prufrock stays locked within the familiarity and security of his fixed image rather than risking the uncertain danger of discovering who he really is. His inner life remains hidden, not just from others, but also from himself.[6]

The conflicting nature of Prufrock's meditations comes to an ironic conclusion with an unfavourable comparison to the heroic stature of another procrastinator, another character whose sensitivity and self-doubt silences his expression of love; Hamlet allows the obstacles of jealousy and betrayal to repress his love for Ophelia, and Prufrock never delivers

---

[6] The mask of conformity to public image implies the existence of a "real" self behind the false façade. The dichotomy between the false and the real self is explored in diverse areas of thought, literature and art. It is particularly central to the work of the psychoanalyst, Donald Winnicot. However, the acceptance of ambivalence in relation to any understanding of the human subject is embraced by all the writers outlined in this study, resulting in a rejection of easy oppositions; Nietzsche expresses his admiration for the construction of masks, and indeed argues for its necessity; Žižek suggests that the initially adopted mask gradually merges with the real self so that it is not possible to separate them. The most noted modernist writer who explores the concept of the mask is Yeats. His theory or doctrine of the mask explores the opposition, conflict and tension between the mask and the inner self, and rather than rejecting the mask or the anti-self, Yeats advocates an embrace and integration of this struggle and antithesis as an essential condition of self-discovery and wholeness.

his love-song. His desire for love is thwarted by his fear of rejection, his fear that he might be misunderstood. Yet the desire for love is the repressed motivation of the entire monologue; this is the primary human need/demand that Freud and Lacan saw as pervading the psychoanalytic encounter, and which seeks its fulfillment as essential to personal healing and happiness. Prufrock turns aside from a full confrontation with his unconscious wishes, he contradicts any new interpretation of his dilemma, and he recoils from an integration of his conflicting and disparate selves. In the words of Raine, he "flinches away from the moment of crisis, with its maximal potential for self-revelation" (Raine, 2006: 68). While Prufrock momentarily confronts the realities of his failure and the sterility of a loveless future, he recoils from the frightening possibilities of a different way of living, and thus settles for a life which he knows is empty and meaningless, where love only exists in the safety and isolation of his private fantasy. He commits the Lacanian crime of "giving ground to his desire". Therefore, he maintains an anti-heroic persona, a fawning politeness, and a ridiculous figure, and he continues to view the possibility of love as a song which he cannot sing or hear: "I have heard the mermaids singing, each to each. / I do not think that they will sing to me" (Eliot, 2004: 16).

Failure of Communication

> Words, after speech, reach into the
> silence (Eliot, 2004: 175).

The emptiness and barrenness of a fragmented psychic experience portrayed through the persona of a particular protagonist in "Prufrock" is explored and universalized through the multitude of anonymous voices which inhabit the world of "The Waste Land". Through a diverse array of human voices selected across conventional divides of time and space, myth and history, gender and age, this poem abides by Eliot's theory of impersonality whereby poetic utterance is "a mode of access to voices and realms of experience beyond the authorial self" (Zilcosky, 2005: 21). This is the impersonality of "the poet who, out of intense and personal experience, is able to express a general truth; retaining all the particularity of his experience, to make of it a general symbol" (Eliot, 1975: 251). The symbol of "The Waste Land" evokes the sense of alienation, fragmentation and isolation which Eliot perceives in the particularities of a post-war Europe, but it simultaneously attempts to give expression to emotional experiences which are universally identifiable even if not easily acknowledged. As David Moody states, "the waste land of the poem is essentially the landscape of an inward desolation. It is the poetic mind or psyche that is as if dead, and which is struggling against its death" (Moody, 1996: 116). The multiplicity of voices clamouring through this barren landscape conveys the fractured variety of the modernist self, and these disparate personalities, in their isolating differences and subtle similarities, merge to express the multi-layered enigma of the modern consciousness. A major feature of this symbolized consciousness is the failure of communication, both within and between individuals: "I can connect / Nothing with nothing" (Eliot, 2004: 70). This resounds with the frustration of failed articulation and the failure of language to translate the deepest introspective experience which confines Prufrock to a meaningless existence: "It is impossible to say just what I mean!" (Eliot, 2004: 16). The "personages" of the waste land share with Prufrock the isolation and passivity of an existence where communication fails; as Moody says, "while they are dramatic voices, they are not involved in any significant action. They are isolated fragments of a static predicament, and the more they speak the more they say the same thing" (Moody, 1996: 150).

The obstacles to connection, with the self and with the other, is a central theme of the philosophy and psychoanalysis explored in this thesis; Buber's work is primarily focused on the relational character of human living, and his concept of the "I – Thou" relationship is developed with an acknowledged awareness of its possible distortions and alternatives; these distortions and their accompanying deceptions are highlighted by Nietzsche in his analysis of human nature; and the insights of psychoanalysis hinge on the ambiguous nature of language as the imperfect vehicle of communication and the source of concealment and misinterpretation. Like Lacan, Eliot acknowledges the incapacity of language to communicate the complexity of human being, especially the innermost depths of emotional experience: "The expression of one's feelings calls for resources which language cannot supply", but he is not deterred from the pursuit of this expression, and he sees in poetry the possibility of this ideal: "While language constitutes a barrier, poetry gives us a reason for trying to overcome the barrier" (Eliot, 1948: etext). The Freudian commentator, Adam Phillips, draws a link between Eliot's reflections and the goal of psychoanalysis. Quoting from "Four Quartets", he portrays the poet's "venture" as "a new beginning, a raid on the inarticulate / With shabby equipment always deteriorating / In the general mess of imprecision of feeling, / Undisciplined squads of emotion" (Eliot, 2004: 182), and he concludes that "A poem is an air raid, a surprise attack, it conquers internal countries of inarticulacy. And it is not worlds apart from Freud's now famous slogan of usurpation, where id was there ego shall be" (Phillips, 2001: 37).

The images of death, sterility, and isolation suggested in the symbolized waste land evoke a spiritual and emotional disintegration as the inhabitants of the poem wrestle with a life devoid of meaning, a longing for escape from a numbed existence, and a fear of the risks which this escape necessitates. Raine agrees with this analysis of the symbolism of the poem: "The desert is a candid, recognizably familiar symbol for spiritual aridity, for the failure of feeling" (Raine, 2006: 83). Risk entails the possibility of pain and failure, and it demands an awakening to the full spectrum of lived experience in contrast to the comforting darkness of a dulled and limited engagement with reality. Eliot suggests the reluctance of the subject to grapple with these difficulties by overturning the traditional poetic associations of Spring; in a startling reversal of conventional expectation, the poet claims that "April is the cruellest month" (Eliot, 2004: 61), because it demands a surrender of the illusory comforts of darkness and denial, and a confrontation with personal realities: "mixing / Memory and desire, stirring / Dull roots with spring rain" (Eliot, 2004: 61). It is cruel in that "what was thought dead is painfully brought to life" (Raine, 2006: 75). Nietzsche also describes the pain of this experience: "My past broke open its grave, many a pain buried alive awoke: they had only been sleeping, concealed in winding sheets" (Nietzsche, 2003a: 182-183). The apparent neglect of "roots" or origins is characteristic of modernism, as the past was increasingly seen as a phenomenon which failed to provide answers, but the significance of memory and psychic origins and their impact on personal experience is central to Freudian psychoanalysis. Without the integration of past and present, memory and desire, root and branch, there is only "A heap of broken images" (Eliot, 2004: 61), a disintegrated personality incapable of connection with self and others.

The failure of communication, with the disparate complexities of the inner self, and with the feared and desired reality of the other, results in a frustrating isolation which precludes the expression of thought and feeling: "I never know what you are thinking" (Eliot, 2004: 65); the possibility of love cannot exist within this vacuum. Feigned attempts at relationship, a woman "hardly aware of her departed lover" (Eliot, 2004: 69), do not diminish the pain of isolation and the unconscious awareness that life in its fullness is blocked and evaded: "each in his prison / Thinking of the key, each confirms a prison / Only at nightfall" (Eliot, 2004: 74). The universality of this predicament, the barriers to love, of self, of other, and of life, is seen by Helen Gardner as the subject of the poem:

Although "The Waste Land" may begin with the 'dilemma of the modern mind', it discovers that the modern dilemma is the historic dilemma…its true subject is ageless…that beneath both beauty and ugliness there lurk in all classes and in all ages boredom and terror; all wars are the same war, all love-makings the same love-making, all homecomings the same homecoming (Gardner, 1968: 88-89).

The boredom, the alienation, and the despair of an unlived life is but one side of this "modern dilemma", as the withdrawal from a fully experiential encounter with reality is perceived as the antidote to the terror which such an encounter evokes. A commitment to avoidance, of self and of others, precludes a living engagement with reality: "I could not / Speak, and my eyes failed, / I was neither / Living nor dead, and I knew nothing" (Eliot, 2004: 62). An openness to life in all its complexity is rejected in favour of a shallow grasping at survival and a gaze averted from life's possibilities: "Sighs, short and infrequent, were exhaled, / And each man fixed his eyes before his feet" (Eliot, 2004: 62). The inability to express anything reflects the inability to feel anything, and this is the deadness of inner desolation depicted in the poem. Passion, love, lust, and all the full expressions of being human are merely mimicked in a parody of encounter and relationship: "His vanity requires no response, / And makes a welcome of indifference" (Eliot, 2004: 68), and the sexual act is followed by relief that another failed attempt at connection has been endured: "Well now that's done: and I'm glad it's over" (Eliot, 2004: 69). In an essay on "Tradition and T.S. Eliot", Jean-Michel Rabaté points to "really astonishing convergences between Lacan and Eliot" (Rabaté, 2006: 219), and the lines quoted above may point to one such convergence. While the context and the intention of the poetic utterance here may differ from Lacan's statement that "there is no such thing as a sexual relationship", the suggested echoes can be heard.

"The partial anaesthesia of suffering without feeling" (Eliot, 2004: 294) is the condition of a life where feeling has been stifled and numbed. In this silencing of the inner world there is nothing real or meaningful to communicate: "And so the conversation slips / Among velleities and carefully caught regrets" (Eliot, 2004: 18). The "slippage" of language is a subject which Eliot consistently revisits, and it is stated pessimistically in "Four Quartets": "Words strain, / Crack and sometimes break, under the burden, / Under the tension, slip, slide, perish, / Decay with imprecision, will not stay in place, / Will not stay still" (Eliot, 2004: 175). Raine perceives a link here with the later insights of Derrida: "Long before Jacques Derrida coined the term "deconstruction' – to define language's

semantic indeterminacy, its insoluble, inevitable and diametric ambiguities
– Eliot was using its slippage very consciously and precisely" (Raine,
2006: 99). In the absence of expression, of thought and feeling, the reality
of the self is diminished, distorted and denied, and a masquerade of
subjectivity engages in a pseudo-dialogue with other masks and pretences.
Communication fails in the tyranny of fear; fear of rejection, fear of being
misunderstood, and fear of confronting the mystery and strangeness of the
self. In his analysis of Eliot's poetry, Shusterman points to "the terrifying
problem of personal communication already poetically expressed in early
works like "Prufrock"", and echoing Nietzsche, he explains:

> the world is always experienced from an individual perspective…An
> individual's mental life consists in a changing series of…finite centres, and
> there is no guarantee that his centres will harmonize with others or even
> with themselves. There is thus no guarantee that one's experience or self
> will be understood by others (or even by one's subsequent self).
> Communication of the inner life is always a courageous act of faith across
> a gulf of privacy and difference (Shusterman, 2006: 35).

The failure of communication is symptomatic of a rejection of reality, and
a negation of complexity and difference, within self and others. The denial
of essential aspects of the self involves a repression of certain feelings and
desires, and in this selective and incomprehensive interpretation of the
human subject the possibility of love, its passion, desire, and experience, is
thwarted and side-stepped.

Loss of Self

> Where is the Life we have lost in
> living?
> Where is the wisdom we have lost in
> knowledge? (Eliot, 2004: 147).

The failure to attempt an integration of the fragmented nature of the self
and the related failure to communicate the reality of one's being, result
from a combination of self-deception or the repression of one's personal
truth, conformity to image as a provider of security and identity, and fear
of risk and vulnerability inherent in exposure of the inner self. A false self-
sufficiency, constructed in fearful caution and withdrawal, precludes an
open and accepting approach to the fluidity and unfamiliarity of self and
others, and this erects a blocking obstacle to the realization of love. The
reality of the self is rejected, disowned, and buried beneath an

accumulated mound of masks and disguises: "Inside my brain a dull tom-tom begins / Absurdly hammering a prelude of its own, / Capricious monotone / That is at least one definite 'false note'" (Eliot, 2004: 19).

The stagnation and paralysis pertaining to the unlived life involves a rejection of life's possibilities. Eliot describes such a retreat and avoidance in the poem "Animula", where life is restricted to meaningless trivialities, "Content with playing cards and kings and queens", an insatiable need for security, "Eager to be reassured", and a repudiation of love and passion, "Unable to fare forward or retreat, / Fearing the warm reality, the offered good, / Denying the importunity of the blood" (Eliot, 2004: 107). The denial of "the importunity of the blood" resounds with Nietzsche's critique of a morality and a way of life which attempts to obliterate or control the passions, and echoes Wordsworth's appeal for the recovery of "the heart" as essential to human life. The anonymity of the subject of the poem, "the little soul", is seen by Raine as suggestive of a life unlived: "the 'little soul' of the title is appropriately nameless because the individual has in effect refused to encounter the forces that shape us as individuals" (Raine, 2006: 2). Life is unlived because there is no self to engage with life; the self has been buried beneath "deliberate disguises" (Eliot, 2004: 85), and has been replaced by a "shadow of its own shadows, spectre in its own gloom" (Eliot, 2004: 107).

Eliot's poetry appears to portray a world of failure; failure to live, failure to love, and failure to express being. Desperation and unease, despair and disguise, alienation and anxiety, and an array of emotional negativity seems to usher from the poetic word. Paradoxically, the entire *oeuvre is* expression, searching, learning and unlearning, an unceasing attempt "to construct something / Upon which to rejoice" (Eliot, 2004: 89). The desire for expression is unquenchable, and Nietzsche links this human urge to the need for love: "Something unquenched, unquenchable, is in me, that wants to speak out. A craving for love is me, that itself speaks the language of love" (Nietzsche, 2003a: 129). Eliot's poetry can be perceived as "a triumph over the waste regions of the self and its world", because as Moody argues, "the most positive and necessary achievements in art and life are those which triumph over what would negate us" (Moody, 1996: 132,133). The human instinct to survive, to create, and to find reasons to rejoice, propels the desire to find meaning, purpose and direction, even in the confrontation with meaninglessness, emptiness and confusion: "But perhaps neither gain nor loss. / For us,

there is only the trying. The rest is not our business" (Eliot, 2004: 182).[7]
Failure does not preclude a new start, apparent impossibility does not
obliterate possibility, and despair does not permanently disable hope.
Herein lies the power of love, according to Hederman: "Negotiating the
storms and the minefields that may always hamper communication, it is
still possible to reach each other in love" (Hederman, 2000: 90). The
embrace of this ambiguity at the root of the human condition is one the
"uses of poetry" according to Eliot: "Poetry...makes us...a little more
aware of the deeper, unnamed feelings which form the substratum of our
being, to which we rarely penetrate; for our lives are mostly a constant
evasion of ourselves, and an evasion of the visible and sensible world"
(Eliot, 1975: 96).

The "unnamed feelings", the unconscious desires and fears, and the
strength and fragility of the psyche, are aspects of the human condition
explored consistently in philosophy and psychoanalysis; from Nietzsche to
Ricoeur, from Freud to Žižek, the conflictual and ambiguous nature of the
human being is both the source and the direction of the search for
understanding. "Poetry attempts to convey something beyond what can be
conveyed in prose rhythms" (Eliot, 2004: 111), and according to Eliot,
there are moments and experiences in the writing of poetry, when habitual
barriers to understanding are capable of being removed. Eliot describes
such moments:

> Though we do not know until the shell breaks what kind of egg we have
> been sitting on. To me it seems that at these moments, which are
> characterized by the sudden lifting of the burden of anxiety and fear which
> presses upon our daily life so steadily that we are unaware of it, what
> happens is something *negative*: that is to say, not 'inspiration' as we
> commonly think of it, but the breaking down of strong habitual barriers –
> which tend to re-form very quickly. Some obstruction is momentarily
> whisked away. The accompanying feeling is less like what we know as
> positive pleasure, than a sudden relief from an intolerable burden (Eliot,
> 1975: 89-90).[8]

The whisking away of obstruction, suggesting the temporary lifting of
inhibition and censorship which seeks to control much thought and
behaviour, is comparable with Freud's description of the liberating power

---

[7] There is a strong echo of the sentiments of these words in Kennelly's poem,
"Begin": "And something that will not acknowledge conclusion / insists that we
forever begin" (Kennelly, 2004: 478).
[8] The sentiments and word choice of this statement resonate with Nietzsche's
commentary on the "genius of the heart" (Nietzsche, 2003: 219).

of the technique of free association. It allows for the attempted representation of failure/lack – in communication, in the real self (in the Lacanian sense), in the possibility of love – while paradoxically sourcing possibility and attainment within this acknowledgement. While Eliot's poetry strips away comforting illusions and traditional conceptions of life and the human subject, to lay bare the realities of desolation, suffering and loneliness, it nevertheless attempts, in the penetration of these experiences, to discover a power which endures and surpasses pain, and which states against all the odds that "All shall be well and / All manner of things shall be well" (Eliot, 2004: 198). This is a power which can integrate the failures and losses, the errors and disappointments, and the despair and deceptions of "Prufrock" and "The Waste Land", with "The moments of happiness", "the sudden illumination" (Eliot, 2004: 186), and the possibility of "love beyond desire" (Eliot, 2004: 195). The enigmatic reference to "love beyond desire" allows for an ambiguity in its interpretation; perhaps the experience of love is more potent than what could be wished for/desired, or it is complete in itself, without desire's unceasing need and demand for more.

The necessity of integration, of past and present, of fear and courage, of melancholy and hope, "compelled [Eliot] to contemplate another vision" according to Gardner: "After "The Waste Land" Mr Eliot's poetry becomes the attempt to find meaning in the whole of his experience, to include all that he has known. To do this, he enters into himself, finding within himself his own music and his own language" (Gardner, 1968: 185). The entry into the depths of the self is the voyage of recovery, it enables the excavation of all that has been camouflaged, repressed and buried, and it involves the use of memory to elucidate "the passage which we did not take / Towards the door we never opened" (Eliot, 2004: 171). This suggests the ongoing creation of a narrative identity as described by Ricoeur, which is open to changing interpretations of oneself and one's relationships with others. Unlike Prufrock's fixed identity, fluidity and transformation enable the experience of love, of oneself as evolving and responding to changing insights, perspectives and horizons, and of others in acknowledgement of their indefinable and ungraspable alterity. Gordon sees this as the task undertaken in "The Four Quartets": "Eliot took up the challenge of his autobiography: to make sense of one's life…to fuse past and future into a single pattern" (Gordon, 2000: 358). As in the psychoanalytic encounter, the past is revisited with the hope of a more comprehensive interpretation, fantasies are traversed, and the familiar vision of the self and the world it inhabits is broadened and unfixed; re-interpretation offers the possibility of a different meaning to experience:

"And approach to the meaning restores the experience / In a different form" (Eliot, 2004: 186). Freud's insight into the pervading influence of past experience, his use of dreams and free association to gain access to repressed memories, and his conviction that an integration of past and present is essential to psychic health, are echoed in Eliot's words: "A people without history / Is not redeemed from time", and the poet elaborates on the necessary direction which integration calls for:

> We shall not cease from exploration
> And the end of all our exploring
> Will be to arrive where we started
> And know the place for the first time.
> Through the unknown, remembered gate
> When the last of earth left to discover
> Is that which was the beginning (Eliot, 2004: 197).

Eliot accepts the difficulty of the endeavour because it means that "every moment is a new and shocking / Valuation of all we have been" (Eliot, 2004: 179), and it entails a mode of conception which differs from the more linear pattern of experience: "And the way up is the way down, the way forward is the way back. / You cannot face it steadily" (Eliot, 2004: 187).

The paradoxical reversion of direction, of discovering the heights of experience in the depths of one's being, is also proclaimed by Nietzsche: "Whence arise the highest mountains? I once asked. Then I learned that they arise from the sea...the highest must arise to its height from the deepest" (Nietzsche, 2003a: 175). The poet acknowledges the pain which inevitably accompanies this honest appraisal of one's life as it inevitably confronts one with shame and guilt:

> And last, the rending pain of re-enactment
> Of all that you have done and been; the shame
> Of motives late revealed, and the awareness
> Of things ill done and done to others' harm
> Which once you took for exercise of virtue.
> Then fools' approval stings, and honour stains
> (Eliot, 2004: 194-195).

The sentiments of these lines resound with Lacan's discourse on philanthropy and altruism and with Nietzsche's critique of traditionally revered virtues, and his assessment of the actual motivation inspiring "virtuous" behaviour; the "re-enactment" of the past and the resulting "awareness" is akin to the challenge of Nietzsche's doctrine of the eternal recurrence, whereby everything is accepted as being an integral part of the whole of a life, and a joyful embrace of the past, even to the point of wishing its recurrence, is an essential prerequisite to love of life in all its manifestations, *amor fati*: "Time present and time past / Are both perhaps present in time future" (Eliot, 2004: 171). This relates to Lacan's view of the situation of our experience as being in the "future anterior": "What is realized in my history is neither the past definite as what was, since it is no more, nor even the perfect as what has been in what I am, but the future anterior as what I will have been, given what I am in the process of becoming" (Lacan, 2006: 84). Nietzsche states it thus: "Our destiny commands us, even when we do not yet know what it is; it is the future which gives the rule to our present" (Nietzsche, 1984: 10), and perhaps anticipating Ricoeur's discussion of narrative identity, he describes the integrative nature of experience: "I am of today and of the has-been; but there is something in me that is of tomorrow and of the day-after-tomorrow and of the shall-be" (Nietzsche, 2003a: 150). Eliot uses the image of the river, moving, changing, flowing, yet containing in its essence all that it has been and will be, to suggest the fluidity of personal integration within the changing circumstances of life: "The river is within us, the sea is all about us" (Eliot, 2004: 184), and this process is an ongoing accommodation of loss and change and growth: "the time of death is every moment" and so "You are not the same people who left that station / Or who will arrive at any terminus" (Eliot, 2004: 188). This is a poetic utterance of Ricoeur's theory of narrative identity, as it captures the differentiation between "two major meanings of 'identity'...*ipse* or *idem*...identity in the sense of *ipse* implies no assertion concerning some unchanging core of the personality" (Ricoeur, 1994: 2).

The recovery of the self, in an acceptance of its vulnerability, fallibility, and fluidity, enables a compassionate love of self and a corresponding openness to the mystery and the shared humanity of the other. This acceptance of mystery, of self and other, is grounded in humility, an acknowledgement of the limits of knowledge: "The only wisdom we can hope to acquire / Is the wisdom of humility: humility is endless" (Eliot, 2004: 179), and this spirit of unknowing and uncertainty allows for a loving approach to the other: "We appreciate this better / In the agony of others, nearly experienced, / Involving ourselves, than in our own" (Eliot, 2004: 187). Eliot's understanding of the human condition as fallible, inscrutable, and paradoxical concurs with the similar visions of all the writers explored in this study, and he humbly asserts that the ideal of love, "a lifetime's death in love, / Ardour and selflessness and self-surrender", is perhaps only achievable "for the saint"; but an ordinary life, flawed and imperfect, can attain at least moments of such love, "hints and guesses", and this is enough to maintain the quest for those "Who are only undefeated / Because we have gone on trying" (Eliot, 2004: 190). In these moments, there is an inter-mingling of self-relationship, "Knowing myself yet being someone other", and a loving response to the other as "Both intimate and unidentifiable" (Eliot, 2004: 193). Here intimacy and distance, sameness and difference, are embraced as characteristics of oneself and the other-than self, and these experiences, transitory and fleeting, encompass Buber's vision of the "I-Thou" relationship, where the other is approached, not as an object foreign to the self, but in the spirit of Ricoeur's dictum of "oneself as another".

The poetry of both Wordsworth and Eliot testifies to a search for transcendence beyond the limitations of the self, beyond the confines of science and knowledge, and beyond what can be apprehended through the structures of language. In each case this search leads to a commitment to love: "Love is the unfamiliar Name…Which human power cannot remove" (Eliot, 2004: 196). For Wordsworth this is the love of nature in all its mystery and power, for Eliot it is the love of a Christian God. Wordsworth's love of nature unfolds the possibility of joy and compassion in the experience of being human through the love of others. Eliot appears to designate an exclusive choice, between divine and human love, and his personal response is to choose the absolute of the divine. As Gordon argues, "Eliot's idea of love does not fit our usual categories, sexual and romantic…Eliot wanted nothing less than perfect love, part of his longing for 'the impossible union'" (Gordon, 2000: 238). This desire for "the impossible union" resonates with Lacan's analyses of the sexual relationship and the inescapability of desire. Moody argues that Eliot's vision of love "never comes to love in the ordinary human way", and he finds it "hard to credit a love of God which is not first of all a love of other beings".[9] However, echoing Nietzsche's perspectivism, Moody interprets Eliot's stance as "one way of being in the world…other ways are possible" (Moody, 1996: 194). Recalling Žižek's confident assertion that "the impossible does happen, that 'miracles' like love do occur", Eliot claims that in spite of all the obstacles, "The broken standards, the broken lives, / The broken faith in one place or another", there exists the possibility of

---

[9] Richard Kearney also questions this separation of divine and human love: "we are compelled to ask here if it possible ever to fully separate out the strands of desire and love that mesh so intimately in the term *eros*…can one desire the infinite – including infinite justice – without first loving the finite beings in front of us? Can one desire the alterity of goodness without loving *human* others?" (Kearney, 2001: 65).

hope and love, because "nothing is impossible, nothing" (Eliot, 2004: 163).

CHAPTER NINE

BRENDAN KENNELLY

The sentiments, questions, and potential conclusions which emanate from the statement that "other ways are possible" (Moody, 1996: 194), serve as an introduction to the theories and concepts associated with the inconclusiveness of the term "postmodernism". Debate continues on the elusive nature of the reference and meaning pertaining to this attempted symbolization of the contemporary period, its situation within a historic framework, and its negation as being merely an extension of modernism or a fleeting phenomenon quickly surpassed by "post-postmodernism". Perhaps it is not feasible to interpret, analyse and label in any objective and cohesive way the immediate experience of life in the world before it has passed from the confinement and unmeasured expansiveness which characterizes subjective engagement with reality. One of the foremost thinkers and commentators on "the postmodern condition", Jean-Francois Lyotard, states that "the general situation is one of temporal disjunction which makes sketching an overview difficult. A portion of the description would necessarily be conjectural" (Lyotard, 1999: 3). Clearly marked epochs of history are only definable in retrospect, and remain open to revision and re-interpretation as distance enhances or hinders present understanding.

The enlightenment, classicism, romanticism, and modernism, are concepts denoting shifts in consciousness relating to social, economic, cultural, political and intellectual development; underlying the changes in understanding within these realms is a corresponding evolution of thought and vision in relation to the individual as the subject creating, experiencing and portraying the visible and invisible, the conscious and unconscious, the signified and wordless effects of "changes" in the world. Yet it is the same subject that is involved and implicated; it is the human being, developing and regressing, evolving and staying the same, adapting and rebelling, who expresses and describes the reality of being in the world at any particular moment, while also being the subject studied and defined. Buber acknowledges this paradox: "The sickness of our age is like that of no other age, and it belongs together with them all" (Buber, 2004: 47). In this sense, there is continuity, and even repetition, discernible in diverse historical periods. Nietzsche explains it thus: "That which an age feels to be evil is usually an untimely after-echo of that which was formerly felt to be good – the atavism of an older ideal" (Nietzsche, 2003: 102). What is constant is the insatiable quest for knowledge and understanding, particularly in relation to questions of truth, justice, happiness and love, expressed in diverse forms according to diverse situations of culture and civilization; the human being continually, uniquely, and personally, attempts to make sense of him/her self and the relationships, to others and to the world, which are the basis of the experience of human life: "The present is a question. / The future is not an answer" (Kennelly, 2006: 17). The disciplines of philosophy, psychoanalysis, and literature, and especially poetry, in exploring these various but constant efforts at understanding and meaning, inevitably return to the concept of love as being central to this experience. The question of love pervades the experience of the human being regardless of time and space. Perennially, established convictions and assumptions are exposed to the interrogation of new insight, wrought through the emergence of original thought and vision or inescapably imposed through confrontation with hitherto unexpected and unimagined manifestations of the natural and human world. According to Nietzsche, this is synonymous with philosophical thought: "It seems to me more and more that the philosopher, being necessarily a man of tomorrow and the day after tomorrow, has always found himself and had to find himself in contradiction to his today" (Nietzsche, 2003: 143). Radically or tentatively, obviously or subtly, quickly or slowly, values, "truths", knowledge and interpretation, are revaluated and revised to accommodate the doubts and questions which have been raised. So it is with the periods explored in this study; from romanticism through to Nietzsche's "perspectivism", from the discoveries of psychoanalysis through to the embrace of modernism, there is discernible an on-going reaction against modes of thought and understanding which are no longer tenable, and a corresponding attempt to initiate new visions and perspectives. [1]

The gradual erosion of certainties and absolutes appears to reach unprecedented proportions in the present age, and the "postmodern" world is characterized by an awareness of the extent and rapidity of this collapse.

[1] The overlapping of thought – interpretation and re-interpretation – between different "epochs" is often discernible in the similarity in arguments and assessments of writers from diverse historical periods; as Kearney notes: "one also witnesses an uncanny commingling of modern and postmodern perspectives in the texts of a writer like Nietzsche, who has exerted as much influence on the deconstructionists as on the existentialists" (Kearney, 1988: 19).

The unfolding of awareness and acknowledgement of the horrors of Auschwitz provided a concentration of horrors spanning twentieth century history and continues to spill over into the present millennium. In the light of the Shoah and more recent atrocities across the world, it is no longer thought possible to definitively ascertain what the human being is capable of, or to provide systematic definitions as to what constitutes the human subject. This is also the conclusion of Buber in his analysis of the first world war, when "man faced the terrible fact that he was the father of demons whose master he could not become. And the question about the meaning of this simultaneous power and powerlessness flowed into the question about man's being, which now received a new and tremendously practical significance" (Buber, 2004: 188). Žižek's argument that the "inhuman" is paradoxically inherent in "the human" is suggested by these reflections, as is Nietzsche's exposition of the commonly distorted view of human nature.

The possibility of love, the evidence of its obliteration in such incontestable terms, and the spectre of reality devoid of its experience, are central issues of concern underlying much of the literature of the present day. Theodor Adorno saw in the horror of Auschwitz the ultimate sign of the impossibility of language to speak the truth and famously declared that after Auschwitz there can be no poetry; this sentiment is understandable in its context, but despite the failures of language, literature, including poetry, continues to testify to the unconquerable urge to express the human quest to make sense of experience.[2] Making sense of life, and of the subject's experience of it, inevitably involves reflection on what is deemed essential to optimum human living, what a human being needs in order to flourish, and what happens when these needs are thwarted and distorted. Any reflection on these issues inevitably addresses the concept of love as a phenomenon that impinges strongly on human being, need, and growth; according to Nietzsche, "kindness and love [are] the most curative herbs and agents in human intercourse" (Nietzsche, 1984: 48), and thus love is a

---

[2] Charles Bernstein argues forcibly for the possibility of this expression:
We can act: we are not trapped in the postmodern condition if we are willing to differentiate between works of art that suggest new ways of conceiving of our present world and those that seek rather to debunk any possibilities for meaning. To do this, one has to be able to distinguish between, on the one hand, a fragmentation that attempts to valorize the concept of a free-floating signifier unbounded to social significance...and, on the other, a fragmentation that reflects a conception of meaning as prevented by conventional narration and so uses disjunction as a method of tapping into other possibilities available within language (qtd. in Cook, 2004: 550).

theme explored, albeit in diverse contexts and from varying viewpoints, in postmodern poetry.

In the postmodern world, meta-narratives, encompassing fixed and absolutist understanding of the human condition in religious, political, social and historical terms, are deemed to be oversimplifications and distortions of complexity, ambiguity, contradiction and diversity, and their proffered interpretations are rejected as being artificially and falsely imposed. For Lyotard, this is a definition of postmodernism: "Simplifying to the extreme, I define postmodernism as incredulity towards metanarratives" (Lyotard, 1999: xxiv). In his discussion of this period, Kearney refers to Lyotard's intention: "to unmask Grand Narrative as a concealment, even suppression, of little narratives", and to envisage "an open culture based on a plurality of narratives...an accumulation of thousands of little histories, futile and serious" (Kearney, 1998: 204, 205). Previously, meaning was associated with grand narratives of religion, history, and nationalism, but now those narratives have become splintered and meaning is unstable. Pat answers are no longer tenable in the face of challenges to orthodox views of reality or meaning; traditional codes of morality are replaced by a plurality of perspectives and interpretations, and the comforting illusions of conformity and security are unmasked. In the absence of the authority of the metanarrative to make sense of the human condition, diverse aspects of this condition are explored without the safety and familiarity of universal and normative judgements. Previously accepted concepts are destabilized; the linguistic construction of such concepts is examined with a recognition of the split between the sign and the referent,[3] a deconstruction of binary oppositions which tend to depreciate the second element, the other, in the pair,[4] and a blurring of the boundaries between the known and the unknown, the internal and external, the subjective and objective.[5]

Thus, postmodernism is associated with the absence of absolutes, especially in relation to issues of meaning, truth, morality, language and subjectivity, and an acknowledgement that "The whole story will never be told" (Kennelly, 2006: 100). This absence can be interpreted and reflected

---

[3] The acknowledgement of that which exceeds knowledge or signification is a central element of Lacanian thought.
[4] This is central to the philosophy of Derrida, as he sees every concept as being susceptible to deconstruction, and thus to multiple and changing meanings and interpretations.
[5] Freud's insights, especially his exploration of the influence of the unconscious, led to a questioning of the validity of these boundaries in an analysis of human experience.

in a negative and cynical response which is variously expressed as nihilism, relativism, and angst, or as a nostalgic yearning for a rehabilitation of what is deemed lost; as Foucault explains, "It is understandable that some people should weep over the present void and hanker instead, in the world of ideas, after a little monarchy" (Foucault, 1997: 327). The surrender of claims of infallibility attributed to the professed certainties of the great authorities of former decades relativizes the truth values of all knowledge. However, absence can also highlight presence as the eclipse of exclusive conceptions of reality and the human opens the way for the emergence of multiplicity and diversity in thought and vision, an acceptance of personal responsibility and reference in the construction of meaning and truth, and a corresponding humility and graciousness in an acknowledgement of the validity and dignity pertaining to different interpretations and different truths. This ideal resounds with Nietzsche's description of "mature freedom of the spirit which is fully as much self-mastery and discipline of the heart, and which permits paths to many opposing ways of thought" (Nietzsche, 1984: 7). Steven Connor sees this possibility as a key question in an understanding of postmodernism: "could it be possible to found postmodernism not just on the negative claim to go beyond the narrowness of particular value systems but in some more positive value-claim of its own?" (Connor, 2004: 15). According to Kristeva, this is the challenge of the present situation: "we are, for the first time in history, confronted with the following situation: we must live with different people while relying on our personal moral codes, without the assurance of a set that would include our particularities while transcending them" (Kristeva, 1991: 195). Connor echoes this sentiment: "It is the attempt to remain responsive to the claims of the other without resorting to the violence of formalization and objectification that characterizes postmodern ethics" (Connor, 2004: 15). Kearney concurs with this "prospect of a postmodern imagination" and suggests that "a postmodern 'poetics of the possible'' entails an 'ethics of the possible'" (Kearney, 1998: 194, 201).

The literature of postmodernism, and especially its poetry, grapples with this duality, avowing the validity of both aspects; it strives to express the ambiguity and fluidity of subjective truth with an acceptance of its corresponding responsibility, and at the same time it challenges the boundaries between subjective and objective, inner and outer, self and other, as it aims to reach through words for the essence of human being which is otherwise beyond words; the "essence" referred to here applies to the particularity of the unique individual and an attempt to discern some universal characteristics of personal experience. It attests to the possibility of meaning in the absence of conventional signification; it seeks to bear witness to that which within our world exceeds our ability to know it. Thus, it attempts an opening to hitherto denied or repressed aspects of the human condition, it risks confrontation with the marginalised, unacceptable, and unuttered complexities of human experience, and it endeavours to embrace ever-new horizons and interpretations of human being.

Kennelly is a poet whose work spans the transition between the temporal periods of modernism and postmodernism, and a reading of his work resists the constraints of both labels. His poetry, like much of the literature explored in this study, is ultimately the expression of a personal response to the private and public experience of his world, but it enables an interrogation and an analysis of this world as something which is shared by the reader. The poetry of Kennelly consistently examines and questions the world in which we live, and while its particular emphasis is on the ambiguities and tensions characteristic of contemporary Irish culture, its honesty, courage, and humour create a fusion between the particularity of the experience of one's nation and the universal concerns with man's life in the world. In this sense, Kennelly fulfils the description of the poetic act articulated by Hans-Georg Gadamer when he says that "poetry makes the universal more visible than any faithful narration of facts and actual events which we call history can ever do" (Gadamer, 1986: 129). Reflecting the ever-changing face of culture and identity within an Irish context, Kennelly's work exposes the deceptions and inconsistencies of popular moral platitudes - a poetic utterance of Nietzsche's re-evaluation of morality - while also giving voice to the unspoken realities of suffering and failure. As Lucy Collins states, "From his earliest work Kennelly has been attuned to the weaknesses and cruelties inherent in human behaviour and has placed these decisively, even relentlessly, in an Irish context" (Collins, 2003: 212). With a plea for openness, his writings invite the reader to confront the uglier side of a national image, the hidden cruelties of self-righteous bravado, and the intolerance implicit in cowardly conformity. Echoing Freud's conviction that honest acknowledgement of the realities of human nature is the only route to personal freedom, and Nietzsche's rejection of moral consensus in favour of the creation of one's own values as the basis of authenticity, Kennelly's poetry enables a greater understanding of ourselves within the larger framework of the contemporary world.

Kennelly's painstaking critique of general complacencies and inhibitions is explored through an equally honest expression of his own vulnerability and weakness, his own limitations and confusions, and his own faltering attempts at self-understanding and self-creation expressed through his poet personas. For Kennelly, this is the basis of poetry; this is his understanding of the poet's activity:

> I believe that poetry must always be a flight from this deadening authoritative egotism and must find its voices in the byways, laneways, backyards, nooks and crannies of the self…a poet, living his uncertainties, is riddled with different voices, many of them in vicious conflict. The poem is the arena where these voices engage each other in open and hidden combat, and continue to do so until they are all heard (Kennelly, 1990: 12).

In accepting the complexity of the human psyche, and the corresponding contradictions of our social world, Kennelly is ultimately honest enough to tell us that he has no answers; in this sense he echoes Rilke's exhortation that we should "try to love the questions themselves" (Rilke, 2004: 31). Out of this openness to experience, and acceptance of uncertainty and contradiction, there emerges for Kennelly the possibility of an affirmative serenity and a joyous celebration of what it is to be human, a determination to persist in a search for what is positive and good, and a belief in the immeasurable potential for hope and love in the human spirit; as Collins states, Kennelly "surprisingly moves towards a celebration of human endurance" (Collins, 2003: 213).

The poetry of Kennelly thus concurs with many of the insights of the theorists explored in previous chapters relating to the possibility of love; the incontestable impact of unconscious influences in personal and societal experience, the repression and distortion of unacceptable realities, the conflictual nature of psychic life, and the inevitable interconnection between ambiguous polarities. It explores the ambiguities pertaining to the possibility of love, the obstacles which mitigate against its experience and communication, and the immeasurable consequences ensuing from its absence in all areas of life; it echoes Freud's sentiment that "In the end we must necessarily start loving if we are not to fall ill, and we must necessarily fall ill if refusal makes us incapable of loving" (Freud, 2006: 370),[6] as it unabashedly exposes the personal and social ills accruing from love's distortions and denials while simultaneously attesting to the significance of love in the creation of a meaningful life.

---

[6] Nietzsche's comment that "We must learn to love, learn to be kind, and this from earliest youth" (Nietzsche, 1984: 251), is also evoked here.

Misreading the Past

Do not distort me, twist me,
misrepresent me,
Let me be truthful as the dance
(Kennelly, 2004: 166).

Echoing the psychoanalytic focus on an examination of the past as a route to an understanding of the present, and Ricoeur's vision of identity as an ongoing narrative of the self which integrates past, present and future, Kennelly reaches for a more comprehensive engagement with contemporary life through a discerning hospitality to historic influences. The finitude of subjectivity is an aspect of temporal and historical contingencies; the subject is limited by spacio-temporal boundaries and is also impacted by inheritance from the past. The question of time, integral to lived experience in the present and also to any understanding of the past, is explored in a unique manner by Kennelly. While accepting the practical necessity of straightforward, chronological, linear, time, he suggests that poetry, like Freud's description of the unconscious, belongs to a less fixed, less rigid image of time, that of "memory and dream, of lightening mental relationship, of surprising, even shocking connection" (Kennelly, 2004: 19). The analogy between poetry and the world of the unconscious is frequently suggested by Kennelly: "Looking back over the poems I've tried to write, they all seemed to be moments, or stabs of memory, or sudden images, and seemed independent of chronological time" (Kennelly, 2004). His *Selected Poems* has "its own necessary architecture", because, he asserts, poetry dictates its own shape and sense of time: "The power of poetry is directly linked to, and measured by, its capacity for surrender. To memory, to difference, to dreams, to what is perplexing or frightening, to diversity, to voices, to history and mythology" (Kennelly, 2004: 18). The word-choice of this statement – "memory", "difference", "dreams", "voices", "history", "diversity" – suggests an index of some of the key ideas of Freud, Nietzsche, and the other theorists outlined previously. In his poetry, Kennelly explores themes of repression, denial, complexity and ambiguity, echoing Freud's theories of psychical conflict and unconscious motivation, and also suggesting Nietzsche's call for a re-evaluation of values and the necessity of creating one's own rules of morality. He acknowledges the significance of "memory, history and forgetting", as outlined by Ricoeur, and he subverts the domination of subtle ideologies as analyzed by Žižek. Kennelly turns to the visionary power of dreams and memory, especially in his epic sequences, "Cromwell", "The Book of Judas", and most recently and most personally, "The Man Made of Rain", to explore and confront personal, national and universal concerns. Kennelly's acceptance and portrayal of reality, as distinct from the more comfortable illusions of pretence and denial, places him in relation to all the theorists explored in this study, and similarly and uniquely, empowers him to reach for a celebratory engagement with life as it is.

In opposition to the ahistoricism that postmodernity is occasionally accused of, whereby the past is deemed to be irrelevant, and the sometimes self-glorifying construction of a one-sided historical interpretation, Kennelly focuses on the past as a way of informing the present. Nietzsche also advocates an examination of the past as a route to greater understanding of the present:

> There are great advantages in for once removing ourselves distinctly from our time and letting ourselves be driven from its shore back into the ocean of former world views. Looking at the coast from that perspective, we survey for the first time its entire shape, and when we near it again, we have the advantage of understanding it better on the whole than do those who have never left it (Nietzsche, 1984: 256).

Nietzsche considers this one of the poet's functions: "Poets...help the present acquire new colours by making a light shine in from the past" (Nietzsche, 1984: 104). Kennelly's poetry seeks, in the exploration of the past, a relinquishment of fixity and closure characteristic of traditional interpretations, and a questioning of the pseudo-unity of grand narratives built on simplistic oppositions of native/foreigner, victim/oppressor, good/evil: "I knew the world is most at ease / With acceptable insanities" (Kennelly, 2004: 351). In this sense Kennelly's work embodies what Richard Kearney terms a "just imagination...which dispels the hegemony of Grand Narrative in favour of little narratives without degenerating into the arbitrary or the cynical" (Kearney, 1998: 209). Kennelly seeks the truth of the past in the "little narratives", the concrete experiences of ordinary individuals which often contradict the accepted ideologies of their time: "He listens to the silence and hears / a revealing story" (Kennelly, 2006: 20). This resounds with Paul Sheehan's discussion of "legitimation" in postmodernity, which is "plural, local, and immanent", as "The death of the grand narrative thus heralds the birth of the local narrative, with its emphasis on diversity and heterogeneity" (Sheehan, 2004: 29).

In seeking a more comprehensive and a more honest appraisal of the influence of history on contemporary life, Kennelly echoes Freud's analysis of the dominant formative influences of one's personal past and

Nietzsche's exploration of the origins of man's attitudes and beliefs. As an uncompromising reader of Irish history, with an openness to its ugliness and deceptions, Kennelly urges us to come to terms with the damaging reverberations of a post-colonial nation which has often substituted an outwardly imposed authority with another of its own choosing. The repressive censorship laws which sought to silence some of the great literary voices of the time[7] are cited by Kearney as an example of lingering colonial influences in the newly-independent state: "The irony is that when Ireland finally achieved her independence in the early decades of this century, the colonial prejudice against the existence of a thinking Irish mind was not immediately disregarded" (Kearney, 1997: 172). The juxtaposition of dearly-won national freedom and comprehensively imposed social suppression is also noted by Collins: "In addressing a culture comparatively recently grown from sexual timidity, Kennelly again places explicit expression against a background of stultifying Catholic morality" (Collins: 2003: 215). The birth of the new state initiated an insistence on a selective and exclusive understanding of Irish nationality, defined as innocent, conservative, and idyllically pastoral, and forced its development through repression and subjugation of dissent and difference.[8] The human experience of love, in all its potential manifestations, was a particular target of forced repression and distortion. The denial of sexual pleasure as innate to human existence, and the resulting frustrations and deceptions, resonate with Freud's pronouncement that most mental suffering has its roots in the perversion and denial of sexual desire. Nietzsche also outlines the deleterious effects of the distortion of human nature:

> Everything natural, to which man attaches the idea of badness, sinfulness (as is still his habit in regard to the erotic, for example) burdens him, clouds his imagination, makes his glance timid, lets him quarrel with himself and makes him unsure, lacking confidence...yet this suffering about the natural is in the reality of things totally unfounded...men have

---

[7] The banning of John McGahern's work is an obvious example.
[8] See article 41, 1, 2, and 3 of *Bunreacht na hEireann,* p.136: "The State recognises the Family as the natural primary and fundamental unit group of society, and as a moral institution possessing inalienable and imprescriptible rights, antecedent and superior to all positive law...In particular, the State recognises that by her life within the home, woman gives to the state a support without which the common good cannot be achieved...The State pledges itself to guard with special care the institution of marriage on which the family is founded, and to protect it against attack".

become worse by labelling the unavoidably natural as bad and later feeling
it to be so constituted (Nietzsche, 1984: 99).

By using his poetry as social protest, Kennelly points to the inordinate
authority and power invested in institutions of state, Church and family,
with the subsequent disempowerment of individuality and opposition. The
attraction of fixed certainties sourced in powerful institutions, had,
according to John McDonagh, in his analysis of Kennelly's work, a
devastating effect on the emotional and intellectual life of the state:

> There were influential elements within the Free State that sought to
> construct a fixed historical interpretation in which the past became a
> simple paradigm of the oppressor and the oppressed, excluding the
> possibility of unstable and shifting interpretations of that history, and it is
> precisely in this framework that Kennelly achieves his critical importance
> (McDonagh, 2004: 103).

The "influential elements", in particular the family, the Church, and the
school, are areas traditionally and romantically associated with ideals of
love, nurturance and care, but Kennelly subverts these comforting images,
and seeks to give voice to a more truthful picture: "May the silence break /
And melt into words that speak / Of pain and heartache" (Kennelly, 2004:
116), because "There's a story behind every pain" (Kennelly, 2006: 15).
The "pain and heartache" associated with the brutal and dehumanising
experience of an Irish education for many children, in which power
translates as violence, and powerlessness is an easy target, is poignantly
portrayed in Kennelly's poem, "The Stick" (Kennelly, 2004: 37). The
calm determination of the school teacher in choosing his weapon of
instruction with a view to its utmost wounding power, "the right size and
shape" (Kennelly, 2004: 37), is echoed in the fearful stillness of the silent
trees, suggesting the unspoken urge to cruelty and aggression inherent in
the intended violence: "How much violence hides in educated voices?"
(Kennelly, 2006: 54). Nietzsche's assertion, repeated by Lacan, that
"moral", altruistic, philanthropic behaviour is often a façade for more
primitive and self-serving drives is suggested here as the brutality of the
teacher is disguised in the name of education and "improvement". The
experience of love, of self and others, is thwarted; in Nietzsche's words
"we suffer little children to come to us, to prevent them in good time from
loving themselves" (Nietzsche, 2003a: 211). The individuality of the
children is subsumed in anonymous categorisations of "farmers, labourers,
even singers, fiddlers, dancers" (Kennelly, 2004: 37). This is in stark
contrast to Buber's description of the "humility of the educator" who

recognizes that "in the manifold variety of the children the variety of creation is placed before him" (Buber, 2004: 112). From Kennelly's perspective, violence insisted that "correct" answers would be reproduced, that curiosity and "thinking" would be punished, and that the price of "learning" would be the loss of human dignity and self-expression. The mind-splitting contradiction between ideology and reality demanded a "double-think" as the perpetrator of terror was "the one-supposed-to-know", the embodiment of the ideals which were to be emulated! Kennelly's portrayal of the distortion of education resounds with the reflections of Buber who states that "Compulsion in education means disunion, it means humiliation and rebelliousness", and who asserts the necessity of integrity in the person of the educator as a simple presence through which the child develops the capacity to learn in his/her own way: "Interference divides the soul in his care into an obedient part and a rebellious part. But a hidden influence proceeding from his integrity has an integrating force" (Buber, 2004: 107).

The actual irrelevance of much of what was being taught to children who would rapidly face the emigrant's world of emotional and cultural disconnection as they confronted the isolation, inferiority, and shaming ridicule of job-hunting queues in the ports and building sites of English cities, is encapsulated succinctly in the incomprehension screaming in Kennelly's question, "What Use?"

> What use is that language to a man out of work?
> A fat bastard of a teacher rammed it down my throat
> For eight years before I could quit
> That school where I learned nothing
> But Sorrowful, Joyful and Glorious Mysteries
> And answers to questions I never understood
> And that damned language bringing tears to my eyes
> Every time I struggled to say a word (Kennelly, 1987: 40).

The reduction of education to a compliant reiteration of imposed doctrines, and the stifling of voices which might have diverged from the inflexibility of the regime, was also central to religious teaching. Images such as "sallyrod", "lashed", "bare legs" and "bled", evoke the powerlessness and humiliation of young boys being force-fed litanies of creed, captured in the poem "Catechism" (Kennelly, 2004: 40). The critique of religion by Freud and Nietzsche as a tool of suppression and subjugation is reiterated in Kennelly's rejection of a passionless and loveless Christianity which negates the affirmation of many aspects of humanity. Repression and fear, resulting in emotional and cultural emigration and alienation, are exposed consistently in Kennelly's poetry, with a simultaneous admiration and compassion for those who were excluded and ignored in the consensus of compliance and denial, the consensus which Nietzsche termed the "herd mentality": "The road of agreed silence / Led to oblivion" (Kennelly, 2004: 254).

For many, the experience of childhood, in contrast to Wordsworth's vision of innocence and bliss, was marred by injustice, cruelty, and rejection, resulting in a diminished sense of self wherein the experience of love continued to be eluded. While he recognises much that was rich and beautiful in the culture of the recent past, such as community, landscape, and boundary, Kennelly refuses to adhere to the false image of idyllic rural innocence and charming achievement of Irish nationality, symbolized in fantasies of loving families and compassionate leaders, but rather strives to portray the realities of life as lived by the individual personalities that were contained in that society. Themes of repression, especially repression of sexuality and passion, the power of unconscious motivation and memories, and the hidden exclusion involved in the repetitive glorification of accepted hierarchies and moralities, are unmasked by Kennelly as essential to an understanding of the present. Reiterating a basic argument of the writers explored in previous chapters, Kennelly's poetry urges a willingness to come to terms with the legacy of the past, a legacy which is open to ongoing interpretation, and which is based on a revaluation of individual and national identities, and on the interweaving of contradictory impulses and desires. In this sense, it resounds with Ricoeur's description of a narrative identity which is open and fluid. Only thus is an understanding of the present, its contradictions and dilemmas, its hopes and fears, its failures and possibilities, approachable and possible.

Crisis of Meaning

> When I cut the lies out of my life
> I still must live as best I can (Kennelly,
> 2004: 100).

This is the background out of which the postmodern culture of contemporary Ireland has emerged, and it is as a critique of this ambivalent phenomenon that Kennelly's poetry is explored by some contemporary commentators, in particular Ake Persson, in his aptly titled work *Betraying The Age*. Persson considers Kennelly's poetry as a window to the challenges and possibilities of this fragmented era. Economic progress, material wealth and technological innovation, coupled with loss of faith in institutional authority, disclosures of corruption and hypocrisy in political and religious affairs, and a tentative rejection of hierarchical and patriarchal assumptions, has led to an apparent vacuum of moral and spiritual guidance and inspiration. The recent social and economic history maps a journey from relative poverty to gaudy prosperity and from the religious to the secular. The inevitable dissolution of metaphysical and religious values, with the corresponding breakdown of absolutes and certainties, is reminiscent of Nietzsche's acknowledgement of a necessary period of nihilism, and Freud's insistence on individual responsibility and freedom, as inescapable challenges in the creation and development of one's personal life. While Kennelly recognises the ambiguities and contradictions of our "unparalleled progress", and the collapse of previously considered "givens",[9] he is determined to celebrate the joy of diversity and deconstruction. In the preface to his collected poems, *Familiar Strangers*, he states that acceptance of the ugliness of reality co-exists with celebration of the gift of life:

> And while poetry must always explore and reveal the realities of this barbarous darkness in a post-colonial land (or anywhere), confronting the violence, cynicism, corruption and "sophistication" that seem to accompany wealth, it must also, somehow, always, cling to a vision of plain human dignity, celebrate the gift of life, the very act of giving that is poetry itself (Kennelly, 2004: 19).

These sentiments subscribe to Nietzsche's assertion of the possibility, and the necessity, of *amor fati* even in the face of its obstacles. Thus Kennelly's poetry embodies a two-fold structure; it is a critique of bland, half-hearted, half-lived complacency which negates the failure and suffering amid the mask of superficial success, but it is also a joyous reception of the challenges and questions forged by this honest appraisal. The avoidance facilitated by protective defences and pseudo-engagement recalls the death-in-life existence of the personas in Eliot's work, but Kennelly envisages the possibility of a passionate and welcoming embrace of life in its fullness, accepting its ambiguities and its mysteries.

In his study of Kennelly's work, Persson argues that the poet "is engaged in social and artistic protest in order to question, challenge and subvert established values and norms in Irish society" (Persson, 2001: 1). The socio-cultural context of many of Kennelly's poems attempts to confront us with the forgotten, the hidden, and the excluded elements of our national image. Referring to the poet's "subversion of established

---

[9] Terms quoted from Paul Lakeland, *Postmodernity: Christian Identity in a Fragmented Age.*

viewpoints", Collins argues that "Kennelly's desire to let the voiceless
speak through his poetry is linked by him to a conviction that poetry is a
force for change, yet one that must accommodate multiple – and often
distinctly marginal – viewpoints within its scope" (Collins, 2003: 213). In
his poem, "The Loud Men", Kennelly parodies the authoritarian and
judgemental assumptions of those who insist on forcing their convictions
on society, "bullies", "politicians", "and bored, truculent men" (Kennelly,
2004: 281). These are the personas of the "experts", the "subjects
supposed to know", which Lacan exposed as fallacious and illusory. The
self-righteousness of moral superiority is only made possible through the
scapegoating and victimisation of the other, the different, the
unassimilated: "My madness is what you fear / to encounter in yourself"
(Kennelly, 2006: 36). This stance of authority and power is, according to
Kennelly, a refusal to acknowledge the reality of their own darkness:
"They proclaim their own emptiness. / Because / by spitting in the eyes of
others / they run like madmen from themselves" (Kennelly, 2004: 281);
what is not accepted within is projected outward. Nietzsche notes that
"inconsiderate thinking is often the sign of a discordant inner state which
craves numbness" (Nietzsche, 1984: 246). Kristeva and Kearney both
explore this human propensity to disown aspects of the self through
defensive projection onto "strangers, gods and monsters", and a refusal to
recognise the foreigner within.[10] This relates to Nietzsche's argument that
"you yourself will always be the worst enemy you can encounter; you
yourself lie in wait for yourself in caves and forests" (Nietzsche, 2003a:
90). The loud self-assertion of the powerful in society is in stark contrast
to the silence of the poor, the wounded, and the ostracised, captured in the
poem through the image of childhood poverty in the person of Sheila
Lehane: "Her suffering would not allow her to be loud" (Kennelly, 2004:
281). Scapegoating of the marginalised and the hidden, whether by
selective labelling, condescending philanthropy, or projective
condemnation, is a superficial response to the darkness of everyday
exploitation, injustice, and the violation of human dignity. Love is not
possible in these circumstances; the other is distorted to embody what
cannot be accepted and so cannot be loved, but the self is also depleted
and reduced by this fabrication because, as Kearney notes, "scapegoating
does not work in the long run…liars can fool others but not
themselves…the projection of inner hostilities onto some outer adversary
is ultimately condemned to fail. The ploy of demonizing others returns to

---

[10] Titles such as *Strangers, Gods and Monsters* (Kearney), and *Strangers to
Ourselves* (Kristeva), open to an exploration of this phenomenon.

plague the inventor" (Kearney, 1997: 66). This resonates with Nietzsche's warning: "He who fights with monsters should look to it that he himself does not become a monster. And when you gaze long enough into an abyss the abyss also gazes into you" (Nietzsche, 2003: 102).

Kennelly's insistence on providing a space and a voice for those in society who may not fit the contemporary ideal of respectability and success is revealed in much of his poetry, and poignantly so in the short poem, "The Good" (Kennelly, 2004: 155). Here he expresses his admiration for a risk-laden, but life-enriching openness to self and the world. This is the risk rejected by Prufrock and the characters of "The Waste Land". The image of the bird in flight suggests movement and vitality, while also hinting at the courage of risk: "They do not think of safety, / are blind to possible extinction" (Kennelly, 2004: 155). The good are not concerned with safety and stability, preferring instead the adventure of possibility. Their willingness to expose their fragile vulnerability, and their acceptance of the reality of failure/extinction, ensures the genuineness and authenticity of self-integration: "And when most vulnerable / are most themselves" (Kennelly, 2004: 155). We have difficulty perceiving these unassuming "Good", because we are blinded by our fixed assumptions, our "casual corruption" (Kennelly, 2004: 155). We prefer to hide behind "The small protective sanities" of group and mask, ensuring that no authentic meeting can take place between ourselves and others (Kennelly, 2004: 156). Buber's vision of the I-Thou relationship is not experienced in a rejection of complexity and difference. In this alienation from the realities of self and others the experience of love is not possible, as human relationships are diminished by the unconscious falsities "that hide men from themselves" (Kennelly, 2004: 156). In contrast, the good risk the nakedness of self-revelation, and though aware of the threat of condemnation and misunderstanding, they still seek the best in life. They embrace the paradox of light and darkness, master and victim, earth and sky, body and spirit, and proclaim through their action the ultimate affirmation, a welcoming acceptance of reality: "Content to be itself" (Kennelly, 2004: 156). This can be read as a contemporary interpretation of Nietzsche's doctrine of eternal recurrence, *amor fati*, and the ideal of the overman, as the paradoxical images of light and darkness, of joy and sorrow, provide a metaphor for the experience of moving towards a fuller and more accepting understanding of the human subject and the human condition, an understanding which enables an affirmative celebration of one's fate. A willingness to trust in the ambiguous beauty of all of life suggests a childlike innocence that is not destroyed by the potentially crushing insights of "maturity". One is here reminded of

Wordsworth's portrayal of the child as the "best philosopher". The good retain the grace of resilience and desire in the face of triumph and disaster, "the vulnerable grace / of any bird in flight" (Kennelly, 2004: 156). Kennelly's tentative assertion that he may have "one or two among his friends" who embody the humanity of the "good" (Kennelly, 2004: 156), is an expression of his admiration for a childlike innocence and sense of wonder which he considers essential to the human spirit:

> I have never surrendered to the language of rational explanation or analysis...I prefer the language of wonder, speculation, outrageous and often hilarious possibility, and this has stayed alive in me. I have therefore in me a child (Kennelly, 1994: 180).

This expressed preference for wonder and possibility resounds with Nietzsche's description of maturity: "Mature manhood; that means to have rediscovered the seriousness one had as a child at play" (Nietzsche, 2003: 94). Kennelly is here rejecting the pseudo-maturity and balanced mediocrity of half-living, the adjustment and conformity to Freud's superego or Žižek's 'big Other', preferring to empathise with those who do not fit neatly into a rational equilibrium, and he is restating Freud's theory that events, memories and desires of childhood are never fully abandoned or fully lost, but are preserved and unravelled as the adult narrator/poet/analysand communes with his younger self. Like Wordsworth, Kennelly refuses to surrender the richness of childish enthusiasm as the price of socially-accepted sophistication and success. He concurs with Nietzsche's claim: "You must yet become a child and without shame" (Nietzsche, 2003a: 168).

The articulation of unvoiced complexities and contradiction in opposition to the silence and betrayal inherent in narrow historical interpretations of events and characters, is attempted in epic proportions in Kennelly's "Cromwell" and "The Book of Judas". Kennelly's preferred adoption of diverse voices within his poetic expression, his rejection of the façade of a unified, fixed identity, and his selection of a variety of personas within his work, is a reflection of his admiration for the Portuguese poet, Pessoa, and his multiplicity of poetic voices. Kennelly's writing therefore concurs with Nietzsche's rejection of a definitive self, and acknowledges the existence of disparate and often conflicting components within the psyche. This accords with Freud's description of the structure of the mind, and the often conflicting needs of the private individual and the culturally influenced super-ego. Through the voices of the disgraced and disparaged characters of Cromwell and Judas, Kennelly uncovers in dreamlike sequence the unconscious and latent meanings concealed in these historical figures. The gradual uncovering of repressed hatred and fear, of learned prejudices and assumptions, and the possibility of attaining a more truthful interpretation of the past, is analogous to the hermeneutical experience of Freud's psychoanalysis, whereby the narration of the past is reviewed and examined, and it also adheres to Ricoeur's vision of narrative as an ongoing interpretation and integration of newly acquired horizons of understanding. In an interview in "The Irish Times" in May 2004, Kennelly urges the expression of darkness as a valid and inescapable component of human experience:

> Think of that marvellous line of Frank O'Connor's: 'celebrate the darkness and the shame'. You don't celebrate shame, but I think poetry does, or it can...how easy hatred is. But if you find out enough about a person, you're bound to find things that you like...this is my idea of celebration, to step outside yourself and find a sympathetic, intelligent place for someone that you were trained to hate (Kennelly, 2004a).

Through the vilified personas of Cromwell and Judas, hitherto confined to "fixed" interpretations, Kennelly articulates the darknesses and frustrations, the cruelties and deceptions, and the cowardice and terror which are projected onto these otherwise silent containers. The projection of the unacceptable, its repression and denial, is rooted in the desire for idealistic images of who we (as distinct from these untouchables) are. The temptation to claim moral rectitude or perfect judgement regarding historical events, the subjugation of one's darkest thoughts and raw impulses, have the effect, according to both Freud and Nietzsche, of extinguishing the vitality and intensity of our connection with ourselves and our past. The experience of love is thwarted in the obliteration of passion and fullness. Kennelly's poetry abandons this duplicitous reading of history, and by giving expression to hitherto silenced voices, it elicits a recollection and resolution of repressed knowledge and truth. Through an imaginative exploration of self and history, the poet enables the possibility of a different interpretation; this is the contention of Kearney in his discussion of these poems. Recalling Freud's theories on dreams and the unconscious, and Wordsworth's belief in the powers of the imagination, Kearney aptly states that "The imagination knows no censorship", and goes on to assert Kennelly's achievement:

> Passing thus through the psychic purgatory of self-analysis, disclosing the ideological memories which drive us to fury and despair, Kennelly is finally in a position to explore a utopian dimension of myth which points beyond the ruins of the past. Having debunked the demons of Cromwell and Buffun – by transmuting them into mock-heroic fictions – the poet

imagines the possibility of another kind of home in history…Once he has
stripped the "old man", "swaddled in lies", of his false mythology,
Kennelly is liberated into a positive ignorance, free to reconnect with
foreclosed dimensions of being (Kearney, 1997: 139-140).

Kennelly's willingness to embrace a more realistic and a more
comprehensive account of human nature, with its triumphs and failures, its
positives and negatives, is a reiteration of Nietzsche's description of the
human subject as "human, all too human", and echoes Ricoeur's
acknowledgement of "fallible man". According to McDonagh, the epic
sequences of these poems allow Kennelly to explore a random selection of
images and events which portray the inevitable conflict between authority
and powerlessness.

> Every story of success is reliant upon a story of failure for its very essence.
> Kennelly is clearly driven towards the latter as a source of inspiration
> because it is largely experiences of betrayal, eviction and brutalisation that
> strip away the veneer of polite hermeneutics to reveal a muddied and often
> brutalised reality (McDonagh, 2004: 140).

Disconnectedness from past and present realities has resulted in a loss of
identity, sense of place, and sense of history, with a tendency to replace
what has been lost with surrogate identities available through material
success. Freud refers to this understandable quest for palliatives in an
effort to alleviate the pain of living, and Ricoeur explores the search for
recognition and identity through modes of power and possession. The
impossibility of satiating spiritual hunger with the material trappings of a
consumerist society is given ironic expression in Kennelly's parody of the
deification of "Money" as the overwhelming metaphor for value:

> You've made me your way, your truth and your life,
> The only God you adore.
> I grant, in return, what your heart most desires;
> More (Kennelly, 2004: 450).

The difficulty of finding meaning in the midst of such contradiction and
uncertainty, and the importance of appearance to the image of success,
often necessitates a masking of vulnerability, loneliness and fear: "Almost
everyone needs a cover" (Kennelly, 2004: 444), and the resulting sense of
alienation and isolation can result in the destruction of meaning altogether:
"Loneliness / has a sleepless bite" (Kennelly, 2006: 8). Kennelly gives
voice to the hidden losses and silent screams of despair and woundedness,
while simultaneously insisting on the indestructible human capacity for

hope and connection: "He hears a voice poised between hope and despair'''(Kennelly, 2006: 27). In an interview with Richard Pine in 1990, Kennelly refers to the spectre of despair and suicide[11] in contemporary society, but insists on the intertwining of nightmare and hope:

> Who knows out of what moody swings or rhythm somebody decides to commit suicide or to live, who knows out of what gelling of emotional rhythms one opts for the assertion of continuity….I think it has to do with that genuinely fundamental and essential tension between the sinking into a bottomless darkness and the desire to rise into a civilized, sharable light, where I know the faces of my friends, where I can share their words, their laughter, where I can once again resume negotiations of friendship and connection. So as a writer I am given to beginnings (Kennelly, 1994a: 174).

The acknowledgement of the significance of interpersonal relationships in the creation of a meaningful (and therefore a liveable) life echoes the philosophies of Buber and Ricoeur, favouring an open-ended understanding of human nature which accounts for self and other, sameness and difference, capabilities and vulnerabilities. References to intersubjectivity, relationship, and the power of love, are suggested in the word choice of the statement quoted above; "sharable", "friends", "words", "negotiations", "friendship" and "connection" evoke an understanding of the human subject as essentially needing to love and to be loved, and the suggestion that life itself may be extinguished if love is absent. A similarly acknowledged need for love is expressed by Nietzsche: "What I have always needed most to cure and restore myself, however, was the belief that I was not the only one to be thus, to see thus – I needed the enchanting intuition of kinship and equality in the eye and in desire, repose in a trusted friendship; I needed a shared blindness, with no suspicion or question marks" (Nietzsche, 1984: 4). The absence of "suspicion" or judgement, the sense of complete acceptance, and the co-existence of solitude and connection, evoke the experience of love, an

---

[11] The questions arising from the concept of suicide are pursued in the three disciplines of philosophy, psychoanalysis, and poetry: Hamlet reflects on the dilemma, "to be or not to be"; Albert Camus claims that suicide is *the* philosophical problem: "Deciding whether or not life is worth living is to answer the fundamental question in philosophy. All other questions follow from that" (*Le Mythe de Sisyphe*, 1942); the Italian poet, Cesare Pavese claims that "no one ever lacks a good reason for suicide", while his compatriot, Antonio Porchia reflects that "truth has few friends and those few are suicides".

experience captured in the lines of a poem from the 13th century Sufi mystic, Rumi:

> Out beyond ideas of wrongdoing and rightdoing,
> There is a field, I'll meet you there.
> When the soul lies down in that grass,
> The world is too full to talk about,
> Ideas, language, even the phrase each other
> Doesn't make any sense (Rumi, 1996: 36).

The necessity of scrupulous self-scrutiny, sometimes facilitated and enhanced by the support and revelation proffered by genuine interpersonal relationships, in the creation of a meaningful life, is akin to Freudian and Nietzshean philosophies: "Now he sees a true friend is a challenge / and a shadowpresence guiding him / across a dangerous bridge" (Kennelly, 2006: 8). Honest introspection and self-scrutiny are central to Nietzsche's writings, wherein he gives expression to the spectrum of drives and emotions, constructive and destructive, which pervade human motivation and behaviour; but Nietzsche also acknowledges the role of relationship in the enhancement of life and sees this need as a central quest in human being: "One seeks a midwife for his thoughts, another someone to whom he can be a midwife: thus originates a good conversation" (Nietzsche, 2003: 100). Kennelly's honesty articulates the multi-faceted composition of the human experience, and through an openness to the nature of memory and mutability, and the relationship between the changing material world and the inner landscape of personal experience, he mirrors Freud's goal of psychoanalysis to interrogate the power of memory and to explore the mysterious otherness of one's self.

Throughout his poetry, Kennelly urges an open-ended understanding of human nature which accounts for self and others, sameness and difference, capabilities and vulnerabilities. Closer perhaps to Freud's pronouncements on the benefits of the dialogical nature of the psychoanalytic encounter than to Nietzsche's reliance on personal introspection, Kennelly suggests that one can make sense of oneself mainly in and through one's involvement with others. Like Buber, Kennelly accepts the difficulties involved in the quest for authentic inter-relationships, and states that his aim is "to try to be truthful to the way your imagination works. Because individual imaginations work in the most extraordinary ways, and we share very little of it with each other" (Kennelly, 2004). Acknowledgement of incommunicability obliterates the authenticity or logic of judgement of self or other, according to Nietzsche: "No experiences of a man...however close he is to us, can be so complete that we would have a logical right to evaluate him in toto. All evaluations are premature, and must be so...the gauge by which we measure, our own nature, is no unchangeable quantity...one ought not to judge at all" (Nietzsche, 1984: 35). The acknowledgement that much of the inner life is incommunicable concurs with the assertions of Lacan and Žižek when they proclaim the impossibility of fully knowing or being known by another. According to Derrida and Irigaray, acceptance of this unknowability and unsharability is the very basis of love. According to this viewpoint, the quest for meaning and worth aims for genuine mutuality, a mutuality based on both our common humanity and our individual uniqueness: "Self knows that self is not enough, / the deepest well becomes exhausted" (Kennelly, 2004: 425); this reflects the philosophical claim of Buber and Ricoeur that there is no unmediated self-understanding: "It is not me you see, but you. / Is there anywhere in the world / you do not meet yourself?" (Kennelly, 2004: 431). Nietzsche offers an answer to this question: "Yet your friend's face is something else beside. It is your own face, in a rough and imperfect mirror" (Nietzsche, 2003a: 83).

Agreeing with Kennelly that "self is not enough", Ricoeur argues that no one alone could be a person, that one can make sense of oneself only in and through one's involvement with others: "Thereby another is not only an other, but my like...man is this plural and collective unity of destination and the differences of destinies are to be understood through each other" (Ricoeur, 1965: 138). The focus on sameness amid diversity is also a tenet of Wordsworth's poetic dictum. Empathy, the willingness to place oneself in the situation of the other, the attempt to recognise the "I" in the "You", resonating with Buber's philosophy of authentic relationship, and the acceptance of the mystery that enfolds the universe in an undeniable inter-connectedness and inter-dependence, is embraced by the poet as the transcendence of the self towards a love of the other. The notion of self-awareness and self-knowledge, in isolation from the direct and indirect influence of past and present relationships, is rejected by Kennelly as he utters his admiration for the integrity evoked in the image of the "island":

> If I ever learn to make what I feel and see
> As a whole
> As the island appears to be
> I shall recognise
> The roots of sadness behind people's eyes
> And link them with my own (Kennelly, 2004: 328).

Like Eliot, Kennelly is willing to undertake the "transient yet upsetting incursions into the mere, messy self which nevertheless remains the truest if murkiest source of poetry" (Kennelly, 2004: 323). The poet, in risking the vulnerability of self-honesty and self-expression, in searching deeply for his own naked truth, and in revealing what is rather than what is wished for, offers glimpses of universal truths and meanings, moments of experience shared in our common humanity: "It coincides with a music I find in myself" (Kennelly, 2004: 337), and in these moments the possibility of love may be glimpsed and experienced.

Celebration of Life

> But from the corruption comes the deep
> Desire to plunge to the true;
> To dare is to redeem the blood,
> Discover the buried good,
> Be vulnerably new (Kennelly, 2004: 370).

The collapse of certainties and absolutes, the deconstruction of previously revered polarities, and the fragmentation of traditional assumptions, can be interpreted as a vacuum in contemporary society, an absence of signposts and direction. This situation may suggest a different interpretation however, as it signals possibilities inherent in viewing life as always new, always in the process of becoming. From this horizon, the absence of pre-given assurances and expectations enables the quest for individual autonomy and self-responsibility. The power of poetry, as evidenced in Kennelly's work, is to stand apart from the isolating dichotomies of good and evil, man and woman, history and status, body and soul, and to initiate an encounter which is truly honest, truly human. Nietzsche's titles, such as *Beyond Good and Evil* and *Human, All Too Human*, resound with these sentiments.

As dialogue, intra-psychic or inter-relational, Kennelly's poetry is a heart-to heart communication and connection, deriving its authenticity from a ruthless abandonment of the superficial and contrived. It is a refusal to comply with what Wordsworth denounced as "the neglect of the heart". In an effort to reveal ourselves to ourselves (in mirroring the revelatory activity of Freudian psychoanalysis and the inclusiveness of Ricoeurian narrative identity), it expresses what is innermost in the human heart; it does not provide tidy summaries; it does not assume answers; rather it rejoices in the immeasurable confusions, contradictions and possibilities of what it means to be human. It embraces Nietzsche's appraisal of human being as rational and irrational, self-seeking and propelled towards the other, and it determines to seek love within and in spite of these realities. Freedom and limitation, urgency and continuity, life and death, co-exist in the humility of the poetic expression of difference and sameness which enables us to see in our unique experience an echo of the universal. In this accommodation of the essentially mysterious nature of life, Kennelly's poetry is created and experienced in humility and tolerance. In tune with Nietzschean doctrines of perspectivism and self-creation, it does not seek to impose diagnoses or solutions; it forces no moralistic dogmatism. In asking his own questions, Kennelly voices our own confusions; and in celebrating the infinite complexity of life, he offers a glimpse of one man's truth. His willingness to confront the ambiguous nature of human life, and his ongoing effort to 2comprehend the incomprehensible", is captured in his dedication of "The Book of Judas" to those who share his task:

> For all good dreams
> Twisted, exploited and betrayed.
> For all those
> Conveniently and mindlessly damned
> By you and me.
> And for all those writing and unwriting
> Poets of humanity
> Who have a bash
> At comprehending the incomprehensible (Kennelly, 1991: Dedication).

The articulation of many voices, and the insistence that they be heard, is in implicit agreement with all the writers previously explored. After reading Kennelly's poetry, with particular reference to these writers, "we are more human than we were before" (Kennelly, 2004: 466). In this spirit of humility and celebration, the experience of love, of self, of others, and of life itself, is sought, glimpsed and at least momentarily attainable; it is integral to human living, and it is possible, even if only in the undramatic, ordinary, unnoted moments of concern and kindness which are felt in simple expressions of being human; what Wordsworth refers to as "that best portion of a good man's life; / his little, nameless, unremembered acts / of kindness and love"(Wordsworth, 2000: 132), and described by Nietzsche as "Goodwill...I mean those expressions of a friendly disposition in interactions, that smile of the eye, those handclasps, that ease which usually envelops nearly all human actions...it is the continual manifestation of our humanity" (Nietzsche, 1984: 48).

Through Kennelly's poetic communication we have access to the ebb and flow of one life in search of truth, meaning, and love, and we take courage and sustenance from his explorations, as they resound with our deepest experiences. An encounter with Kennelly's work confronts us with the reality of limitation and possibility; historical, biological, environmental and anthropological influences, intertwined with the often unforeseeable and uncontrollable vicissitudes of human relationships, inevitably impact on the subject's mental, emotional, and physical make-up. However, an acceptance of these determining factors does not negate an acknowledgement of the potential freedom co-existing within this framework, a freedom which is based on the ongoing pursuit of ever-changing truth and possibility. This acceptance of the paradox inherent in the human condition is central to Kennelly's poetry, and in his welcoming reception of the questions and contradictions of human living, in his willingness to forego certainties and stagnation, he insists on our freedom to create and re-create ourselves and our lives. Central to this creative act is the possibility of love.

As a critique of the vanities and repressions of our contemporary world, the poetry of Kennelly also exposes the potential for Nietzsche's *amor fati* and Freud's ideal of self-acceptance as providing the basis of authentic hope and genuine joy. In this sense, love is possible, when the subject is willing to embrace the reality of paradox and ambiguity in human life. To love one's fate, to "keep on going", to lose and to find meaning over and over again (eternal recurrence), is to live with an intimate appreciation of simply being alive; such is the determination to continually seek to transcend the limitations that confine us, a determination which is asserted in the imagery and symbolism of the celebratory poem, "Begin" (Kennelly, 2004: 478). Here Kennelly embraces the birth and death at the core of every experience when the poet persona states that, "every beginning is a promise / born in light and dying in dark", he recognises the "bridges linking the past and future", and he admits the necessity of "the loneliness that cannot end / since it is perhaps what makes us begin" (Kennelly, 2004: 478). The sentiment of these lines is close to Nietzsche's admiration of a fervour "for seeking the truth, a search that does not tire of learning afresh and testing anew" (Nietzsche, 1984: 264). The mystery of hope in the face of despair, the resilience of restarting after failure, and the belief in love as something worth striving for, combine in the poet's confident assertion that life is meaningful, and that the search for that meaning is in itself worthy of our effort:

> Though we live in a world that dreams of ending
> That always seems about to give in

> Something that will not acknowledge conclusion
> Insists that we forever begin (Kennelly, 2004: 478).

The insistent tone of persistence and affirmation of these lines is a statement of belief in humanity's potential to overcome the limitations and frustrations of determined positions, and fulfilment of Kennelly's hope that "sometimes a poem becomes a sharable moment of light" (Kennelly, 1990: 11), perhaps akin to the "sharable moment" of insight which is Freud's goal in psychoanalysis. The temporary failure of love does not prevent the innate human search for its possibility, and the conviction that the quest is worthwhile and capable of fulfilment.

CONCLUSION

> Your task is not to seek for love, but
> merely to seek and find all the barriers
> within yourself that you have built
> against it (Rumi, 1999: 84).

This study has approached a concept which, it asserts, defies definitive description or definition. Although a universal experience, across history, geography, chronology and gender, the question of love resists analyses and conclusions which are universally valid or applicable. The modest aim of this work has been to examine this question through a selected reading of the works of writers and thinkers who have impacted at least to some degree on how the human condition is understood, and particularly on how the experience of love, as a significant aspect of that condition, is explored and illuminated. The argument put forward has been that such exploration and illumination is enhanced through the trans-contextual and interdisciplinary nature of the selected readings. The enhancement asserted by the method and focus of this particular study is based on the evidence provided that the question of love's possibility is a central, essential, inescapable concern of human existence as depicted in the three disciplines of philosophy, psychoanalysis and poetry, and across different historical dimensions.

The Interdisciplinary and Trans-Historical Centrality of Love

The work of all nine writers explored in this work attests to the centrality of love in any attempt to approach an understanding of the human being. The literature studied across the disciplinary and historical dimension of the study abounds with exploration, observation, analysis and interpretation of the phenomenon of love. Each of the writers offers a unique portrayal of the diverse manifestations of the need/desire to love and to be loved which may be discerned in the conscious or unconscious motivations underlying human behaviour.

Nietzsche posits "will to power" as the principle thrust of human life, whereby the organism continually seeks to overcome and overpower resistances and limitations. The insatiability and progressive thrust of this drive as described by Nietzsche resounds with Freud's analysis of how the pleasure principle, while inevitably modified by the reality principle, is essentially superseded by the strength and the persistence of the death drive which impels the organism towards its own destruction as it paradoxically seeks to overcome itself. The impossibility of permanent satisfaction or equilibrium within the living organism is also suggested in Lacan's exposition of desire as the unquenchable ground of human being. Žižek firmly concurs with this appraisal of the key significance of desire in human living, while Buber and Ricoeur discuss the intricacies of desire in relation to happiness, power and self-fulfilment. The three poets also give expression to the onward thrust which propels the urge to life; each of the poets, in similar and differing ways, engages with this "development thrust" (Lear, 1998: 220).

As a conclusion of the research outlined in the previous chapters, this work offers a possible interpretation of the variously described force which permeates human life - will to power, desire, growth, overcoming - as the expression of love, its necessity, its persistence, and its indomitable impact, in diverse forms. For Wordsworth it is the spur towards love of nature and of others, concomitant with a love and an acceptance of self; for Eliot it is an unpredictably changing focus and direction that ultimately leads beyond the self and the confines of humanity towards a religious or divine love; and for Kennelly it is the impetus demanding and enabling an ever-recurring attempt to "begin again" as the self seeks continually, in spite of failure and disappointment, to express and to receive love. From this analysis, each of the poets approaches the concept of love both as the motivating thrust towards transcendence, of the self, the known world, and relationship between the two, and as the means, attainment and experience of such transcendence. From this interpretation, it is argued that the possibility of love is a central concept underlying the philosophies, theories and expressions of all nine writers explored here; it is a thread which links the disciplines of philosophy, psychoanalysis and poetry across a historical spectrum; and consequent to this argument, the reflection is proffered that perhaps this is the key question which underlies the search for truth, or truths, and its expression, which lies at the heart of these studies.

The Primary Obstacles to Love

The obstacles to love which are highlighted by the unique focus of the research fall into three main categories: fear, failure of communication, and self-deception. These are variously explored by the different writers as potentially thwarting the possibility of love, its desire, its experience and its communication. The three categories, like all the variables of human nature, are not distinct and separate, but rather originate in and through each other and are variously manifested in diverse combinations and permutations. Consensus and divergence is discernible in the unique commentary, analysis and insight offered by the individual writers into these impediments, but an attempted overview enables discussion and conclusion regarding insight and illumination which may be furnished therein.

The pervasive presence of fear in the experience of human living, in personal, social, national and global realms, is reflected and explored by all the writers. Accordingly, it is manifested in psychoanalytic terms as "anxiety", "repression", "trauma", and as filtered through the super-ego and the big Other. Nietzsche and Buber identify fear as the underlying force behind the phenomenon of herd-mentality and compliance with the crowd; an understanding of the phenomenon is advanced through Freud's elucidation of the child's fear of loss of love, a fear which is intermittently repressed and denied, but which continues to motivate behaviour throughout life; this fear translates variously as that of rejection, abandonment, judgement, and exclusion. Ricoeur explains the fear implicit in seeking recognition from another, and the ensuing threat to the subject's sense of identity. The poets illuminate the experience of fear pertaining to love and loss, and all the uncontrollable facets of human experience. The fear of the solitary and the existential aloneness of the human subject is poetically explored in the work of Wordsworth, and in all the works reviewed in this study the dichotomy between solitude and connection is acknowledged and assessed. According to these reflections, the self is essentially alone; there are recesses within the self which cannot be shared. On the other hand, Buber and Ricoeur also stress the inter-subjectivity of human existence and argue that the self cannot be a self without mediation and encounter with others.[1] Kennelly reiterates this paradox. Fear of confronting human solitude results in many impediments to love, as a basic reality of self and other is denied. The desire for connection, security, certainty and control belies a fear of openness to risk and vulnerability, and precludes a genuine encounter with self and others

---

[1] The title of Judith Butler's exploration of ethics in the contemporary world, *Giving an Account of Oneself,* resounds with Ricoeur's notion of narrative identity. Here, she echoes the sentiments of Buber and Ricoeur regarding the self and the other: "One seeks to preserve oneself against the injuriousness of the other, but if one were successful at walling oneself off from injury, one would become inhuman" (Butler, 2005: 103).

which is prerequisite to the experience of love. The rejection of risk and vulnerability, and the ensuing withdrawal from life and from love, is documented especially in Eliot's "Prufrock", but it is also explored by the other writers. All concur with the analysis of fear as a reluctance to encounter the flawed, imperfect, ambiguous reality of the self and of the other, an attempted avoidance of uncertainty and incomprehension relative to the human condition, and an effort to evade the existential aloneness which characterizes human being. All the writers acknowledge the understandable nature of these fears within the complexities of human living, though Nietzsche is more adamant in his insistence on the necessity of overcoming the restrictions imposed through a passive acceptance of fear's power. His exhortations calling for self-creation, self-responsibility and self-empowerment do not stress the corresponding necessity of relationship, attachment and recognition as forcibly as the other writers.

The subject's enmeshment in the structures and the laws of language, as outlined clearly by Lacan and Ricoeur, entails an acknowledgement of the failure of language to fully express human being. Eliot concurs with this analysis of the limitations of language, and the ensuing difficulties pertaining to communication, meaning, and relationship. The experience of being human is closely bound to the existence, acquisition and use of language, but paradoxically, the complex needs of human expression often lie beyond the power of language to articulate and communicate. Thus, faced with this inevitable predicament, the subject resorts to alternative expressions of need, desire, thought and feeling, described by Freud and psychoanalysis generally as symptom formation, displacement, transference, duplicity and repetition, with the ensuing relational difficulties of communication and interpretation. At this point, as argued by Buber, human relationships are diminished, reduced to pseudo-encounters, intersecting monologues replace authentic dialogue, and the self is alienated from itself.

The loss of the self precludes the possibility of love, because, as portrayed especially in Eliot's poetry, the vacuum is filled with desperate attempts to obliterate the emptiness; performance, duplicity, subterfuge, and a host of image-making manoeuvres, are efforts to substitute an acceptable persona for the feared, denied, and lost self. As outlined by the writers, the subject, as a speaking being, strives to give expression to itself, physically, intellectually, and emotionally, and a significant instrument of this attempted expression is the use of language in order to mediate and relate, both within the self and between the self and others. The attempt to accomplish what Lacan refers to as "full speech", to articulate the inner world as the poets strive, and to create and to share a Ricoeuerian narrative of the self, are aspects of human being which are observed and investigated by the philosophers, psychoanalysts and poets who are the focus of this research. All the literature which has been explored here situates love at the centre of the self which seeks expression, and when language fails to articulate this essence, through the many ambiguities, repressions, fears and conflicts inherent to human nature, as outlined and analyzed in various ways by the writers, the possibility of love is thwarted and diminished. Language often fails to communicate the desire for love, the commitment to love, and the experience accruing from both: "I have phrases and whole pages memorized / but nothing can be told of love" (Rumi, 1996: 224). Love cannot be captured/interpreted/explained/portrayed/expressed fully in language; indeed, the being of humanness cannot be articulated; however, this does not mean that it cannot be approached, its meaning experienced, its truth lived.

However, perhaps the most significant aspect of the failure of language, in relation to love's possibility, lies in its propensity to deception, of others, but more significantly, of the self. All the writers under review take cognizance of this phenomenon, as it is manifested in diverse relationships between the disparate elements of the self, in interpersonal encounters, and in historical, biographical and sociological misrepresentation and misinterpretation. Ricoeur and Žižek outline the problems posed in any attempt to attain an honest and unprejudiced narration of the past, the other, and the uncomfortably unfamiliar. These problems are portrayed poetically by Kennelly through his investigation into the common erection of scapegoats and villains as convenient receptacles of human evil and destruction that enable the self-deception of an individual or group. Throughout the study, the phenomenon of projection has been addressed through various terms applied by the individual writers; Jews, Nazis, Muslims, Cromwell, Judas, the foreigner, the other.

The subjective nature of truth, while always a contentious issue, is a characteristic acknowledged with varying definitiveness by all nine writers, and a corollary of this is the acknowledgement that conflict, horror, disgust, and many other "negative" attitudes towards outer realities have their source in personal experience, albeit an experience often denied or repressed out of consciousness. The paradox of self-deception emerges as a constant of human nature, and is explored by all the writers. Nietzsche and Freud particularly attest to the ability, the willingness, and the determination of the subject to deceive him or herself. Nietzsche points to factors such as fear, pride, image, and the irresponsibility attendant on accepting external sources of value and judgement, as enabling the adoption of deception within the self, while Freud seeks an understanding of repression and denial, compulsion and repetition, and the multiple manifestations of self-deception observable in "neurotic" and "normal" behaviour, by attempting to discover the hidden and unconsciousness origins of the subject's current situation. The work of the three poets is a courageous exploration towards self-discovery, and as such, it continually encounters, highlights, and seeks to understand the allure of deception. An overview of this topic, as explored through all the writers under review, suggests that deception, of self and of others, is a major obstacle to authentic relationships, to the possibility of love; the self cannot be loved as a mere caricature of its reality, and the other cannot be loved by a subject whose self is camouflaged.

The reality of deception asserted by all the writers necessitates a corresponding discourse on the nature of truth, and it is the conclusion of this study that the philosophers, psychoanalysts and poets are in full agreement on the subjective nature of truth. It is not within the domain of this work to explore the vastness and the complexity pertaining to a concept such as "truth", but it is asserted that there is agreement and coherence between all the writers outlined, as they refute universal or absolutist depictions of this concept. The relationship between love and truth is approached directly or indirectly by all the writers, and their various reflections lead to the conclusion that love is impossible in the absence of personal truth.[2] Truth is the main casualty of each of the obstacles to love discerned through the research; fear, deception and the failure of communication are inextricably linked, causally and impactfully, and without personal truth, conceptualized variously by the different writers, the possibility of loving and being loved is threatened and diminished.

Glimpses of Love's Possibility

It has been argued in this study that the question of love's possibility is a (or *the*) motivating force in the theoretical, analytic and creative writing of philosophy, psychoanalysis and poetry, as these areas are represented by the writers selected and explored. Asserting that the question of love is a common and central thread uniting all three disciplines may seem to

---

[2] The Greek philosophers variously define the object of love as "the beautiful" and the "good". Keats' dictum, "beauty is truth , truth beauty" (Keats, 2006: 906), suggests a correlation, or even an equivalence between love as love of beauty and love as love of truth.

suggest a nebulous connection, but this study claims that the identification of a common thread, that weaves gently through the thought of all the thinkers under review, has important implications for the way we view the knowledge of what it is to be human. Exploring the literature of those who have influenced, not only their own discipline, but arguably the thinking of their historical epoch and beyond, through the lens of the apparently narrow and particular focus of the centrality of love, illuminates these individual and diverse writings, and shows that the interconnection and disconnection between these (and other) disciplines is fundamentally what may enable a greater understanding of human existence. A central aspect of this understanding is an acknowledgement of the significance of love, its necessity, its experience, and its frustration, in human living. The research has firmly asserted this claim. It has argued that the question of love is central to all the literature studied, that at least some of the obstacles to love's possibility are identified through the focus of the exploration, and it concludes with an overview of the conditions of love's possibility glimpsed or highlighted through the study.

A condition of love asserted by all the writers is a willingness to approach a realistic appraisal of human nature in the place of idealistic and theoretical abstractions, which deny the complexity and multiplicity inherent in the concept. Only thus can a real, flesh and blood person love an other in an open embrace of incompleteness, incomprehension, separateness, and possibility. Acknowledgement of the complexity of self and other necessitates a tolerance for ambiguity, a relinquishment of certainties, and an openness to vulnerability and unpredictability. The integration of the full spectrum of human being, including its less attractive and less consoling attributes, is portrayed by Nietzsche as an essential prerequisite to the experience of love, of self, of others, and of life. The honesty and courage implied by this attempted integration is urged by all the writers; it forms the basis of psychoanalytic practice as explicated by Freud, Lacan and Žižek, it is deemed essential to authentic dialogue and relationship as outlined by Buber and Ricoeur, and it is a compelling motivation and inspiration of the poetic works explored. Wordsworth undertakes a searching discovery of himself, and finds therein an ability to love himself and his fellow human-beings; Eliot seeks the illumination of what is hidden, buried, or disguised within the self, and the ensuing growth of compassion and love which this difficult encounter enables. Kennelly gives expression to his own vulnerability and that of others, he acknowledges his uncertainty and fallibility, and he directs his praise towards the embrace of risk which love demands. Resounding with the other writers, Kennelly welcomes the ambiguity of apparent contradictions that lie beneath concepts such as good and evil, hope and failure, solitude and connection, and self and other. The traditional opposition between love of self and love of the other, between selfishness and altruism, is questioned and critiqued by all the writers under review. While Nietzsche and Freud insist on the persistence of at least some traces of narcissism in all experiences of love, and avow the drive of self-preservation in all human behaviour, writers such as Buber and Ricoeur suggest the possibility of self-love co-existing with a genuine and unconditional love for others. All writers concur on the essential necessity of self-love and self-acceptance as a condition of the ability to love another and to receive the other's love. They point to the distortions and misinterpretations which ensue when this condition is not met, and to varying degrees, they posit love of self and of others as intricately and essentially linked.[3]

A corollary of tolerance and acceptance of ambiguity in human nature, as suggested by the research, is the humility inherent in an ongoing process of openness to self and to others. This *humility* is sourced in an acknowledgement that full self-knowledge or self-transparency is not possible; this reality of the human condition is explicitly asserted through the insights of Freud and Nietzsche, with particular reference to their reflections on morality, the unconscious, repression and duplicity. The narrative identity of the subject as outlined by Ricoeur entails a constant openness to revision and reinterpretation, and echoes Nietzsche's reference to the "process" of becoming. The humility which enables an avowal of ignorance with regard to the self is also essential in a loving approach to the difference and incomprehension of the other. Lacan and Žižek argue that the acknowledgement of this incommensurability is essential to the possibility of love, and that it is indeed a central aspect of love's experience. They both point to the dangers pertaining to an assumption of knowledge regarding others, and like Ricoeur, suggest a relation between such a conviction and the justification of power which may be exercised under euphemistically-termed motivations. Complete self-knowledge is exposed as a fantasy, and the demand to fully know or

---

[3] The ability and willingness to love the self is therefore deemed essential to the possibility of inter-subjective love, by all the writers outlined. However, the question remains open as to how the human subject acquires this ability; is it inherent in being human? Is it a natural aptitude which is sometimes "educationally" modified or removed by external rules and expectations? Is it something which can be only be attained after it is experienced through the reflection and love of an other? These questions are posed through the research without definitive or categorical conclusion.

understand, self or an other, can result in convenient conclusions and grandiose generalizations.

While all the writers explored in this study assert the prevalence and endurance of love's impediments and failures, each writer is equally committed to the portrayal of love's possibility within the constraints and complexities of human living. The testimony of the failure of love provided through this study, its impermanence, its volatility, its proximity to hate, and all the vicissitudes which assail the possibility of love, does not negate the conviction expressed by the writers that love can be experienced, given, and received. The affective experience of hatred and annoyance can co-exist with a continued commitment to love, which can integrate "negative" experiences and emotions without denying them. Love is most clearly portrayed in the concrete, momentary, and transitory encounters of human living, and Buber especially insists on centring the reality of love in the experiential encounter of "I" and "Thou". Nietzsche also suggests that the "affect", the emotion, underlying love, cannot be commanded or promised. However, this does not negate the possible endurance of love. It is the conclusion of this work that the concept of love emerging from the study is something greater than an emotional, intellectual, sexual, physical or theoretical experience; it is all of these and more, and its possibility persists in spite of its recurrent impossibility. This conclusion is particularly supported by the expression of the three poets in their unique and personal accounts, and the poetic word appears to be capable of overcoming the dilemmas and conflicts posed in relation to the question, as it surrenders claims to certainty and knowledge, and is satisfied with offering glimpses whereby the truth of love may be approached.

"Late Fragment"

And did you get what
You wanted from this life, even so?
I did.
And what did you want?
To call myself beloved, to feel myself
Beloved on the earth (Carver, 2002: 456).

BIBLIOGRAPHY

Armstrong, John, 2003. *Conditions of Love: The Philosophy of Intimacy*. London: W.W. Norton & Company Ltd.
—. 2006. *Love, Life, Goethe: How to be Happy in an Imperfect World*. London: Allen Lane.
Assoun, Paul-Laurent, 2000. *Freud and Nietzsche*. London: Continuum.
Astley, Niall, ed. 2002. *Staying Alive: Real Poems for Unreal Times*. Northumberland: Bloodaxe Books Ltd.
Auden, W.H., 1994. *Collected Poems*. London: Faber and Faber.
Badiou, Alain, 2000, "What is Love?" in *Sexuation*, ed. Renata Salecl. Durham: Duke University Press, pp. 263-281.
—. 2006, "Lacan and the Pre-Socratics" in *Lacan: The Silent Partners*, ed. Slavoj Žižek. London: Verso, pp. 7-16.
Barthes, Roland, 1979. *A Lover's Discourse*. New York: Hill and Wang.
Beer, John, 1978. *Wordsworth and the Human Heart*. London: The Macmillan Press.
Berry, Donald, 1985. *Mutuality: The Vision of Martin Buber*. Albany: State University of New York Press.
Blake, William, 2004. *Selected Poems*. London: Collector's Poetry Library.
Bloom, Harold, 1976. *Poetry and Repression: Revisionism from Blake to Stevens*. London: Yale University Press.
Boothby, Richard, 2001. *Freud as Philosopher*. New York: Routledge.
Bradbury, Malcolm, and James McFarlane eds. 1978. *Modernism: A Guide to European Literature 1890-1930*. London: Penguin Books.
Bromwich, David, 2000. *Disowned by Memory: Wordsworth's Poetry of the 1790s*. Chicago: Chicago University Press.
Brooks, Cleanth, 1965. *Modern Poetry & the Tradition*. Chapel Hill: The University of North Carolina Press.
Buber, Martin, 1999. *Martin Buber on Psychology and Psychotherapy*, ed. Judith Buber Agassi New York: Syracuse University Press.
—. 2002. *The Way of Man*. London: Routledge
—. 2004. *Between Man and Man*. New York: Routledge Classics.
—. 2004a. *I and Thou*. London: Continuum.
Bullock, Allan, 1991, "The Double Image" in *Modernism: A Guide to European Literature 1890-1930*, ed. Malcolm Bradbury and James

McFarlane. London: Penguin Books, pp.58-70.

Burston, Daniel, 1996. *The Wing of Madness: The Life and Work of R.D. Laing*. London: Harvard University Press.

Butler, Judith, 2005. *Giving an Account of Oneself*. Fordham: Fordham University Press.

Campbell, Matthew, ed., 2003. *The Cambridge Companion to Contemporary Irish Poetry*. Cambridge: Cambridge University Press.

Camus, Albert, 1957. "The Nobel Prize in Literature 1957: Banquet Speech". Available:[nobelprize.org/nobel_prizes/literature/laureates/1957/camus -speech-e.html - 24k -], accessed 20/11/07.

Carver, Raymond, 2002. "Late Fragment" in *Staying Alive: Real Poems for Unreal Times,* ed. Niall Ashley. Northumberland: Bloodaxe Books Ltd.

Childs, Peter, 2000. *Modernism*. London: Routledge.

Chiesa, Lorenzo, 2007. *Subjectivity and Otherness: A Philosophical Reading of Lacan*. Cambridge: MIT Press.

Clark, Maudmarie, 1990. *Nietzsche on Truth and Philosophy*. Cambridge: Cambridge University Press.

Collins, Lucy, 2003, "Performance and Dissent: Irish Poets in the Public Sphere" in *The Cambridge Companion to Contemporary Irish Poetry,* ed. Matthew Campbell. Cambridge: Cambridge University press, pp. 209-228.

Connor, Steven ed., 2004. *The Cambridge Companion to Postmodernism*. Cambridge: Cambridge University Press.

Cook, Jon, 2004. *Poetry in Theory: An Anthology 1900-2000*. Oxford: Blackwell Publishing Ltd.

Curran, Stuart, ed., 2005. *The Cambridge Companion to British Romanticism*. Cambridge: Cambridge University Press.

Dawson, P. M. S., 2005, "Poetry in an Age of Revolution" in *The Cambridge Companion to British Romanticism,* ed. Stuart Curran. Cambridge: Cambridge University Press, pp.48-73.

Day, Aidan, 1996. *Romanticism*. London: Routledge.

Derrida, Jacques, 1981. *Writing and Difference*. London: Routledge and Kegan Paul Ltd.

—. 1994. *Given Time: 1. Counterfeit Money*. London: The University of Chicago Press.

—. 1996. *The Gift of Death*. London: The University of Chicago Press.

—. 1998. *Resistances of Psychoanalysis*. Stanford: Stanford University Press.

—. 2004, "Che cos'è la Poesia?" in *Poetry in Theory: An Anthology 1900-*

2000, ed. Jon Cook. Oxford: Blackwell Publishing Ltd, pp.533-537.

—. 2004a. *Deconstruction in a Nutshell: A Conversation with Jacques Derrida*. New York: Fordham University Press.

—. 2005. *The Politics of Friendship*. London: Verso.

Dilman, Ilham, 1998. *Love: Its Forms, Dimensions and Paradoxes*. London: MacMillan Press Ltd.

Dunne, Joseph, 1996, "Beyond Sovereignty and Deconstruction: The Storied Self" in *Paul Ricoeur: The Hermeneutics of Action*, ed. Richard Kearney. London: Sage Publications Ltd., pp 137-157.

Edmundson, Mark, 2007. *Towards Reading Freud: Self-Creation in Milton, Wordsworth, Emerson, and Sigmund Freud*. Chicago: University of Chicago Press.

Eliot, T.S., 1948. "The Nobel Prize in Literature 1948: Banquet Speech". Available: [nobelprize.org/nobel_prizes/literature/laureates/1948/eliot-speech.html], accessed 24/04/2007.

—. 1975. *Selected Prose of T.S. Eliot*. Orlando: Harcourt Inc.

—. 2004. *The Complete Poems & Plays*. London: Faber and Faber Limited.

Erikson, Erik, 1994. *Identity and the Life Cycle*. New York: W.W. Norton & Company.

—. 1998. *The Life Cycle Completed*. New York: W.W. Norton & Company.

Fingarette, Herbert, 2000. *Self-Deception*. Berkeley: University of California Press.

Foucault, Michael, 2000. *Ethics: Essential Works of Foucault 1954-1984 Volume 1*. London: Penguin.

Frankfurt, Harry G., 2006. *The Reasons of Love*. Princeton: Princeton University Press.

Freud, Sigmund and Carl Jung, 1974. *The Freud/Jung Letters*. Princeton: Princeton University Press.

Freud, Sigmund, 1985. *The Complete Letters of Sigmund to Wilhelm Fliess: 1887- 1904*. ed. Jeffrey Masson. London: Harvard University Press.

—. 1988. *Five Lectures on Psychoanalysis*. Translated by James Strachey. New York: W.W. Norton & Company.

—. 1991. *Introductory Lectures on Psychoanalysis*. Translated by James Strachey. London: Penguin Books.

—. 1995. *The Freud Reader*. ed. Peter Gay. New York: W.W. Norton & Company.

—. 1997. *The Interpretation of Dreams*. Translated by A.A. Brill. Herfordshire: Wordsworth Editions Limited.

—. 2002. *Civilization and Its Discontents.* Translated by David McLintock. London: Penguin Classics.

—. 2003. *An Outline of Psychoanalysis.* London: Penguin Classics.

—. 2005. *On Murder, Mourning and Melancholy.* Translated by Shaun Whiteside. London: Penguin Classics.

—. 2005a. *The Psychopathology of Everyday Life.* Translated by Anthea Bell. London: Penguin Classics.

—. 2006. *The Penguin Freud Reader.* ed. Adam Phillips. London: Penguin.

—. 2006a. *The Psychology of Love.* London: Penguin.

Friedman, Maurice, 2002. *Martin Buber: The Life of Dialogue.* London: Routledge.

Fromm, Erich, 1995. *The Art of Loving.* London: Thorsons.

—. 2003. *Man for Himself.* London: Routledge.

Gadamer, Hans-Georg, 1991. "The Conflict of Interpretations: Debate with Hans-Georg Gadamer" in *A Ricoeur Reader: Reflection and Imagination,* ed. Mario J. Valdes, Toronto: University of Toronto Press, pp.216-241.

—. 1996. *The Enigma of Health: The Art of Healing in a Scientific Age.* Stanford: Stanford University Press.

---. 2004. *Truth and Method.* London: Continuum.

Gardner, Helen, 1968. *The Art of T.S. Eliot.* London: Faber and Faber Limited.

Gay, Peter, 1998. *Freud: A Life for Our Time.* London: W.W. Norton & Company.

Gordon, Lyndall, 2000. *T. S. Eliot: An Imperfect Life.* London: W.W. Norton & Company.

Gill, Stephen, 1991. *Wordsworth: The Prelude.* Cambridge: Cambridge University Press.

Gill, Stephen, ed., 2003. *The Cambridge Companion to Wordsworth.* Cambridge: Cambridge University Press.

Green, Andre and Gregorio Kohun, 2005. *Love and Its Vicissitudes.* New York: Routledge.

Greenblatt, S., et al. eds. 2006. *The Norton Anthology of English Literature, Volume 2, eighth edition.* New York: W.W. Norton & Company.

Hall, William David, 2007. *Paul Ricoeur and the Poetic Imperative: The Creative Tension between Love and Justice.* Albany: State University of New York Press.

Harari, Roberto, 2004. *Lacan's Four Fundamental Concepts of Psychoanalysis: An Introduction.* New York: Other Press.

Hayes, John, 1988. "Freud's Philosophical Roots", *Irish Philosophical Journal,* Volume 5, pp. 46-77.

Heaney, Seamus, 1995. "Crediting Poetry". Available: [nobelprize.org/nobel_prizes/literature/laureates/1995/heaney-lecture.html] accessed 11/7/07.

—. 2004, "The Redress of Poetry" in *Poetry and Theory: An Anthology 1900-2000,* ed. Jon Cook. Oxford: Blackwell Publishing Ltd., pp. 567-573.

Hederman, Mark Patrick, 2000. *Manikon Eros: Mad, Crazy Love.* Dublin: Veritas Publications.

Hobes, Aubrey, 1972. *Encounter with Martin Buber.* London: Allen Lane The Penguin Press.

Hyde, G. M., 1991, "The Poetry of the City" in *Modernism: A Guide to European Literature 1890-1930,* ed. Malcolm Bradbury and James McFarlane. London: Penguin Books, pp. 337-348.

Irigaray, Luce, 2002. *The Way of Love.* New York: Continuum.

Jones, John, 1970. *The Egotistical Sublime: A History of Wordsworth's Imagination.* London: Chatto & Windus.

Joy, Morny, ed. 1997. *Paul Ricoeur and Narrative: Context and Contestation.* Calgary: University of Calgary Press.

Jung, Carl, 1998. *The Essential Jung.* London: Fontana Press.

—. 2004. *Modern Man in Search of a Soul.* London: Routledge Classics.

Kaplan, David, 2003. *Ricoeur's Critical Theory.* Albany: State University of New York Press.

Kaufmann, Walter, 1974. *Nietzsche: Philosopher, Psychologist, Antichrist.* London: Princeton University McGraw-Hill.

—. 1980. *Discovering the Mind, Volume III: Freud Versus Adler and Jung.* New York: McGraw-Hill.

—. 1992. *Discovering the Mind, Volume II: Nietzsche, Heidegger and Buber.* London: Transaction Publishers.

Kay, Sarah, 2003. *Žižek: A Critical Introduction.* Cambridge: Polity Press.

Kearney, Richard, 1997. *Postnationalist Ireland: Politics, Literature, Philosophy.* London: Routledge.

—. 1998. *Poetics of Imagining: From Modern to Postmodern.* Edinburgh: Edinburgh University Press.

—. 2001. *The God Who May Be.* Bloomington: Indiana University Press.

Kearney, Richard and David Rasmussen, eds. 2001a. *Continental Aesthetics: Romanticism to Postmodernism.* Massachusetts: Blackwell Publishers Ltd.

Kearney, Richard, 2002. "Strangers and Others: From Deconstruction to Hermeneutics" in *Critical Horizons* Volume No. 3:1, pp. 7-36.

—. 2003. *Strangers, Gods and Monsters: Ideas of Otherness.* London: Routledge.

—. 2004. *On Paul Ricoeur: The Owl of Minerva.* Aldershot: Ashgate Publishing Limited.

Keats, John, 2006. "Ode on a Grecian Urn" in *The Norton Anthology of English Literature, Volume 2, eighth edition.* S. Greenblatt et al, eds. New York: W.W. Norton & Company, p. 906.

Kennelly, Brendan, 1987. *Cromwell.* Newcastle upon Tyne: Bloodaxe Books Ltd.

—. 1990. *A Time for Voices: Selected Poems 1960-1990.* Newcastle upon Tyne: Bloodaxe Books Ltd.

—. 1991. *The Book of Judas.* Newcastle upon Tyne: Bloodaxe Books Ltd.

—. 1994. *Journey into Joy: Selected Prose.* Newcastle upon Tyne: Bloodaxe Books Ltd.

—. 1994a. "'The Roaring of Your Words': Brendan Kennelly in conversation with Richard Pine" in *Dark Fathers into Light,* ed. Richard Pine, Newcastle upon Tyne: Bloodaxe Books Ltd.

—. 1998. *The Man Made of Rain.* Newcastle upon Tyne: Bloodaxe Books Ltd.

—. 2002. *Glimpses.* Northumberland: Bloodaxe Books Ltd.

—. 2003. *Martial Art.* Northumberland: Bloodaxe Books Ltd.

—. 2004. *Familiar Strangers: New & Selected Poems 1960-2004.* Northumberland: Bloodaxe Books Ltd.

—. 2006. *Now.* Northumberland: Bloodaxe Books Ltd.

—. 2006a. *When Then is Now.* Northumberland: Bloodaxe Books Ltd.

—. 2004a, qtd. in *The Irish Times,* May 22nd.

Kinsella, Thomas, 1996. *The Collected Poems 1956-1994 (Oxford Poets).* Oxford: Oxford University Press.

Kristeva, Julia, 1987. *Tales of Love.* New York: Columbia University Press.

—. 1991. *Strangers to Ourselves.* New York: Columbia University Press.

—. 1992. *Black Sun: Depression and Melancholia (European Perspectives: A Series in Social Thought and Cultural Criticism).* New York: Columbia University Press.

Lacan, Jacques, 1991. *The Seminar of Jacques Lacan: Book 1: Freud's Papers on Technique 1953-1954.* London: W.W. Norton & Company.

—. 1997. *The Ethics of Psychoanalysis: 1959-1960. The Seminar of Jacques Lacan, Book VII.* London: W.W. Norton & Company.

—. 1999. *On Feminine Sexuality, the Limits of Love and Knowledge: Encore: The Seminar of Jacques Lacan, Book XX.* New York: W.W. Norton & Co.

—. 2004. *Écrits: A Selection.* Translated by Bruce Fink. London: W.W. Norton & Company.

—. 2007. *The Other Side of Psychoanalysis: The Seminar of Jacques Lacan Book XVII.* London: W.W. Norton & Company.

Laing, R.D., 1967. *The Politics of Experience.* New York: Pantheon Books.

—. 1972. *Knots.* New York: Random House, Inc.

—. 1990. *The Divided Self.* London: Penguin Books.

—. 1999. *Self and Others.* London: Routledge.

Lakeland, Paul, 1997. *Postmodernity: Christian Identity in a Fragmented Age.* Minneapolis: Fortress Press.

Larkin, Philip, 1988. *Collected Poems.* London: Faber & Faber.

Laurence, D.H., 2002. *Complete Poems of D.H. Laurence.* Hertfordshire: Wordsworth Editions Ltd.

Lear, Jonathan, 1998. *Love and Its Place in Nature.* Yale: Yale University Press.

—. 2001. *Happiness, Death, and Remainder of Life.* Harvard: Harvard *the* University Press.

—. 2005. *Freud.* New York: Routledge.

Lessing, Doris, 1995. *Under my Skin: Volume One of My Autobiography, to 1949.* New York: Harper Perennial.

Levenson, Michael ed., 1999. *The Cambridge Companion to Modernism.* Cambridge, Cambridge University Press.

Lewis, C.S., 1988. *The Four Loves.* New York: Hartcourt Inc.

Lyotard, Jean-Francois, 1999. *The Postmodern Condition: A Report on Knowledge.* Minneapolis: University of Minnesota Press.

McDonagh, John, 1998. *'Narrating the Nation': Post-Colonial Perspectives on Patrick Kavanagh's The Great Hunger (1942) and Brendan Kennelly's Cromwell (1983).* PhD Thesis, The University of Warwick.

—. 2004. *A Host of Ghosts.* Dublin: The Liffey Press.

McEwan, Ian, 2007. *On Chesil Beach.* New York: Vintage.

McFarlane, James, 1991, "The Mind of Modernism" in *Modernism: A Guide to European Literature 1890-1930*, eds. Malcolm Bradbury and James McFarlane. London: Penguin Books, pp. 71-93.

McGahern, John, 2006, qtd. in *The Irish Times,* November 25th.

Mays, J. C. C., 2006, "Early Poems: from 'Prufrock' to 'Gerontion'" in *The Cambridge Companion to T. S. Eliot*, ed. David Moody. Cambridge: Cambridge University Press, pp. 108-120.

Mitchell, Juliet, and Jacqueline Rose, ed. 1982. *Feminine Sexuality: Jacques Lacan and The École Freudienne.* London: MacMillan Press

Ltd.

Moody, A. David, 1996. *Tracing T.S. Eliot's Spirit.* Cambridge: Cambridge University Press. Cambridge: Cambridge University Press.

Moody, A. David ed., 2006. *The Cambridge Companion to T.S. Eliot.* Cambridge: Cambridge University Press.

Moran, Dermot, 2002. *Introduction to Phenomenology.* London: Routledge.

Murdoch, Iris, 1993. *Metaphysics as a Guide to Morals.* New York: Penguin Books.

Myers, Tony, 2004. *Slavoj Žižek. (Routledge Critical Thinkers).* London: Routledge.

Nehamas, Alexander, 1985. *Nietzsche, Life as Literature.* Harvard: Harvard University Press.

Nicholi, Armand M., 2002. *The Question of God. C.S. Lewis and Sigmund Freud Debate God, Love, Sex, and the Meaning of Life.* New York: Free Press.

Nietzsche, Friedrich, 1968. *The Will to Power.* Translated by Walter Kaufmann and R. J. Hollingdale. New York: Vintage.

—. 1974. *The Gay Science.* Translated by Walter Kaufmann. New York: Vintage.

—. 1984. *Human, All Too Human.* Translated by Marion Faber and Stephen Lehmann. Harmondsworth: Penguin.

—. 1998. *On the Genealogy of Morality.* Translated by Maudmarie Clark and Alan J. Swensen. Indiana: Hacket Publishing Company, Inc.

—. 2003. *Beyond Good and Evil.* Translated by R. J. Hollingdale. London: Penguin Books.

—. 2003a. *Thus Spoke Zarathustra.* Translated by R. J. Hollingdale. London: Penguin Books.

Nussbaum, Martha, 1992. *Love's Knowledge: Essays on Philosophy and Literature.* New York: Oxford University Press.

—. 1994. *The Therapy of Desire: Theory and Practice in Hellenistic Ethics.* Princeton: Princeton University Press.

—. 2001. *The Fragility of Goodness.* New York: Cambridge University Press.

Pascal, Blaise, 1999. *Pensées and Other Writings (Oxford World Classics).* Translated by Honor Levi. New York: Oxford University Press.

Persson, Ake, 2000. *Betraying the Age: Social and Artistic Protest in Brendan Kennelly's Work.* Goteborg: Parajett AB.

Phillips, Adam, 2002. *Equals.* New York: Basic Books.

—. 2002a. *Promises, Promises: Essays on Poetry and Psychoanalysis.*

New York: Basic Books.

—. 2005. *Going Sane: Maps of Happiness.* New York: Harper Collins.

—. 2006. *Side Effects.* London: Penguin Books.

Pine, Richard ed., 1994. *Dark Fathers into Light.* Newcastle upon Tyne: Bloodaxe Books Ltd.

Porchia, Antonio, 2003. *Voices.* Washington: Copper Canyon Press.

Quiller-Couch, Arthur Thomas ed., 1919. *The Oxford Book of English Verse: 1250-1900.* Oxford: Clarendon.

Rabaté, Jean-Michel, 2006, "Tradition and T. S. Eliot" in *The Cambridge Companion to T. S. Eliot,* ed. David Moody. Cambridge: Cambridge University Press, pp. 210-222.

Raine, Craig, 2006. *T.S. Eliot.* Oxford: Oxford University Press.

Rawls, John, 1971. *A Theory of Justice.* London: Oxford University Press.

Reginster, Bernard, 2006. *The Affirmation of Life: Nietzsche on Overcoming Nihilism.* Cambridge: Harvard University Press.

Rich, Adrienne, 2004, "Blood, Bread, and Poetry" in *Poetry in Theory: An Anthology 1900-2000,* ed. Jon Cook. Oxford: Blackwell Publishing Ltd, pp.503-513.

Ricoeur, Paul, 1970. *Freud and Philosophy.* New Haven: Yale University Press.

—. 1991. *A Ricoeur Reader: Reflection and Imagination.* ed. Mario Valdes. Toronto: University of Toronto Press.

—. 1992. *Oneself as Another.* Chicago: The University of Chicago Press.

—. 1995. *Figuring the Sacred: Religion, Narrative, and Imagination.* Minneapolis: Fortress Press.

—. 1996. *The Hermeneutics of Action.* ed. Richard Kearney. London: Sage Publications Ltd.

—. 2002. *Fallible Man.* New York: Fordham University Press.

—. 2004. *Memory, History, Forgetting.* Chicago: The University Of Chicago Press.

—. 2005. *The Course of Recognition.* London: Harvard University Press.

—. 2006. *On Translation.* London: Routledge.

Rieff, Philip, 1966. *The Triumph of the Therapeutic: Uses of Faith after Freud.* Florida: Harcourt.

—. 1979. *Freud: The Mind of the Moralist.* Chicago: The University of Chicago Press.

Rilke, Rainer Maria, 2004. *Rilke on Love and Other Difficulties.* New York: W. W. Norton & Company.

Roth, Philip, 2007. *Exit Ghost.* London: Jonathan Cape.

Roudinesco, Elisabeth, 1997. *Jacques Lacan.* Cambridge: Polity Press.

Rumi, Jalal al-Din, et al, 1996. *Essential Rumi.* New York: Harper Collins.
—. 1999. *Whispers of the Beloved.* London: Thorsons.
Salecl, Renata, 2000. *Sexuation.* Durham: Duke University Press.
Santas, Gerasimos, 1988. *Plato & Freud: Two Theories of Love.* Oxford: Basil Blackwell Limited.
Sartre, Jean-Paul, 1969. *Nausea.* New York: New Directions Publishing Corporation.
—. 1992. *The Reprieve.* New York: Vintage.
—. 1992a. *Being and Nothingness.* Washington: Washington Square Press.
Sedlmayr, Gerold, 2005. *Brendan Kennelly's Literary Works: The Developing Art of an Irish Writer.* New York: The Edwin Mellen Press, Ltd.
Sexton, Anne, 1999. *Love Poems.* New York: Mariner Books.
Shapira, Avraham, 1999. *Hope for Our Time: Key Trends in the Thought of Martin Buber.* New York: State University of New York Press.
Sheehan, Paul, 2004, "Postmodernism and Philosophy" in *The Cambridge Companion to Postmodernism,* ed. Steven Connor. Cambridge: Cambridge University Press.
Shusterman, Richard, 2006, "Eliot as Philosopher" in *The Cambridge Companion to T. S. Eliot,* ed. David Moody. Cambridge: Cambridge University Press, pp. 31-47.
Singer, Irving, 1987. *The Nature of Love 1, 2, 3.* London: The University of Chicago Press.
Soble, Alan, ed., 1989. *Eros, Agape, and Philia: Readings in the Philosophy of Love.* St. Paul: Paragon House.
Solomon, Robert, and Kathleen Higgins, 2000. *What Nietzsche Really Said.* New York: Schocken Books.
Storr, Anthony, 1997. *Solitude.* London: HarperCollins.
Styron, William, 1981. *Sophie's Choice.* London: Corgi Books.
Tracy, David, 1996, "Ricoeur's Philosophical Journey: Its Import for Religion" in *Paul Ricoeur: The Hermeneutics of Action,* ed. Richard Kearney. London: Sage Publications Ltd., pp. 201-203.
Wagoner, Robert, E., 1997. *The Meaning of Love: An Introduction to Philosophy of Love.* Westport: Praeger Publishers.
Wall, John, 2005. *Moral Creativity: Paul Ricoeur and the Poetics of Possibility.* New York: Oxford University Press.
Webster, Richard, 2003. *Freud.* London: Weidenfeld & Nicolson.
Wordsworth, William, 1858. *The Poetical Works of William Wordsworth.* London: Routledge and Sons.
—. 1888. *The Complete Poetical Works.* London: MacMillan and

Company.
—. 1984. *William Wordsworth: The Major Works.* Oxford: Oxford University Press.
—. 2007. *Wordsworth: A Life in Letters.* ed. Juliet Barker London: Penguin.
Wu, Duncan, 2003, "Wordsworth's Poetry to 1798" in *The Cambridge Companion to Wordsworth,* ed. Stephen Gill. Cambridge: Cambridge University Press, pp. 24-35.
Yeats, W. B., 1967. *Selected Poetry.* London: MacMillan.
Zilcosky, John, 2005. "Modern Monuments: T.S. Eliot, Nietzsche, and the Problems of History" in *Journal of Modern Literature.* Vol. 29, No. 1, pp. 21-23
Žižek, Slavoj, 1997. *The Plague of Fantasies.* London: Verso.
—. 1997a. "The Big Other Doesn't Exist". *Psychomedia: Journal of European Psychoanalysis.* Spring-Fall. Available: [mhtml:file://E:\%20PSYCHOMEDIA%20%20JOURNAL%20OF%2 0european], accessed 7/2/'07.
—. 1999. *The Žižek Reader.* Eds. Elizabeth Wright and Edmond Wright Oxford: Blackwell Publishers Ltd.
—. 1999a. "Human Rights and Its Discontents". *Lacan Dot Com.* Available: [mhtml:file://E:\Slavoj%20 Žižek –Bibliography Human%20Rights%20and%20its%20Dis], accessed 14/2/07.
—. 1999b. "The Superego and the Act". *The European Graduate School Faculty.* Available: [mhtml:file://E:\Slavoj%20Žižek,%20The%20Superego%20and%20th e%20Act], accessed14/2/07.
—. 2001. *Enjoy Your Symptom!: Jacques Lacan in Hollywood and Out.* New York: Routledge.
—. 2001a. "The One Measure of True Love Is: You Can Insult the Other". *Lacan Dot Com.* Available: [mhtml:file:/E:\Slavoj%20 Žižek-Bibliography-The%20One%20Measure%20of%20True…], accessed 14/2/07.
—. 2001b. "Self-Deceptions: On Being Tolerant and Smug". *Die Gazette.* Available: [mhtml:file://E\Slavoj%20Žižek-Bibliography-Self Deceptions-Lacan%20Dot%20Com], accessed 14/2/07.
—. 2001c. "Welcome to the Desert of the Real". *Free Speech.* Available: [mhyml:file://E:\ Žižek%20on%20Chomsky.mht], accessed 14/2/07.
—. 2004. *Conversations with Žižek (Conversations).* Cambridge: Polity Press.
—. 2004a. "Burned by the Thing". *Psychomedia –Journal of European Psychoanalysis.* Available: [mhtml:file://E\%20PSYCHOMEDIA%20-

%20JOURNAL%20OF%20EUROPEAN%...], accessed 7/2/07].
—. 2004b. "Death's Merciless Love". *Lacan Dot Com.*
Available:[mhtml:file://E:\Slavoj%20 Žižek-Bibliography-
Slavoj%20Žižek%20Death's%20Merciless...], accessed 14/2/07.
—. 2005. *The Neighbour.* London: University of Chicago Press.
—. 2005a. "Freud Lives". *London Review of Books.*
Available:[mhtml:file://E:\LRB%20%20Slavoj%Žižek%20%20Freud
%20Lives..], accessed 10/2/07.
—. 2006. *How to Read Lacan.* London: Granta Books.
—. 2006a. *Interrogating the Real.* London: Continuum.
—. ed., 2006b. *Lacan: The Silent Partners.* London: Verso.
—. 2006c. *On Belief (Thinking in Action).* New York: Routledge.
—. 2006d. *The Parallax View.* London: The MIT Press.
—. 2006e. "Nobody has to be Vile". *London Review of Books.* Available:
[mhtml:file://E☺LRB%20%20Slavoj%20   Žižek
%20%20Nobody%20has%20to%20be%20...], accessed 10/2/07.
—. 2006f. "Freud Lives!". *London Review of Books.* Available:
[mhtml:file://E\LRB$%20%20Slavoj%20
Žižek%20%20Freud%20Lives..], accessed 10/2/07.
—. 2007. *The Universal Exception.* London: Continuum.
Zupancic, Alenka, 2003. *The Shortest Shadow: Nietzsche's Philosophy of
the Two.* Cambridge: The MIT Press.

INDEX

transference, 13, 108-9, 127, 160, 175, 253

unconscious, 11, 16, 45, 48, 50, 63, 73, 89-91, 93, 95, 101-2, 107, 112, 119, 124-30, 135, 139, 146-7, 154, 166, 170, 174, 184, 189, 193, 203, 207, 210, 214, 220, 224, 227-8, 233, 237-9, 249, 257

vulnerability, 30, 38, 50-1, 61, 81, 98, 110, 132, 142, 148-9, 156, 176, 182, 188, 190, 204-5, 212, 217, 226, 236, 241, 244, 252, 256

will to power, 3, 9, 16, 27, 130-1, 190, 204, 250
wisdom, 3, 5, 15, 22, 96, 124, 132, 139, 174, 185, 212, 217

Yeats, W.B., 24-5, 50, 120, 202, 206, 270